Berserkers, Cannibals &

Essays in Dissident Anthr

By Stone Age Herbalist

Copyright

Dedication

This book is dedicated to those anons closest to me, you know who you are.

Without your friendship, encouragement, humour and generosity this book would never have happened.

My special thanks to my friends, Pygmy Glottochronologist for his superb contributions to this collection and to Raw Egg Nationalist for the cover art and invaluable advice.

"Comedies, in the ancient world, were regarded as of a higher rank than tragedy, of a deeper truth, of a more difficult realisation, of a sounder structure, and of a revelation more complete. The happy ending of the fairy tale, the myth, and the divine comedy of the soul, is to be read, not as a contradiction, but as a transcendence of the universal tragedy of man.... Tragedy is the shattering of the forms and of our attachments to the forms; comedy, the wild and careless, inexhaustible joy of life invincible."

Joseph Campbell

Content

Introduction

If you ever take an introduction to animal tracking course, one of the first things they will teach you is how to recognise the general outline prints of different types of animals. The elongated oval of the hoofed prey, the square box of the mustelid and so on. The idea is to train the mind to see these fuzzy horizons long before you hone in on the details. This sensation has become all too familiar to me in the last few years since acquiring a twitter account, I can see a vague impression of something just ahead, something which needs patience and work to bring into focus. The general state of academia feels like a sinking ship, or a bleeding animal, exhausted from the chase. What it once was has been exsanguinated, its vitality drained. As a so-called 'junior researcher' my own sense is of being one hungry tick among millions, all scrambling to feed on a rotten carcass. The fight to even gain a career in a university is so intense it takes decades to accomplish, and if one should be so lucky you will find yourself stretched over the rack of endless bureaucratic demands, the rounds of conferences, the churning paper-mill of citations and publications. The reality is clear, real genuine research - undistracted and focused - is dead now. While we do see new and interesting publications every week, what is lacking is any real and innovative thought. Universities are cashing in the last gasps of intellectual capital painstakingly built over centuries in the West and the few genuinely independent thinkers are rapidly approaching the grave. What I see happening instead is the abandonment of this system by those interested in ideas and research for its own sake. Anyone driven by enthusiasm and passion for a subject will find themselves drawn towards like-minded people, and this is happening elsewhere now. Everyday I meet and see people online who take a deep and abiding joy in history, linguistics, archaeology, literature, science, anthropology. They read old books, they cross-compare disciplines, they ignore academic distinctions between time periods and places and genres, they despise the straightjackets of formal writing and conventions, they dismiss credentialism and reward novelty and creativity. I have been in higher education and research for over a decade, but I have never been so intellectually challenged and stimulated as when I engaged with the strange collectives of thought happening anonymously online. Somewhere between the blogs, the groups chats, the posts, the videos, the back and forth over the finer points of an arcane topic, somewhere here is the fuzzy footprint of a formidable beast, one with the raw talent to reshape the intellectual landscape. Writing for myself and my supporters over the last year has been a joy and a privilege. With anonymity comes the freedom to pursue topics which get no attention and it has been a genuine delight to find that others have also found these interesting - Australian prehistory, modern human sacrifice, palaeolithic seafaring, the biology of berserker warriors, Chinese cannibalism. If this year of writing has shown me anything, it is that a hunger exists out there for content which is not hectoring, condescending or moralistic. People rightly sense in the tone of academic works that researchers don't care for their concerns and worse, that modern scholarship is constantly in the process of critiquing, undermining, deconstructing all that is sacred or healthy. I sense a new era of challenge to their authority and I stand on the shoulders of many anonymous intelligent friends who are constantly learning, constantly striving to put together ideas out of fragments of academic publications, where we read between the lines and follow citation trails back centuries to make sense of the world. It has been a revelation to me to discover that the best and most creative thinking has come from outside the institutions which purportedly exist to do just this. So I humbly present a year of writing from within this world. These articles and essays do not reflect my actual day to day work, but rather reflect the stimulating maelstrom of ideas I discovered online. I always intended them to be somewhere between a counter-academia and an outlet for my own thoughts, I hope you find them interesting.

Disclaimer - these essays were for the most part written for Substack and other online platforms. Many articles originally contained images, maps and diagrams, which cannot be transferred to a book without permission. I have made minor alterations where necessary to ensure the text flows, but if you wish to read them with images then please visit my Substack page at https://stoneageherbalist.substack.com/. They are all free to read.

Part One - Current Affairs & Politics

Human Sacrifice in the Modern World

Murder for divine fortune and appeasement in Uganda and India

Human sacrifice, the intentional killing of a person as part of a religious ritual, is usually explored in the past tense. The infamous civilisations of Central America, of Carthage, of the Celts, can be safely discussed at a distance, the remove of time rendering the reality more of a gentle titillation than a gut wrenching horror. But is this entirely true? Although we tend not to frame certain violent killings as 'sacrifice', there have been decades of reports and cases of ritualised satanic murders, brutal acts of savagery in conflict zones and odd cultic insantities, usually best left to hyperbolic television shows. Does this mean though, that there are no parts of the world where the practice is formalised? Are there traditions, inherited meanings and deep subterranean psychological impulses that continue to exist, out of the glare of the camera? The Wikipedia page for human sacrifice has a number of cases from all over the world, often linked to cults and specific individuals. But a few places jump out as struggling with sacrifice as a commonplace problem - Uganda and India, and it's to those I want to turn to explore what modern sacrifice looks like.

Child Sacrifice in Uganda

Africa in general has a huge problem with human, particularly child, sacrifice. The dominant motivation is to utilise body parts to create 'muti' or 'juju' medicines. Internal organs, heads and limbs are particularly prized by herbal practitioners, traditional healers, witch-doctors and grifters for the production of potions and remedies, as well as amulets, charms and rituals for good luck and fortune. A horribly typical scenario might involve a local businessman working with a politician to build a new hotel or restaurant, they would commission a child to be kidnapped and murdered so they could offer their body parts along with money for good luck in their commercial venture. A specific case the world is more familiar with is the hunting down and sacrifice of albinos, particularly in Tanzania. A 2013 report documented 106 reported incidents, 34 of them survived the attack, along with 15 grave robberies. A standard attack involves masked men breaking into a family home in the middle of the night and hacking off a child's limbs before running away into the dark. Sometimes the child might survive, often they do not. While Tanzania has the highest number of cases, the targeting of albinos occurs across Africa, from Mali to Zimbabwe, with body parts crossing many borders to get to the customer. Sometimes these killings are to order, other times the demand is high enough to make it worthwhile for the killers.

Outside of albino specific murders, some countries more than others have sunk to the point of an institutionalised problem of child sacrifice. Uganda has become notorious for the disappearance of children, many sacrificed ritually at secret shrines. A study in 2012 estimated that at a minimum, one child was being sacrificed every week in the country. One district especially, the Buikwe District, appears to have become synonymous with witchcraft and child murder. The Ugandan government has taken the almost unheard of step of forming the 'Anti-Child Sacrifice and Mutilation Committee', demonstrating exactly how serious the problem is. The committee runs a number of projects, including the 'Community Amber Alert Against Child Sacrifice' (CAAACS) project in Buikwe. This organised a series of community alerts and protocols for quickly raising the alarm in the district when a child goes missing. A multimedia approach, everything from text messages, radio stations and traditional drums are used to get people out of their houses and searching for the child, often with positive results. A further mind boggling project of the CAAAACS has been to target formal institutions like churches and schools and have them publically take the 'raise your hand campaign' pledge to never engage in child sacrifice or the products of child sacrifice. That such measures are considered at all shows the strength of traditional belief in sacrificial medicine. A quote from the report shows the necessity of teaching children at school what to do if and when they are kidnapped:

"The boy had this to say, "When they were performing their rituals, they took me to a large hut. They untied me thinking I was still unconscious due to chloroform. I quickly ran into a sugarcane plantation nearby as they followed me with spears…" Upon hearing the alert on megaphones, community members began to search for him. When the abductor heard the announcements, they fled. The boy was later discovered at around 12:40PM the next day. According to the boy, he was able to escape his abductors because of the community sensitisations they had had at school. At school, children were taught on what to do when caught up in such a critical situation."

Of course, not all children are so lucky and fortunate as to escape. Many disappear and are never found, sometimes buried alive on construction sites or in building foundations, while others come to a grisly end and their tormentors are never caught. Three rare survivors of an attempted sacrifice, Kanani Nankunda, George Mukisa and Allan Ssembatya, all young boys, testify to the brutality of the process. Two were castrated, somehow managing to survive the ordeal, one of them bears a huge scar across his neck where his assailants attempted to bleed him out. One regained consciousness next to the decapitated body of his sister. All three children are now looked after by the Kyampisi Childcare Ministry, the only dedicated organisation in Uganda which cares for child sacrifice survivors. Pastor Peter Sewakiryanga has dedicated his life to helping protect these children and to eradicate the phenomenon.

Sadly Uganda has been exporting this cultural practice out into the world. Since 2007 authorities in the UK have known of children smuggled into the country for the purpose of blood sacrifice. The BBC obtained the figure of 400 children in 2011, roughly equivalent to two children a week every year being brought into Britain. Sometimes they are killed, often they are bled to make bespoke potions or healing charms for customers. The network of contacts running from Kampala to London is well organised and capable of moving children quickly from Uganda on request.

India

Stepping up from Uganda, India might be the epicentre for human sacrifice in today's world. More specifically, the regions of northern India like Uttar Pradesh have a long history of human sacrifice. The modern apparatus of ritual killings here is obviously underground and illegal, but both the numbers of deaths and the shocking kinds of violence that are inflicted on victims makes it an institution of a sort. A quick list of some of the biggest cases in recent years highlights the scale of the problem:

A man in Odisha state beheaded his 12 year old sister to appease the Hindu goddess of war Durga

A man in Andhra Pradesh state kidnapped and beheaded a four year old boy in honour of the goddess Kali, seeking 'divine powers'

A group kidnapped and tortured to death a six year old boy in Maharashtra state. The boy had needles inserted into his eyes, a hole in his skull from a cordless drill and his throat slit.

A pregnant woman in Bihar conspired with a 'sorcerer' to have an eight year old girl killed, her blood and eyes made into an amulet to protect her unborn child

A woman in Uttar Pradesh kidnapped and mutilated a three year old boy, cutting off his nose, ears and hands during a protection ritual in which he bled to death

In Assam, two brothers sacrificed their children in order to receive divine guidance to buried treasure

A man in Madhya Pradesh beheaded his wife in front of his children in order to appease the gods

Cases like this abound in India, particularly in rural and poor parts of the country, where healthcare is non-existent and a long tradition of human sacrifice has persisted. India has only recently begun to take these deaths seriously, with the National Crime Records Bureau starting to record sacrificial deaths in 2014 (51 cases between 2014-16) and the creation of the 'Maharashtra Prevention and Eradication of Human Sacrifice and other Inhuman, Evil and Aghori Practices and Black Magic Act', in 2013. This bill specifically targets practitioners and con-men who make use of magical powers and encourage violence and degradation towards others. The bill outlaws such practices as:

"Assault, torture, forced ingestion of human excreta, forced sexual acts, branding etc. on the pretext of exorcising ghosts from an allegedly possessed person"

"Claiming to be related to a person from a previous incarnation and coaxing them to sexual acts, and claiming to have supernatural power to cure an impotent woman and having sexual relation with the woman"

A common denominator in these cases is the presence or encouragement of a 'holy man' or 'sorcerer'. Note in the bill's full title above the word 'Aghori'. The word refers to an esoteric and largely shunned religious practice, an offshoot of Shaivism, which looks to break the cycle of reincarnation by engaging in highly taboo and unorthodox acts. Aghoris seek out dead bodies, using human skulls to drink alcohol or burn cannabis. They may eat rotting flesh, faeces and drink urine, smear human ashes across their faces and meditate sitting on top of corpses. The relationship between Aghori and Tantra is complex, but many articles and interviews surrounding human sacrifice talk of a Tantrik or an Aghori Tantrik, who either performed or suggested that a person needed to be sacrificed. An article from the Irish Times discussed the Kamakhya temple in Assam, where monks, including Aghori Tantric priests, vowed to end the practice of human sacrifice. While the majority of Tantric priests have been publicly appalled at the murders which happen in their name, clearly a small minority are devoted to the older rituals and continue to suggest to the desperate and the unhinged that killing a child is their only option.

India has attempted to crack down on this phenomenon and the 2013 Bill has directly influenced a similar 2020 law in Uganda, titled 'The Prevention and Prohibition of Human Sacrifice Bill', which makes human sacrifice a capital or lifelong imprisonment offence. How effective either will be remains to be seen.

Final Thoughts

Researching this article was a journey into some very disturbing and unpleasant realities and many cases didn't make the final edit. It struck me that the act of killing a child in a ritual manner seems so barbaric to the modern mind, and yet has persisted in almost all cultures across all of human history. Something about the innocence and the uncorrupted nature of an infant or a child presents them as a worthy offering to whatever may control the fate of a people's life. Untarnished by the world, they seem more spiritually charged and at one with the deeper forces of the cosmos. The Aghori refer to the propensity for children to play in the dirt and in filth without shame, and see this innocence about society's rules as an enlightened state. Since children come into the world with less preconceptions and with less inhibitions about human behaviour and social norms, they are a target for any line of thought which sees society, civilisation, modernity as a force which disfigures that purity. Ideologies and religions of all stripes have viewed children as a plastic force, one which can be moulded into an ideal type. The fact that in parts of the world, the oldest type of sacrifice to an ideal future still continues should be a sobering reminder that human nature is not easily changed.

Based Eco-Militias & Green Violence

Armed Environmentalist Groups Around The World

We're all horribly familiar with militia groups, paramilitary and mercenary units and terrorist organisations committing violence in the name of some ideological or religious vision, but we are less familiar with similarly armed groups who fight in the service of an environmental cause. I've decided to call these groups 'based', since they largely fall outside of the traditional left-wing activist approach to ecological politics that dominates the Western world. To most people left-wing and environmentalism are one and the same, hand-in-glove, some call it a 'watermelon ideology'. This is a shame, because there is no inherent reason for eco-politics to belong to one camp or the other. It fits comfortably into right wing, indigenous, nationalist, internationalist, localist and technocratic approaches. I leave it up to the reader to decide whether my selections truly are based, or whether they are just outside of the mainstream conception of environmentalism. They are a mixture of radicals, government backed projects, organised political groups and tribes. I believe it's necessary to expand what we mean when we talk of green solutions - tracking and killing poachers or enforcing mining regulations with intimidation may be more effective than being left up to NGOs and corrupt politicians. I therefore invite you to enjoy this tour of the 'other' side of environmentalism, one which the mainstream media is unlikely to ever show or endorse.

"Eco-Fascism"

One of those monsters under the bed of modernity is the fear of fascism drawing strength from a primitivist strain of ecological thinking. Dubbed 'Eco-Fascism', there aren't really any examples of it influencing politics in a serious and sustained way. Much like its anarcho-primitivist mirror image, any adherents to eco-fascism are usually lone individuals or small friendship groups, and fail to gather any larger momentum. Despite this, the irrational terror of neo-Nazism in general across the western chattering class means that even the small organisations that do exist will be hysterically portrayed as something much larger and different than they really are.

Enter Tsagaan Khas, or 'white swastika'. If you type the name of this ostensibly Mongolian Nazi organisation into a search engine you find titillating articles such as "*A Mongolian Neo-Nazi Environmentalist Walks Into a Lingerie Store in Ulan Bator*" and "*Why Asia may not be immune to far-right terrorism*", the latter a laughable piece trying to link the appearance of Pepe the Frog in Hong-Kong to some shadowy global far-right takeover bid. Tsagaan Khas is just about the only direct connection one can make between European Neo-Nazism and Asia. They are a small group, likely numbering no more than a hundred members, set up in the 1990's by an eccentric man called Ariunbold Altankhuum. The media coverage of them looks amusingly staged, with swastikas everywhere, portraits and tattoos of Mongolian warriors and everyone in dark blue uniforms. Personally I think it looks like an excellent exercise in trolling a gullible media, but I could be wrong.

Their *modus operandi* appears to have switched from the standard 'boots on the street' approach to far-right organising, something not really seen in the West since the 1980's, to a focus on mining and environmental pollution. Aside from the exoticism of Mongolian Nazis, their main claim to fame is this switch towards an environmental and regulation enforcing stance. Again, this is seen in Western reporting solely through the lens of a spectre of eco-fascism, but even a basic level of journalistic curiosity would reveal that Mongolia has had decades of issues with mining companies. Since the collapse of the USSR, Mongolia has sought to use its mineral wealth as a means to attract foreign investment. The early 90's saw a literal gold rush for companies to exploit the sparsely populated landscape. The 1997 Mineral Law created a very weakly regulated environment and well over 60% of licences issued were for gold mining, alongside the tens of thousands of small scale artisanal miners. By 2001, nomadic pastoralists living around the Ongi River were severely threatened by drought and lack of water access for their animals as mining companies sucked up vast quantities of water in their search for gold. Later that year the Ongi River Movement was formed, led by Tsetsgeegiin Mönkhbayar, the chair of the local citizen's council, aiming to stop illegal mining practices and rampant pollution. Mönkhbayar was later arrested and sentenced for opening fire in a government compound, but he succeeded in forcing the State to take action against the companies. 36 out of 37 licences were revoked on the Ongi River and wider national river campaigns have been built. Notable in this struggle was the commitment by local rural people - not urbanites - who saw their environmental struggle, not as an abstraction, but as part of a concrete national reality. As nomads the grasslands are both life-giving and a core feature of their cosmological universe, part of what makes Mongolia unique. Therefore it differed from many contemporary eco movements in that it aroused nationalist and patriotic sentiment. Also notable was the role the movement played in directly confronting and challenging the mining companies in lieu of weak government oversight. From this unique blend of nationalist, direct action environmentalism, Tsagaan Khas draws its inspiration.

Aside from claims that Tsagaan Khas has attacked Chinese migrants and shaved the heads of Mongolian women accused of sleeping with Chinese men, the group has a reputation for visiting the areas of mining operations and demanding to see legal papers and checking that they comply with legislation. While they claim to be non-violent in their methods, they are affiliated with a number of smaller eco-nationalist groups which have begun to ramp up the use of violence over the issue of illegal mining. In 2013 a demonstration in Ulaanbaatar saw members of Gal Undesten (Fire Nation) plant bombs and bring hand grenades and firearms to show their seriousness (this was the demonstration where Tsetsgeegiin Mönkhbayar was arrested). The group, and similar nationalist groups, have been labelled 'eco-terrorists' and various members prosecuted for attacking LGBT people, including for kidnapping a trans woman in 2019 and releasing a video to the media describing gay people as paedophiles. In the bigger picture it looks like Mongolia is really at the beginning of a series of profound social changes, both relating to how its economy was structured in the post Soviet era and how it will relate to China in the coming decades. A rural, right-wing or nationalist movement, which seeks to place Mongolia and its natural resources first, might be best placed to provide a counterweight to the usual globalist suspects.

Anarcho-Primitivist

If eco-fascism is the romantic, deep ecology answer to the right, then anarcho-primitivism is the natural end point to the left. Or at least a particular kind of left. Anarcho-primitivism has never fit into the mainstream left or even any 'orthodox' anarchist current, despite being a major influence on the intellectual trajectory of anarchism since at least the 1990's. A full discussion of the history and tributaries of the movement would demand another article, but the bare bones of the ideology are: civilisation and agriculture are synonymous, both are destroying the biosphere and alienating humans from their evolutionary telos, the solution is to return humans and the planet to a state of wild nature, where humans live as hunter-gatherers. Despite the mammoth task that primitivists set for themselves, they have managed to make themselves felt in the wider culture through a number of political strategies - animal rights advocacy and liberation, tree spiking and anti-road protests, attacking fur farms, industrial animal agriculture and the 90's moment of 'ecoterrorism' or 'green terrorism'. The latter was mostly the result of a number of groups - Earth First! and the Earth Liberation Front, conducting arson attacks on industrial developments, like ski resorts. While these were clamped down on by the FBI in some dubious 'counter-terrorism' operations, the impulse from primitivists to attack 'civilisation' has never gone away.

In 2008 a group of anarchists were arrested in France for sabotaging high speed railway lines. They became known as the 'Tarnac 9' and were widely suspected of being part of the anonymous collective 'The Invisible Committee', responsible for writing the left wing hit, *The Coming Insurrection* in 2007. The book is a call to arms for a certain kind of disaffected youth, one who is alienated from all traditional politics, especially the left wing and union movements. Around this time a number of violent primitivist and insurrectionary anarchist organisations began targeting scientists and engineers working in biotechnology and nuclear power, along with more general arson and political violence. In 2013 in Greece, the group called 'The Conspiracy of the Cells of Fire' planted a bomb underneath the car of prison director Maria Stefi, destroying the vehicle. The same group claimed responsibility for placing homemade explosives in shopping malls, at the houses of politicians, for a drive-by shooting at the office of the Prime Minister and for launching several RPG attacks on the US Embassy and the offices of far right parties. In 2012 alone there were 527 arson and bomb attacks in Greece, most pinned to anarchist organisations. In Italy the

Informal Anarchist Federation kneecapped Roberto Adinolfi, a CEO of a nuclear power company, and sent bombs to embassies, banks and power plant owners. Across the world a similar militant style of informal primitivist/insurrectionist anarchist cells have burnt down police firearm centres (UK), bombed nanotechnology workers (Mexico), used dynamite on military barracks (Bolivia) and travelled to Syria to join the Kurdish defence forces fighting Islamic State.

Much of this seems far away from any environmental concern, and on one level this is true. There is little gain for biodiversity when an embassy is hit with a rocket propelled grenade. But the underlying ideology of this strain of anarchism places itself against *the totality of modern life,* and therefore sees practically every manifestation of civilisation as a legitimate target. Pragmatically of course there has always been a consensus that shooting local business owners or burning family cars is a poor tactic - much better to aim for symbolic and practical targets. This is why high speed rail, nuclear power, police facilities, car dealerships, banks, political figures, military installations and STEM research centres are often the sorts of target, rather than everyday people. However, this consensus broke down when one of the strangest and most unclassifiable groups emerged in 2011 in Mexico - *Individualistas Tendiendo a lo Salvaje,* often translated as 'Individuals Tending to the Wild' or 'Individuals Tending towards Savagery' (ITS). ITS is an unusual phenomenon - a primitivist cell which glorifies the pre-Columbian Aztec mythology and way of life, while taking inspiration from European anarchist violence and communicating primarily with the North American 'green anarchist' scene. Their initial activities were focused on sending bombs to individual researchers at various universities and research centres, the majority causing substantial non-fatal injuries. In 2012 Ted Kaczynski himself wrote a scathing communique and condemned the group's actions. In 2014 ITS announced a new phase in their project and appeared to be promoting a totally nihilistic philosophy. They claimed responsibility for several unprovoked murders, of young women, of backpackers in the woods, pushing a form of 'eco-extremism' (their terminology). Their rambling statements took on a new and unhinged inflection, identifying themselves with the doomed and savage warriors who fought the Spanish after the fall of the Aztec Empire:

"For one can firmly state that the Mixton War (1540-1541), the Chichimeca War (1550-1600), and the Guamares Rebellion (1563-1568) were all authentic wars against civilization, technology, and progress. The savage Chichimecas did not want a new or better government. They neither wanted nor defended the cities or centres of the defeated Mesoamerican civilizations. They did not seek victory. They only desired to attack those who attacked and threatened them. They sought confrontation, and from there comes their battle cry: "Axkan kema, tehualt, nehuatl!" (Until your death, or mine)."

The group launched online attack after attack, announcing that anarchists were "fucking faggots", praising ISIS and declaring that "every human being deserves extinction". A large number of anarchist and primitivist groups worldwide condemned ITS and distanced themselves, but a single journal, 'Atassa', and a handful of North American anarchists decided to keep publishing their communiques and disseminating 'eco-extremist' ideas. The publisher 'Little Black Cart' became briefly infamous for allowing ITS to praise indiscriminate murder, rape, homophobia and fascism. From this point on ITS began taking responsibility for a wide number of random actions, almost none of which originated with them. Bombs, arson attacks, shootings, vandalism and other acts, claimed by ITS, but police in many countries declared as unrelated acts. ITS are on no terrorist watch list, despite claiming violence in Scotland, Chile, Brazil and Mexico. Within primitivist circles a furious debate opened up, arguing over interpretations of anthropology (did rape exist before the State?), how much and what kind of violence is justified in resisting civilisation and why do so many primitivists end up sounding like fascists? These are questions which are still playing out today in obscure corners of the internet.

State Rangers & Tribal Militias

The final group I want to turn to is a broad selection of players - tribal and ethnic groups in South America and anti-poaching Rangers in Central and Southern Africa. Their goals are broadly to prevent, halt and defend against some outside force, including extractive industries, poachers and governments.

The first of these are the Amazonian tribal militias which have appeared in recent years, primarily to prevent illegal logging, an activity which has devastated the rainforest. In 2012 a group called 'the Guardians' formed in the NE state of Maranhão in Brazil, made up from the Guajajara tribe. Several more Guardian groups have been founded nearby, including one by the Ka'apor tribe. Their objective has been to make life difficult for illegal loggers by enforcing the law. Armed with shotguns, bows and arrows, machetes and using drone imagery and traditional tracking methods, they follow loggers into the forest and physically detain them. They often deliver these bound and cuffed men to the nearest police stations, after torching their lumber and vehicles. Other tactics include creating checkpoints on dirt roads to enforce only licensed logging. Their activity has massively reduced logging in their regions - nearly 130 trucks a day were leaving the state, packed with trees. Now less than 15 make it out. Despite these successes, the groups are in running battles with the loggers, who aren't afraid to use lethal force to shut down the Guardians. In a similar vein, but more forcefully, are the actions of the Chilean Mapuche terrorist group 'Coordinadora Arauco-Malleco' (CAM). CAM grew out of the indigenist movement in the 90's, a blend of Mapuche nationalism and left wing politics and have claimed responsibility for attacks on forestry operations, mining companies and even fish farms.

A second group of national 'defenders' are the anti-poaching militias and rangers, focused around central and southern Africa. Some of these work for national governments, others actually work on behalf of large NGOS. In the latter category is a fairly secretive operation run primarily by the World Wildlife Fund (WWF), who have positioned themselves as the protectors of the Central African rainforests. WWF works with a number of logging companies, such as the French giant Rougier, who have licences to fell across millions of hectares of forest in Cameroon and the DRC. WWF have been accused of arming and allowing 'anti-poaching' militias to attack the Pygmy tribes who live in the forests of Central Africa. The charity Survival has documented extensively the violence against the Baka Pygmies. Who exactly constitutes these 'anti-poaching' groups is hard to say, but they seem to be tasked with making life in the forest almost impossible for the Baka, thus creating a 'human free zone' which the WWF can manage as part of its portfolio of 'sustainable stewardship'.

Away from the WWF we have state backed armed groups who are tasked with apprehending, disrupting and, if needs be, shooting poachers who target rhinos and elephants, among other species. Between 2010 and 2012, around 100,000 elephants were killed across the African continent, sparking worldwide concern about the survival of the species. In 2013 around 25 forest elephants were slaughtered by a Sudanese gang with AK-47s. They had travelled to the Central African Republic (CAR), in part because its a lawless zone for poaching. Today the CAR is a bloody ethnic mess, but elephants are protected by trained rangers who are authorised to shoot poachers. The CAR isn't alone here, there's been an explosion of ex-military companies providing training and resources for

African ranger units, so much so that academics shout about 'Green Militarisation'. As a recent Atlantic article complains:

"Meanwhile, Joaquim Chissano, the former president of Mozambique, alleges that 476 Mozambican poachers were killed by South African rangers between 2010 and 2015. South African authorities are cagey about releasing official figures, but research on organized crime estimates that between 150 and 200 poachers were killed in the Kruger National Park alone during the same period. In neighboring Botswana, anti-poaching action has reportedly resulted in dozens of deaths, and the country's controversial "shoot to kill" policy—which gives rangers powers to shoot poachers dead on sight —has drawn allegations of abuse."

Personally I won't lose any sleep over the deaths of poachers, driving the last rhinos, lions and elephants to extinction. But it does highlight the shift in attitudes of world governments, members of whom not 100 years ago would have been happily travelling to shoot elephants themselves. Now we have British soldiers training Malawian rangers and American veterans teaching tracking to Indonesian police. The escalating violence and death count also shows the willingness to engage in lethal force over issues of conservation, something unthinkable until recently. The burnout rate of these rangers is very high, living in primitive conditions, away from home for months on end. The violence towards the animals they protect takes its toll, with horrific stories of rangers finding still-living rhinos with their faces hacked off. For now the trend toward militarisation is increasing, with drones, armed helicopters and special forces being deployed to protect the vulnerable animals in such enormous national parks. Time will tell whether the money will continue to flow to support these activities.

Conclusions

There were other groups I wanted to discuss here, particularly the heavily armed militias of the Niger Delta, but to do justice to the complexity and number of actors would have required this article to go to ridiculous lengths. As it stands I hope this gives a flavour of the spectrum and activities of different armed groups around the world who fight for some form of environmentalist cause - be it the eco extremism of ITS, the anti-mining activity of Mongolian Nazis, the Amazonian anti-logging tribes or the state backed drone operators in Kruger National Park - the use of violence is widespread and global. This should really be a challenge to our neat conception of ecology as solely a professionalised left-wing NGO topic. Ecological problems affect every community in every country and often involve exploitation by powerful actors. There is no reason for ecology and environmental politics to be limited to the left or to forms of 'ethical consumption'. I leave it up to you, dear reader, to think about whether these methods are acceptable and what other forms of ecological politics are possible in the future.

The Forest People

Life and Death under the Green Revolution

One of the oldest myths impressed into the minds of modern people is the image of the wild, virgin forest. The twisted, gnarled and dense trees, complete with ancient ferns, silent deer and patches of sunlight through gaps in the canopy.

In this vision there are no people, and this is a striking feature of what we mean by 'wilderness'. We have decided that humans are no longer a natural part of the wild world. Unfortunately, these ideas have real world consequences for those remaining people who do call rainforests and woodlands their homes. Approximately 1,000 indigenous and tribal cultures live in forests around the world, a population close to 50 million people, including the Desana of Colombia, the Kuku-Yalanji of Australia and the Pygmy peoples of Central Africa and the Congo. This is a story about those people of the Congolese forests, about how their unique way of life is threatened by the very people who should be defending them and how rainforests actually thrive when humans adapt to a different way of life.

The Democratic Republic of Congo has to be amongst modernity's greatest tragedies. Almost no-one knows that the 'Great African War', fought between 1998 and 2003, saw 5.4 million deaths and 2 million more people displaced. Very few can grasp the bewildering complexity of armed groups, of the ethnic and political relationships between the Congo and Rwanda or the sheer scale of the conflict, which at its height saw 1000 civilians dying every day. And yet this is also a country of staggering beauty, a sanctuary to the greatest levels of species diversity in Africa. It is home to the mountain gorilla, the bonobo, the white rhino, the forest elephant and the okapi. Roughly 60% of the country is forested, much of it under threat by logging and subsistence farming expansions.

The Congolese Pygmy peoples have been living here since the Middle Stone Age, heirs to a way of life over 100,000 years old. A note here on naming – the term Pygmy is considered by some to be offensive and the different people grouped under the title prefer to call themselves by their ethnic identities. These include the Aka, the Baka, the Twa and the Mbuti. The Congolese Pygmy people are grouped under the Mbuti – the Asua, the Efe and the Sua. In general these all refer to Central African Foragers who have inherited physical adaptations to life in the rainforest, including shortened height and stature.

The Mbuti people are hunters, trappers and foragers, using nets and bows to drive and catch forest animals. They harvest hundreds of kinds of plants, barks, fruits and roots and are especially obsessed with climbing trees to source wild honey, paying no heed to the stings of the bees. In many ways theirs is an idyllic antediluvian image of carefree hunter-gatherers, expending only what energy they need to find food and make shelters, preferring to spend their lives dancing, laughing and perfecting their ancient polyphonic musical tradition. Of course, this is an edenic view and the reality of their lives is much more complex and far more tragic, but it is worth highlighting the key environmental role they play as stewards and denizens of the forests. The Mbuti have been in the Congolese forests for tens of millennia, living within the carrying capacity of the land and developing sophisticated systems of ecological knowledge, based on their intimate familiarity with the rhythms and changes of the wildlife and the plants. Despite other groups of hunter-gatherers eating their way through large herds of megafauna, the Mbuti can live alongside elephants, rhinos and okapi without destroying their numbers.

In spite of this, the Mbuti and other Pygmy peoples have been attacked and evicted from their forests for decades. In the 1980's, the government of Congo sold huge areas of the Kahuzi Biega forest to logging and mining companies, forcibly removing the Batwa people and plunging them into poverty. To this day, many of their descendents live in roadside shanties, refused assistance from the State, denied healthcare and even the right to work. Many have since fled back to the forests. Alongside the mining and logging companies, conservation charities have been targeting the Baka peoples for evictions.

In particular the World Wildlife Fund (WWF) has been lobbying to convert the Messok Dja, a particularly biodiverse area of rainforest in the Republic of Congo, into a National Park, devoid of human presence. This aggressive act of clearance is rooted in the idea that a 'wilderness' area should not contain any people, thus rendering the original inhabitants of the forests as intruders, invaders and despoilers of 'Nature'. The charity Survival – an organisation dedicated to indigenous and tribal rights – has been campaigning for WWF to stop their activities. In particular Survival has successfully documented numerous abuses committed by the Park Rangers, whose activities are funded by WWF and others:

> "notwithstanding the fact that Messok Dja is not even officially a national park yet, the rangers have sown terror among the Baka in the region. Rangers have stolen the Baka's possessions, burnt their camps and clothes and even hit and tortured them. If Baka are found hunting small animals to feed their families they are arrested and beaten"

Outside of the forest, the Baka and other Pygmy peoples face widespread hostility and discrimination from the majority Bantu population. Many are enslaved, sometimes for generations, and are viewed as pets or forest animals. The situation is no better within the Democratic Republic of Congo (DRC), where the endless cycles of violence have seen the most shocking abuses against the Mbuti populations. Even in the most peaceful areas, park rangers regularly harass and abuse Mbuti hunters and villagers, illegally cutting down trees for charcoal or shooting animals for meat. In some places the Batwa people have formed militias, often armed with little more than axes and arrows, to defend themselves against slaving raids by the neighbouring Luba people.

The worst events for the Mbuti people in recent years began during the Rwandan genocide, where the Hutu Interahamwe paramilitaries murdered over 10,000 Pygmies and drove a further 10,000 out of the country, many of whom fled into the forests of the DRC. Later, between 2002 and 2003, a systematic campaign of extermination was waged against the Bambutis of the North Kivu province of DRC.

The Movement for the Liberation of Congo embarked on a mission, dubbed *Effacer le tableau* – 'cleaning the slate', which saw them kill over 60,000 Pygmies. In part this was motivated by the belief that the Bambuti are subhumans, whose flesh possesses magical powers to cure AIDS and other diseases. Many of the victims were also killed, traded and eaten as bushmeat. Cannibalism against the Pygmy peoples has been reported throughout the Congolese Civil Wars, with almost all sides engaging in the act.

Unsurprisingly under these pressures, the Mbuti and other groups have been displaced, broken up and scattered throughout Central Africa. In part this has always been the intention of these campaigns, for the Congo region is not an isolated backwater of the modern world, but an integral part of the material economy of advanced modernity. In particular Central Africa has been cursed with an abundance of precious and important metals and minerals, including:

tin, copper, gold, tantalum, diamonds, lithium and, crucially, over 70% of the world's cobalt. The intensive push for electric vehicles (EVs) by the EU and the USA has seen prices for battery components skyrocket. Cobalt in particular reached $100,000 per tonne in 2018. Tantalum is also heavily prized, as a crucial element for nearly all advanced electronics and is found in a natural ore called coltan.

Coltan has become synonymous with slavery, child labour, dangerous mining conditions and violence. Almost every actor in the endless conflicts in DRC have been involved in illegally mining and smuggling coltan onto the world market, including the Rwandan Army, who set up a shell company to process the ore obtained across the border. Miners, far from food sources, turn to bushmeat, especially large primates like gorillas. An estimated 3-5 million tonnes of bushmeat is harvested every year in DRC, underlining the central role that modern electronic consumption has on the most fragile ecosystems. In this toxic mix of violent warlordism, mineral extraction, logging, bushmeat hunting and genocide, the Mbuti people have struggled to maintain their way of life. Their women and children end up pounding lumps of ore, breathing in metal dusts, they end up as prostitutes and slaves, surviving on the margins of an already desperate society.

In Mbuti mythology, their pantheon of gods are directly woven into the life of the rainforest. The god *Tore* is the Master of Animals and supplies them for the people. He hides in rainbows or storms and sometimes appears as a leopard to young men undergoing initiation rites deep in the trees. The god of the hunt is *Khonvoum*, who wields a bow made of two snakes and ensures the sun rises every morning. Other animals appear as messengers, such as the chameleon or the dwarf who disguises himself as a reptile. These are the cultural beliefs of a people who became human in the rainforest, adapted down to the bone to its tempos and seasons. They are a part of the ecosystem, as much as the gorilla or the forest hog. Their taboos recognise the evil of hunting in an animal's birthing grounds, or the importance of never placing traps near fresh water.

Breaking these results in a metaphysical ostracism known as *'muzombo'*, a kind of spiritual death and sometimes accompanied by physical exile from the village. As far as their voice has counted for anything under the deluge of horror that modernity has unleashed upon them, they want to be left alone, to hunt and fish in their forests, to live close to their ancestors and to raise their children in peace and safety.

The expansion of the 'Green New Deal' and the rise of 'renewable' industrial technologies may be the death knell for these archaic and peaceful people. Make no mistake, these green initiatives – electric vehicles, wind turbines, solar batteries – are actively destroying the last remaining strongholds of biodiversity on the planet. The future designs on the DRC include vast hydroelectric dams and intensive agriculture, stripping away the final refuges of the world. Now, more than ever, the Mbuti and other Pygmy peoples need our solidarity, an act which can be as simple as not buying that next iPhone

Archetypes Of Power: Anarcho-Fascism, Monarchism & Primitivism

As a change of pace from my usual writing I thought I'd spread my intellectual wings and engage with a little niche political thought. Anarchism is one of those fringe adolescent movements which maintains itself on rebellious energy but does have some history of serious writing and theory. Like all fringe movements it has splintered into numerous, and quite dull, subsects: syndicalism, green, communism and so on, each trying to stick the appendage 'anarcho' onto something more outlandish. You might ask then why I'd be interested in three utterly insane sounding ideologies, two of which sound oxymoronic. I think all three represent some deep archetypes about 'organicism' - the interest in how societies and organisations develop naturally, rather than through imposed ideological blinkers. This to me represents a subterranean question or fault-line running through our political life, is it possible to rationally or ethically 'create' or 'design' a society from scratch? The fundamental conservative Burkean insight is that human life must move from where it currently sits, with all its own histories, baggage, prejudices, assumptions, mores, cultures and tendencies. For the reactionary there is no Ground Zero of history, only zealots attempting to level and destroy. Personally I am ambivalent on whether this form of conservatism is always to be followed, so I offer these three positions on political violence as topics of reflection - reform, creation and destruction.

Notes On Anarchism

There are two approaches one could take when considering the history of anarchism. The first is the 'official' history of the anarchist labour movement in the 19th century, that mixing of liberal and socialist thought, with a healthy dollop of romanticism. The second is the more diffuse and deeply historical look at what we could call the 'anarchist tendency', that instinct to rebel, to be sovereign, to create life outside the walls of the city. For me this is the more interesting of the two by far. I see anarchism from this perspective as the youthful, violent, impulsive need to be away from authority, from parents and priests, to let Life ascend and to not only 'be' free, but to create it and forcefully take that freedom if necessary. Here I depart from any traditional left-wing understanding of the term. I include pirates, war-bands, adventurers, explorers, the Indo-European *koryos*, Junger, Nietzsche, Polynesian island hunters, prophets, cattle-raiders and nomadic steppe tribes in my vision of what anarchism means, spiritually understood.

Scholars of anarchist history, who tend to be activists themselves, have an irritating habit of looking back into history and drag-netting everything which they see as having any spirit of independence and liberty, claiming it as some 'prehistory of anarchism'. This is intellectually sluggish and turns all of human history into a linear approach to the apex of 19th century thought, when the Word could finally break through and an independent and self-aware 'anarchism as ideology' crown itself as the inheritor of all human freedoms. In this way Taoism, Socrates, the Khirijites and the Anabaptists were all just signposts on the road to modern sociology departments. My argument with these modern scholars is that the impulse of anarchism, to be without a ruler, is too rigid and modern an understanding of power. I think it is possible to see the desire to throw off a particular type of ruler or regime as only part of the concept, and that what could fill the void could certainly involve a hierarchy and authority, but of a kind or degree. With this qualification in place I think we can turn to the first of the three 'organic impulses'.

Anarcho-Monarchism: 'with the King and the True Commons'

> My political opinions lean more and more to Anarchy (philosophically understood, meaning the abolition of control not whiskered men with bombs)—or to 'unconstitutional' Monarchy. I would arrest anybody who uses the word State (in any sense other than the inanimate real of England and its inhabitants, a thing that has neither power, rights nor mind); and after a chance of recantation, execute them if they remained obstinate! If we could go back to personal names, it would do a lot of good. Government is an abstract noun meaning the art and process of governing and it should be an offence to write it with a capital G or so to refer to people.

This quotation from J.R.R Tolkien, taken from a 1943 letter to his son, is one of the only written examples of anything that could resemble anarcho-monarchism. Tolkien's instinctively English love for both Saxon liberty and the organic, dishevelled institution of constitutional monarchy is the crossover point in the seemingly contradictory venn diagram of anarchism and monarchism. Clearly on first reading the two seem polar opposites - how could a philosophy which rejects hierarchy be compatible with belief in a divinely chosen sovereign? In Bronze Age Pervert's essay, *The Biology of Kingship,* published in Asylum Magazine, he posits the 'monarchical instinct' in man, building on Schopenhauer's description of monarchy as a natural force. This instinct is built around the physical body of the king, in his blood and descendants, originating in his power as a warrior and ruler of his war-band. He argues that any belief in the divine institution of monarchy, of the king as anointed by God, is a secondary development and justification. The primary claim to kingly rule is the organic majesty of the warrior.

> Monarchy thus appears as political manifestation of the principle of blood or heredity or breeding, as these are the only ways known to mortal humans to cultivate and transmit quality across generations. The continuity of monarchy rests on the presence of a culture of biological breeding, even if this should be limited only to the warband and its lineages, meaning to the nobility. The king exists as king—and not, for example

as a cloistered figurehead—only so long as he remains "the most noble of the nobles," the head of his warband. It is this type of ruler especially who is able to be the target of the people's passions, to "trigger" the monarchical instinct in the people, who are able to respond to his remote powers and spontaneously organize themselves in orbit around him. **It could be added also that it is only through the king and his retinue that a nation in the proper sense exists as a political as well as organic unity**. Outside of this there are only agglomerations of individuals vying for supremacy, but no political or hive order.

That monarchy is an organic instinct, which binds the political community together, is a good place to start for understanding how it relates to anarchism. In keeping with my earlier description of anarchism as not merely the rejection of authority - but the rejection of a *certain kind of authority* - I believe Tolkien's magnetic attraction to both philosophies makes sense. The organic contract between the king and his people embodies a form of order whereby the two are bound together through mutual obligations and inheritances. To my mind there is no greater example of this than the so-called Peasants' Revolt of 1381.

The open rebellion of the English Commons in the 14th century seems a strange place to find evidence for the organic contract between sovereign and ruled, but too often people misunderstand exactly what the aims and grievances of the rebellion were. The yoke of serfdom, imposed from 1066 onward, had largely come to an end by the 1370's. In its place was a complex and typically mediaeval mixture of loyalty, obligations, dues, laws and customs. The historian Dan Jones, in his book *Summer of Blood*, describes the situation thus:

> Yet despite the occasional irritations, and the intrusions of life's grimmer realities, the various strata of English society had lived in relatively peaceful coexistence since at least the days of the Conquest. Medieval life was acutely hierarchical, with a sense of place in the world inseparable from ideas of Christian duty and the belief in a divinely ordained order of the universe. Charity and paternalism on the lords' side was largely reciprocated by deference and respect for authority on their tenants'. Villages could not be policed in the sense that we would understand it now, and a sensitive lord understood that he had to work his estate management and local government through the existing village hierarchies. More senior men in the village were needed to perform administrative tasks for the lord, and to broker potentially unpopular lordly demands with the lesser men of their communities.

The ravages of the Black Death and the subsequent attempts by Parliament to introduce wage caps to maintain social order ripped into this social fabric. New taxations and demands for money began to be aggressively imposed, a situation which essentially broke the social contract between King and Commons. When the villages began to assert their ancient rights and resist these impositions, tensions reached boiling point and exploded in an orgy of violence. Intriguingly the Anglo belief in their ancient liberties was evident even then, as over 100 villages applied for a copy of the Domesday Book in order to apply for tax exemption, on the basis that many were granted freedom nearly 300 years ago from "lordly claims on their labour and wealth". When the rebellion began in earnest, the target of their fury was not the king himself, but rather his advisers and the entire class of lawyers and administrators:

> Even among the chaos and rioting, then, a clear statement of ideology was emerging. The rebels fixated on the cult of kingship, but despised all those dripping poison into the king's ear and spreading rot through the timber of government by their self-serving use of royal positions and power. And they saw themselves as the voices of true moral justice, on a mission to restore the natural order of things to the realm. They were the true commons indeed.

As the barricades went up, the watchword across England was simple and clear:

The rebels' watchword, 'With whom holds you?'-answerable by 'With King Richard and the true commons'-was in their minds a clear badge of loyalty.

There is no need here to describe all the events of the Rebellion, but it is evident from an objective reading of the history that the rebels meant in the first instance to *restore* the correct organic relationship between themselves and the king, not destroy it. They were the true commons, not Parliament, and it was only after they were stymied by an inexperienced young king and his inept advisers that the situation turned dangerous for the monarch.

This I suggest is the archetypal vision of anarcho-monarchism, a philosophy which seeks to maintain the ordered and hierarchical system of relations between king and commons. Far from the simple revisionism that the peasantry had always wanted to be free from authority, what they craved was the right and true form of authority, the one which protected them and upheld its duties and responsibilities. I submit that this is the monarchical instinct. People will gravitate towards the figure of the king who in turn will provide order and justice.

Anarcho-Fascism: Donovan & the Koryos

Fascism is probably the most misunderstood political theory in a crowded market. The historian and paleoconservative Paul Gottfried, in his book *Fascism: The Career of a Concept*, goes to great lengths to divorce fascism and Nazism in his reader's mind. That the two have become conflated, he argues, is the result of decades of political propaganda and sloppy thinking. 'Generic fascism' looks something like Italian fascism, a distinctly Latin phenomenon which drew far more from the philosophy of the left than people care to admit. Gottfried argues that fascism is a right wing collectivist movement which arose in response to the domination of the Communist left. Many will take issue with this description and fascism will always remain a contested theory, but what is clear is that anarchism should equally be divorced from its total association with the left. Strains of right wing anarchism have existed, and traditions which energise it go back millennia.

The right wing writer Jack Donovan exhorts in a short article for Counter-Currents magazine:

> With no more frontiers to explore, save space–which can only be allowed, even in fantasy, as a neutered bureaucratic project–the modern, effeminate, bourgeois "First World" states can no longer produce new honor cultures. New, pure warrior-gangs can only rise in anarchic opposition to the corrupt, feminist, anti-tribal, degraded institutions of the established order. Manhood can only be rebooted by the destruction of their future, and the creation of new futures for new or reborn tribes of men. It is too late for conservatism. For the majority of men, only occupied structures and empty gestures remain.

The way of men can only be rediscovered in Night and Chaos.

Ur-fascism is the source of honor culture and authentic patriarchal tradition.

Ur-fascism is a response to anarchy.

The political position of *The Way of Men* is "anarcho-fascist."

This anarcho-fascism is not an end; it is hungry for a new beginning.

In Donovan's reading, anarcho-fascism is the condition of total war and chaos, out of which comes the war-band of warrior men, their vitality and violence being the necessary precursor for any form of later order. What we have here then is not a political programme or conception of the Good, but rather the set of preconditions which leads to something else. The anarcho of anarcho-fascism for Donovan is the swirling disorder which provides the raw material for the correct kind of man to rise up. Whether he believes that this Hobbesian war is part of a cycle of collapse or whether we should be pushing for it is beside the point, the man of power is born in conditions of anarchy, wherein he can engage in the fascistic struggle for himself and his own.

A traditional source of inspiration for right-wing thinkers is the Indo-European tradition of the youthful warrior band, the *koryos,* the

Männerbund. Common to many Indo-European cultures and literature is the presence of a group of young men who achieve manhood by leaving their homes in order to raid, steal cattle and women and prove themselves men through deed and valour:

> The Greeks in later times did not think that out-of-control warriors had a place in the phalanx formation. Individual, berserk-acting warriors do not make good soldiers and are, consequently, obscured in the written sources during classical times… The evidence gravitates around two interconnected points, the terrifying aspect of the warriors and the use of animal skins. These points find parallels among other IE young warriors. For instance, the Germanic Harii, whose name is etymologically built on the IE root *koryos,* were, according to Kershaw, contingents of young men more than a separate tribe. Tacitus mentions in section 43 of the Germania that "their shields are black, their bodies dyed. They choose dark nights for battle and strike terror by the horror and gloomy appearance of their death-like army. No enemy can bear their strange and almost infernal aspect"

In a similar way to Donovan's conviction that a state of anarchism allows for the flourishing of the primal male instincts, the history of the *koryos* suggests that its unpredictable and wild nature was at odds with the later development of professional warfare. Only in those spaces where the State does not control can such a warband flourish, it is antithetical to any form of external governance, hence the *koryos* being expelled from the lands of their people. But what exactly is fascistic about this?

The academic Daniel Woodley sees fascism as promoting an ethic of violence for its own sake. In his work *Fascism and Political Theory* he writes:

> Fascism is distinguished from liberalism by the aestheticization of struggle and the glorification of paramilitary violence as primary features of political action. Whereas liberals seek to isolate or minimize the disruptive impact of violence – seeing war as the distinctive activity of military specialists – for fascists 'creative violence' is contrasted with the insipid cowardice of liberal intellectualism: violence is not just a means to an end, but an intrinsic value in itself.

Some have argued that fascism inherited this value from the Victorian theory of Social Darwinism, but this feels like weak sauce. The celebration of violence as a critical means for a man to prove himself is ancient, and collective violence organised by a tribe or a state has rarely been seen as a wholly negative attribute throughout human history. Wars and conflicts are the testing ground, the real physical way to ensure one can achieve a goal outside of words and the worship of logocentrism. In this way anarcho-fascism is a condition of war where the celebration of violence can be at its zenith. As Cormac McCarthy's Judge famously declares:

> "It makes no difference what men think of war," said the judge. "War endures. As well ask men what they think of stone. War was always here. Before man was, war waited for him. The ultimate trade awaiting its ultimate practitioner. That is the way it was and will be. That way and not some other way… war is the truest form of divination. It is the testing of one's will and the will of another within that larger will which because it binds them is therefore forced to select. War is the ultimate game because war is at last a forcing of the unity of existence. War is god."

This is the second archetype of our list of three, the man who thrives in the absence of external authority, who gives himself over to his comrades and the greater cosmic authority of war and violence. War alone in this way is the ultimate sovereign and the warrior who becomes stronger through this test can impose his will upon others. If left wing egalitarian anarchism is the struggle to liberate all, then anarcho-fascism is the struggle of a select few to impose their will upon the herd-like many.

Anarcho-Primitivism:

> Personally, I am pleased that these anarchists are blowing up fire extinguishers, burning buses, and

giving themselves over to violent action. Their devotion to these works is very respectable (as in the case of anyone carrying out violence). So let's see if those with big mouths start putting their money where their mouth is, stop writing their entries on their blogs and start making devices... faggots. I am only stating this for the sake of the war so that it's not extinguished, so that the anarchos of the future will see that they just didn't devote themselves to talking shit... But for now the Mafia will not take one step back, and neither will the politically-incorrect propagandists. Let the war against civilization and the modern human continue in the South and North!

Atassa Vol 2 - Readings in Eco-Extremism

Anarcho-primitivism is probably the most coherent and popular of the three strands of thought in this essay - barely coherent by any other measure. Simply put, it seeks to eradicate civilisation and return humans, and the rest of the world, to a wild or savage state. Primitivists argue that civilisation is a form of human domestication, brought about through the twin forces of agriculture and the State. Humans once existed in a free condition, and this ended when we committed ourselves to the bondage of the field and taxman. Although this seems an extreme take, it is merely the next step after identifying agriculture as a sort of cosmic mistake, a wrong turn in our potential future, and this is not far away from being a mainstream opinion. Popular writers like Jared Diamond, James C Scott and Yuval Noah Harari have described agriculture as the worst blunder in the history of the human species, citing health, disease, labour, freedom, inequality and warfare as the consequences of adopting farming. I'm not unsympathetic to this argument myself, but the notes sounded here are all too familiar - what anarcho-primitivists argue is that *domination itself* as a form of human relation was essentially created alongside agriculture. Prior to this, reading from simplistic anthropological views of the San Bushmen and the Mbuti Pygmies, humans were egalitarian, free from gendered divisions of labour, peaceful, cooperative and ecologically minded. If this sounds fanciful, it's because it truly is.

However, it would be a mistake to think that primitivism stops here in its assault on civilisation. The author John Zerzan takes the root cause of human alienation with the natural world back to symbolic thought itself:

> Culture is a fairly recent affair. The oldest cave art, for example, is in the neighborhood of 30,000 years old, and agriculture only got underway about 10,000 years ago. The missing element during the vast interval between the time when I.Q. was available to enable symbolizing, and its realization, was a shift in our relationship to nature. It seems plausible to see in this interval, on some level that we will perhaps never fathom, a refusal to strive for mastery of nature. It may

be that only when this striving for mastery was introduced, probably non-consciously, via a very gradual division of labor, did the symbolizing of experiences begin to take hold.

For Zerzan and other primitivists, civilisation begins with domestication- of animals, plants and humans. Splitting up the gestalt of the world into utilitarian functions and parts has enabled humans to exploit and commit violence against it. The activist-author Kirkpatrick Sale goes so far as to argue that *Homo sapiens* themselves are a creature evolved on cruelty and domination, and that our *erectus* forebears lived simple, peaceful lives of harmony. To go this far is to wish for a levelling of such a great degree that even cave art and clay figurines represent a radical split in the world. Better that we almost abolish consciousness itself, in order not to be separated and alienated from nature.

But whilst this tendency towards nihilism through the obliteration of the mind exists within primitivist thought, so too does a far more violent and bloody vision of the state of nature. Anthropologist Pierre Clastres, in his research amongst Amazonian tribes, conceived of a new form of political philosophy, one where the equation of the State with violence is a mistake. For Clastres, primitive violence was not the proto-State beginning to assert itself, but rather the opposite - the State abhors violence and does everything possible to reduce it:

For [Hobbes], the social link institutes itself between
men due to "a common Power to keep them all in
awe": the State is against the war. What does primitive
society as a sociological space of permanent war tell us
in counter-point? It repeats Hobbes's discourse by
reversing it; it proclaims that the machine of dispersion
functions against the machine of unification; it tells us
that war is against the State.

Under the Clastrian conception of war, the State can be held at arm's
length through the deliberate use of violence, in order to prevent
power from coalescing. Even torture, mutilations, executions and
humiliations all serve the purpose of keeping men in a state of war.
Clastre's thought had a profound impact on some anarcho-
primitivists, who have continued to hold that violence is an essential
tactic to destroy the State and prevent another from arising. In
language that comes flirtatiously close to fascism, primitivists and
so-called 'eco-extremists' have turned to Nietzsche, anthropologies
of steppe warriors and early Islam and Indo-European paganism to
make sense of the primitive mind. In an essay called *The Return of
the Warrior,* primitivist Ramon Elani writes:

Clastres demonstrated that what is desirable,
substantive, and eminently deserving of emulation in
primitive society is precisely due to and constituted by
ever-present, permanent violence. We must refuse to
shy away from the importance of violence in the

creation of community. **We must acknowledge, in fact, that violence alone, properly understood, is the only means to achieve the kind of society we desire.**

Some primitivists have followed these thoughts to their logical conclusion and also rejected the entire 'moralistic' and 'humanistic' framework upon which leftist anarchism is built. Obscure anonymous journals like *Atassa* contain a plethora of writing rejecting feminism, egalitarianism and even the principle that human life has any inherent worth. These self-described 'eco-extremists' place 'wildness' and nihilism as their ultimate goal, casually turning towards homophobia and the celebration of rape, bride capture and arbitrary murder. This is unsurprising in many ways, since someone who rejects civilisation but believes in egalitarianism is fooling no-one. A response piece to this new primitivist tendency - *Of Indiscriminate Attacks and Wild Reactions* - highlights exactly where anarcho-primitivists cross the line into anarcho-fascists:

> It's easy to imagine that Elani's Warrior possesses qualities resembling the ideal of warbound Aryans and eager *Freikorps* a century ago, or any number of young neo-fascists of today. Before the name change to "Wild Reaction" and their intensifying spiral of bigotry (hearkening back to the positions of former leading light Kaczynski) there were already strong authoritarian commitments evident in this group who so badly wanted to see its name in lights in its contest

with the establishment, a fight now recalibrated to hone in on those most hated targets: anarchists and random women. Furthermore, their identity could shift to an explicitly ethnic one, their rhetoric could become suffused with a heroic folkish realism, and their spirit could end up falling closer to the Traditionalism of arch-fascist philosopher Julius Evola.

Thus anarcho-primitivism is a hopeless mess of left-wing ideas trying to engage with the realities of anthropology, confused about where and why domination and violence arose, lost in the thicket of accusations and denunciations. If there is a binding element here, it is in the rejection of domesticated life and the destruction of the natural world, but attempting to square this circle while retaining the exceptionally novel ideas of left-wing anarchism seems a fool's errand. In many ways this makes primitivism a wellspring of ideas which belongs to neither left nor right, but rather an archetypal refusal to be shackled to the cage of civilisation.

Conclusion

In the three philosophies I have attempted to describe we can see perhaps three approaches to violence: *Violence to restore order, violence to create order and violence to destroy order*. The monarchist seeks an organic and perhaps divine hierarchy; the fascist seeks an organic order through struggle and the primitivist seeks to sweep away the civilised world and return to a primordial order. The anarcho-prefix is the recognition of the state of flux we find ourselves in, a transition zone between here and the desired outcome. While none of them offers a blueprint or ideological mission statement, I think that this is precisely the point. Rational designs fail to ignite the passions needed to drive change and struggle, rather a conception or pre-rational image of aesthetics and war is what stokes the human heart to action. This is why I find these philosophies attractive, they offer a glorification of struggle in which one can become something greater. An invitation to overcome. Maybe they will do the same for you as well.

Modern Witchcraft in the UK

I had seen some pretty tough things during my time in
Africa, but for a second I felt sick. O'Reilly cleared his
throat. He'd seen the expression on my face.

'Obviously we all find this . . . distressing . . .' he said.
'We have next to nothing to go on, Dr Hoskins. We
don't know who the child is, or where he comes from.
We're guessing that he's of African or Caribbean
extraction. We don't know exactly what happened to
him. According to our home office pathologist, Dr
Mike Heath, the cut to the neck is very precise. He
thinks it was made from back to front, and that his
body was drained of its blood – though you must keep
that information completely confidential. We haven't
released it to the press.'

When the torso of a young African boy was fished out of the Thames
in September, 2001, the UK public was already aware of the barbaric
murder of another African child just a year earlier - Victoria Adjo
Climbié. The mood was one of confusion and disgust. Fatal child
abuse cases were depressingly common (averaging 78 a year since
the 1970's), but the added elements of witchcraft, mutilation and
even ritual sacrifice placed both cases into a new category of horror.
These types of crimes are now classified as CALFB - 'Child Abuse

Linked to Faith or Belief' - a typically bland modern euphemism for often intensely gruesome acts of torturous exorcisms, beatings and deaths, where the parents or guardians of a child believe that inflicting violence will help cure them of a supernatural affliction. Despite decades of awareness and incident after incident making national headlines, UK law enforcement seem powerless to stop this steadily growing trend of immigrant related crime. Between 2000 - 2006, 38 specific witchcraft related child abuse cases had been documented. By 2018, 1,950 cases were being reported per year, with the Telegraph quoting local councils as saying "40 cases a week". This trend shows no signs of slowing down. My aim here is to outline the landscape of the past 20 years, the major cases and responses, and to demonstrate how the UK has utterly failed to stamp out this particular form of crime. The inevitable conclusion is that UK law enforcement is simply incapable of policing African immigrant enclaves, especially in London, and that this is yet another imported cultural crime which will never be properly tackled.

The Murder of Victoria Climbié

Victoria's story is set in the context of European and African immigration and welfare systems. She was born on the 2nd of November 1991 in Abobo, Ivory Coast, and by all accounts was an intelligent and promising child. The villain in this story is her great-aunt, Marie-Thérèse Kouao, her father's aunt. She was born in 1956 and had attained French citizenship, living on benefits in Paris with her sons and husband. She returned to the Ivory Coast in October 1998 for her brother's funeral, planning on returning to France with another little girl called Anna. Her motive appears to have been to use the child in order to gain more welfare at home, but Anna or her parents changed their minds. Kouao convinced the Climbiés to allow her to take Victoria in her place on Anna's passport, promising her a fine French education. The parents agreed. Between November 1998 and April 1999 Victoria lived with Kouao in Paris, where the authorities had already noticed her absenteeism from school. The French benefits agency was pursuing Kouao and Victoria's school had issued a Child at Risk Emergency Notification following obvious signs of abuse and mistreatment. Kouao then fled to the UK on her French passport, allowing her to disappear under the radar with ease. They arrived in London on April 24th, Victoria sporting a wig with a shaved head to pass as the photograph of Anna in her passport.

From this point on Victoria's tale becomes a litany of spiralling abuse, social service incompetency and administrative farce. Kouao managed to secure housing and employment, then a boyfriend, Carl Manning. Between April 1999 and February 2000 Kouao and Victoria saw dozens of housing officers, welfare and social service workers, police officers, medical practitioners and child protective service staff. Kouao contacted and visited Ealing social services 18 times and Victoria visited a GP and was admitted to hospital twice, both times with serious injuries stemming from physical abuse.

The full horror of what Victoria endured only became apparent when she was finally rushed, unconscious, to St Mary's hospital with hypothermia, organ failure and severe malnutrition. After her death the pathologist documented 128 separate injuries, calling it the "worst case of child abuse" she had ever seen. For the short time she had been in the UK she had been beaten, scalded with boiling water, burnt with cigarettes, starved, deprived of water and subject to astonishingly degrading and humiliating practices. Her fear of her great-aunt and her boyfriend caused her to wet the bed at night, which was punished by her being made to sleep in a bin liner in the bath, her hands tied and deprived of any blankets.

Aftermath: Laming Inquiry

The details of the case were to be exposed over a long public inquiry, the most expensive in British legal history. The inquiry was damning in its verdict about institutional failure, noting 12 separate events where someone should have intervened to save her life. Following appeals, all the relevant social workers, doctors and police officers kept their jobs and right to work with children. The point made early on in the inquiry, that all the key social workers and officers were black, and made inappropriate judgement calls regarding cultural differences, was shouted down as racist. A number of recommendations led to the typical sprawling 'blob' approach of British governance, with a new (and largely pointless) Children Act of 2004, the creation of Local Children's Safeguarding Boards and the Office of the Children's Commissioner for England, which explicitly fights to have the United Nations Convention on the Rights of the Child incorporated into British law. The fact that Kouao took Victoria to see several African church pastors and informed them that she was suffering from demonic possession didn't seem to be particularly noteworthy to the inquiry.

The Boy in the River

If Victoria's death was an anarchic hellscape of cruelty and incompetence, then the murder of the Boy Called Adam could not have been more different. On 21st Sept 2001, the torso of a young West African boy was fished out of the Thames. The initial result revealed that his arms, legs and head had been carefully and expertly removed and his blood drained from an incision in his neck. This was not the insanity of a woman beating a spirit-riddled child, this was a methodical and well-planned ritual murder. To quote from Richard Hoskins, a religious anthropologist who worked on the case:

> 'I don't believe Adam was butchered for his body
> parts,' I said. 'His genitals and internal organs were all
> intact. He was not killed agonisingly slowly, but
> quickly – at least fairly quickly – by precise cuts to the
> throat, his body held horizontally or upside down until
> it was drained of blood. And the body was dressed in
> orange-red shorts after death and placed in the river.
> For all these reasons, it is my conviction that Adam
> was the victim of a human sacrifice...

'Let me go further,' I said. 'Given that Adam was almost certainly African, he was probably sacrificed as an offering to one of the gods or deities of West Africa. Why West Africa? In my opinion, it's only there that sufficiently sophisticated religious and ritual systems exist that could account for the complexity of the awful ceremony to which he was subjected...

If I'm right about that, then many aspects of this disturbing crime fall into place. The colour of the shorts will prove to be important, and similarly the deposition of the body in water. Also the precise way the killing was carried out. And the timing: the fact that the body was dressed in the shorts only after death. We do not know yet why they wanted to sacrifice a child in London, but they obviously felt they needed power for something major, which as yet is unknown to us...

But identifying the particular god or goddess is no easy task – there are literally hundreds in the West African pantheon. I will be looking further at deities associated with both the colours orange and red, and with water – especially those in the Yoruba tradition and surrounding ethnic groups'

The contents of Adam's stomach also make for grim reading. Clay pellets, full of gold and quartz, consistent with West African river deltas, plus an assortment of animal bone, charcoal and plant matter. Hoskins identified this a traditional pre-sacrifice potion, made by cooking down powerful and unusual ingredients over an open fire. The smoking gun was the presence of the calabar bean. This bean, also known as the ordeal bean, is highly poisonous. Given in small doses the practice of witchcraft accusation rested on whether the offender vomited or died. In very small amounts the toxins produce a numbing or even paralysing effect. Adam's shorts were also a mystery. They turned out to be a specific brand sold only in Germany and Austria, suggesting perhaps that Adam had spent time in Europe before being moved to the UK. This suspicion was confirmed by several arrests and leads in the following years which placed Adam in Germany with a Yoruba cult prior to his ritual murder in London. The colour of the shorts, plus the fact he was dressed after his death and placed into water strengthened the case for a Yoruba sacrifice.

To this day the mystery of Adam's death has not been solved and his killers remain free. What this careful, premeditated ritual killing suggests is that the UK had one or more Nigerian groups which planned for similar sacrifices, and that Adam is far from the only victim.

Blood & Sacrifice

In the wake of Victoria and Adam's murders, the Metropolitan Police Force began surveying African communities and churches, looking for clues and evidence that might reveal the scale of the witchcraft and sacrifice problem. In 2005 a leaked internal report confirmed the worst fears - an unknown number of African children were being smuggled into the UK for the express purpose of blood harvesting and human sacrifice. Within the toxic brew of beliefs around witchcraft, including the Congolese belief in *kindoki* and the West African belief in *ju-ju* magic, a number of different issues were emerging as specific threats to children:

> Church pastors who encouraged a belief in demonic and spiritual possession which may require physical abuse and violence to be inflicted on the child in order to cure them.

> Children being sent back to different African countries for violent exorcisms.

> The production of magical and healing potions and mixtures by witch-doctors which may require the blood of particular children. These children may be kept alive for long periods to harvest this blood.

> Children being trafficked from African countries, in particular Uganda, for the purposes of blood harvesting and sacrifice.

Gallingly, some African community charities and organisations demanded a robust police response and decried the lack of action.

Debbie Ariyo, the director of Africans Unite Against Child Abuse, is quoted as saying:

> "The way forward is for the government to sit up and realise that something horrible is going on and do something concrete about it. We know definitely there is an increasing number of children being trafficked. Now is the right time for the government to accept there is a problem."

'Child B' & Project Violet

In November 2003, a group of council wardens discovered an 8 year old child shivering in the stairwell of a Hackney flat. The child, known only as 'Child B', turned out to be an orphan from Angola, smuggled into the UK by her aunt - who hasn't been named - in 2002. During her time in Britain, Child B was subject to vicious and brutal acts of torture from at least three adults: her aunt, Sita Kisanga and Sebastian Pinto. Child B gave harrowing testimony, describing how she was beaten with belts, cut with knives and had chilli peppers rubbed into her eyes. This was only discovered in January 2004, after social services sent the girl to hospital - she had been mistakenly returned to her aunt by the authorities over Christmas. The three abusers had planned to drown the girl in a canal, zipped up in a laundry bag, but had backed out at the last moment. The police discovered that the aunt was insistent the girl was infected with *kindoki*, a Congolese form of witchcraft, and that her pastor at the Church of Spiritual Warfare had identified her as a witch, an *ndoki.*

In the wake of Victoria Climbie's murder, the Victoria Climbie Foundation (VCF) had been established by her parents to act as a grassroots charity, campaigning to ensure such deaths never happened again. The London Safeguarding Children Board, itself set up on the recommendation of the Laming Report, worked with the VCF and the Met Police to pioneer community projects aimed at understanding child abuse amongst African and South Asian communities. This led to the creation of Project Violet, a police initiative to gather intelligence, evidence and train officials on spotting signs of religious or ritual abuse. The Met Police also created the Community Partnership Pilot Project. This consulted African and Asian communities in two parts of London, discussing 'possession in children' - it was clear that the belief that children can be possessed was widespread and could certainly lead to abuse.

In 2006 the *Child Abuse Linked To Accusations of Possession and Witchcraft* report was published by Eleanor Stobart. This aimed to collate all known cases of witchcraft related child abuse in the UK and revealed at least 38 confirmed cases involving 47 children. As expected, all but one case involved children of African immigrants, in particular from the Democratic Republic of Congo. In many instances the children were living with step-parents or other relatives and many showed signs of learning difficulties, epilepsy, autism or other disabilities.

The Murder of Kristy Bamu

The murder of 15 year old Kristy Bamu on Christmas Day 2010 was the next serious high profile case of witchcraft related deaths in Britain. Kristy Bamu was one of five children, his oldest sister Magalie Bamu lived in London with her boyfriend Eric Bikubi. Both Bikubi and the Bamus originally came from the DRC and Bikubi had been reared by his father with a profound terror of *kindoki,* bordering on the schizophrenic. Similar to the case of Victoria Climbie, the Bamus seem to have either French citizenship or immigration rights in France, allowing them to move freely to Britain. Magalie had invited her siblings to visit her and Bikubi over Christmas and they travelled from Paris, excited to spend the holiday with her.

Almost immediately upon arrival Bikubi locked them in their flat and accused all the children of bringing evil spirits into his house. They were denied food and water, beaten and made to stay awake for days, praying all night. Several of the youngest children confessed to being *ndoki,* to make the tortures stop, but Kristy refused. The children begged their elder sister to protect them, but she refused. Kristy wet the bed, after which Bikubi decided that he was the source of the problem. Turning on him he encouraged the youngsters to join in a frenzy of violence against the teenager - smashing ceramic tiles across his head and back, beating him with a metal bar which was forced into his mouth and down his throat, breaking his teeth and hands with a hammer, mutilating his ears with a pair of pliers and more.

On Christmas Eve, Kristy managed to phone his parents and informed them he was going to be killed. Pierre and Jacqueline Bamu began racing from Paris to save their son, but it was too late. On Christmas Day, Bikubi forced all the children into the bathtub and hosed them down with icy water. Kristy pleaded with his tormentors to "let him die." He got his wish. After nearly four days with no sleep and over 130 injuries to his body, Kristy was exhausted and broken. He slipped under the water and drowned, his siblings forced to sit on his chest as Bikubi sprinkled them with water from the bath. The paramedics arrived at a chamber of horrors - the prosecutor described broken tiles and blood everywhere, naked, hysterical children screaming in French and the ghastly disfigured body of Kristy Bamu, every limb broken and bloody.

Where Are We Now?

12 years on from Kristy Bamu's death and 22 years after Victoria Climbie's, it seems as though little has changed. The cases continue to pile up and the transnational networks of child trafficking have only grown. Almost every few years another headline declares "officers to be given specialist training in detecting witchcraft child abuse", to little avail. The most recent initiative, Project Amber, has plunged headlong into the standard progressive response to immigrant related crime - ensuring we don't stigmatise and reinforce harmful tropes. As the project founder, Trinity Junior Research Fellow Dr Naomi Richman says:

Witchcraft beliefs and spirit possession practices are common in so many societies around the world and are not in themselves at all harmful. They can simply be ways of explaining misfortune or resolving interpersonal disputes. In the UK, we have sadly witnessed an increase in children being accused of witchcraft, or of being possessed, which is then used to sanction child abuse. . . We are seeking to develop understanding of this complicated and sensitive area, and so the goal of the Amber Project is to equip audiences with the tools to recognise this type of harm whilst correcting the numerous misperceptions surrounding it, including ideas around witchcraft and possession only belonging to some groups.

The message is clear - there is nothing inherent to the African immigrant community worth investigating, witchcraft beliefs are benign and ordinary, we must correct misperceptions and taboos... After reading report after report from the last two decades it is clear the language has become more diffuse and bureaucratic, a shift from direct speech to "equipping audiences with tools", "improving trust and confidence within the communities which we serve through effective safeguarding", "harm reduction through stakeholder engagement" and so on.

What seems to be obvious as an outsider looking in, is that each high profile crime prompts a new expansion in semi-official, community based charity and advocacy groups, rather than a focus on policing methods and approaches. We now have the Victoria Climbie Foundation, The Churches' Child Protection Advisory Service, Children and Families Across Borders, Africans Unite Against Child Abuse, the Centre for Social Work Research and the Congolese Family Centre amongst others. This sprawling web of unaccountable organisations has formed a blob-like mesh which constantly redefines and redirects the aims of policing towards other goals. The job of the police is to detect and prevent crime by enforcing the law, but reading through the literature on faith-based child abuse, one would be forgiven for thinking their job was to solve poverty, enforce UN declarations across Africa and act as a strange mediating referee amongst African communities in the UK.

What many of these cases have in common is: the ability for African immigrants to leave and enter the UK undetected; the ability for people to hide and move around big cities like London without suspicion; the proliferation of African churches and witch-doctor services with little to no oversight and the total cultural, linguistic and religious divide between new immigrant communities and the host nation. Personally, I see no way for the police to do their job in this environment- assuming they wanted to. We will never know how many children have been brought into the country to be bled for potions, sacrificed to a deity, used as a slave or violently killed for being a witch. We are blind as to the extent of connections between the DRC, Uganda, Nigeria and the UK. We get glimpses of children being sent back for genital mutilation or exorcisms, we get hints that children disappear to order and reappear in London, but we don't have the means to prevent it from happening. It's only a matter of time before the next Victoria, Adam, Child B or Kristy appears on the news.

Part Two - Biology

The Celtic Curse: Haemochromatosis & Agriculture

Irish Population Genetics & The Biological Impact Of The Famine

Haemochromatosis, or 'iron overload' is one of a cluster of iron processing disorders with their roots in the Agricultural Revolution. Prior to the over-reliance on cereal grains, humans ate a more meat based diet, which provided enough heme iron to keep the body healthy. Something changed with the Neolithic adoption of wheat and other plants and one of the results was the transmission of iron metabolic problems into the general population of Europe and the rest of the world. For the Irish, haemochromatosis is known as the 'Celtic Curse', disproportionately affecting populations of Celtic descent. This is the story of how and why this metabolic problem was selected for, but also the story of how agriculture and its associated problems led to persistent and still destructive issues with processing dietary iron today.

What Is Haemochromatosis?

Haemochromatosis is the condition where the body receives and stores excess iron, the results of which can be fatal and include: heart attack, liver disease, arthritis, loss of libido, diabetes and skin problems. Excessive iron can come about in a number of ways, such as blood transfusions, iron supplementation or a hereditary genetic disorder known as 'Hereditary Haemochromatosis Type-1'. For the purposes of this article, we will just be focusing on this form of the condition. Humans lack any ability to naturally excrete excess iron, except through menstruation or blood loss, which makes the persistence of this disorder intriguing from a population genetics standpoint - especially given the very high levels in Celtic, English and Scandinavian peoples, Celtic in particular.

The most common genetic mutation for haemochromatosis is the C282Y allele of the 'Human homeostatic iron regulator protein' or 'HFE protein' controlled by the *HFE* gene - located on the short arm of chromosome 6 at location 6p22.2. The Irish population carry this C282Y mutation at around 10%–11%, the highest known frequency in the modern global population. Although there are over 100 known mutations that lead to iron overload, the C282Y variant is the most common by far. The recessive allele leads to the above mentioned conditions when two copies are inherited in an individual. Iron toxicity has also been implicated in neurological damage, Alzheimer's disease and other brain related disorders.

The origins of C282Y are murky, but a 2004 paper suggests the following:

"The mutation responsible for most cases of genetic haemochromatosis in Europe (HFE C282Y) appears to have been originated as a unique event on a chromosome carrying HLA-A3 and -B7. It is often described as a "Celtic mutation"—originating in a Celtic population in central Europe and spreading west and north by population movement. It has also been suggested that Viking migrations were largely responsible for the distribution of this mutation. Two, initial estimates of the age of the mutation are compatible with either of these suggestions… **We conclude that the HFE C282Y mutation occurred in mainland Europe before 4,000 BC**."

While this paper is useful, the field of prehistoric European population genetics has raced along with little pause to consolidate the data. Certainly more studies looking at how specific mutations have arisen and moved with populations are sorely needed.

The Biology Of Iron Metabolism

To really understand how this mutation works and why it might have been selected for and preserved in certain populations, we need to turn to the topic of how iron is processed and metabolised by the body.

Iron is a crucial element in human health, primarily due to iron's ability to accept or donate electrons. This makes it important in redox (reduction and oxidation) reactions where electrons are transferred, in particular in red blood cells as heme in haemoglobin and for cellular respiration in the cell. Crucially the difference is between iron as an electron donor: **ferrous state (Fe2+)** and as an acceptor: **ferric state (Fe3+).** The difference between these two forms of iron has profound consequences.

In general the metabolism of iron is a strictly controlled and well regulated system. An adult male stores around 4000mg of iron, held in haemoglobin, iron proteins and macrophage immune cells. Roughly 1-2mg of iron a day is lost through cellular sloughing in the intestinal wall, while menstruation can account for 3mg a day. Given that the average European diet nets around 15mg of iron per day, one might wonder how we don't accumulate iron very quickly. The answer is that only about 10% of consumed iron is actually absorbed into the body and put to use, the remainder is simply left to pass through the body. Why? The body can only absorb iron in its ferrous Fe2+ state or as an iron-protein like heme. Ferric iron has to be converted to ferrous, a process which is significantly helped by consuming ascorbic acid (vitamin C) at the same time.

Thus iron consumption and use is highly dependent on the type of foods being eaten. A number of compounds such as oxalates, phytates, tannins and fibre will hinder the absorption of nonheme iron, a problem which will bring us on to agriculture shortly. So whilst high meat diets, such as hunter-gatherers, will have no problem providing enough heme iron, other diets which rely heavily on ferrous and ferric iron run the risk of iron deficiency.

Anaemia and Agriculture

Despite iron overload being associated with the onset of the Neolithic, in fact the opposite problem is the more significant result from the adoption of agriculture - a deficiency of iron causing a decrease in red blood cells. The effects of anaemia are devastating and global. In a paper entitled *A systematic analysis of global anemia burden from 1990 to 2010,* the authors conclude that "Global anaemia prevalence in 2010 was 32.9%" and accounted for "8.8% of the total disability from all conditions in 2010".

To quote from another paper looking at the evolutionary logic behind anaemia:

> "In the developing countries, prevalence of IDA [iron-deficient anaemia] is **estimated to be 56% among pregnant and 41% among non-pregnant women**. In South Asia, **more pregnant women have IDA (62%) than a normal hemoglobin level**; this is also true for women and children in some African countries. Although many reports have not excluded other causes of microcytic anemia that could lead to overestimation of the prevalence of IDA, **in many parts of the world the prevalence of IDA is sufficiently high to be considered a "statistical normality".**"

The reasons for this are many, but an agricultural diet is amongst the top contributors. Agriculture does two things simultaneously, it decreases the amount of heme-iron rich foods - in particular red meat - it also increases the amounts of compounds in the diet which interfere and block the absorption of what little iron can be found in domesticated plants - phytates in cereals, lactoferrin and calcium in milk, lactoferrin in eggs and tannins in nuts, tea and other plants. The switch from a forager to agricultural diet therefore, was a vast biological selection process which utterly transformed the metabolic processes of the previous two hundred thousand years at least. On top of this, the Neolithic Revolution also increased the birth rate, increased the frequency of conflict and warfare and the amount of parasites and infectious diseases in human populations, all extra risk factors for people suffering with chronic iron shortages.

Interestingly, both low and excess iron have adaptive properties. We'll discuss the benefits of iron overloading later, but anaemia does also seem to protect the individual against chronic parasitic and bacterial infections. All microorganisms require iron for their own metabolic processes, so when a person suffers from an infection, one response is to increase the production of an intestinal protein called *apoferritin*. This sequesters free iron and binds it in an unavailable form to any infectious bacteria or parasites. Many bacteria have their own mechanisms for securing iron from their hosts - in the case of *Helicobacter pylori* it has surface molecules for acquiring human iron-proteins; for the plague-causing *Yersinia pestis,* it steals iron using human binding proteins, and for *streptococcus* it actively destroys iron storing cells to acquire free iron. Lower free iron levels in the case of anaemia are therefore adaptive against chronic and persistent infections, essentially hiding iron from pathogens and potentially decreasing mortality.

Parasites such as hookworm and malaria also play an important role in evolutionary history. Bizarrely infections of hookworms and malaria often coincide, but where a person suffers a high level of hookworm infestation, their risk of death from malaria *decreases*. Despite the fact that 25% of the world's population being infected with hookworms sounds atrocious, this has been postulated to be an adaptive and beneficial mutualism, since hookworms decrease free iron and help prevent the lethality of the malarial parasite:

> "A protective effect of iron deficiency against malaria has been supported by studies of animals and humans. Iron-supplementation treatment of anemia increases the risk of P. vivax malaria.
>
> In contrast, anemia-inducing parasites, including particular helminths and nematodes, appear to offer a benefit against malaria to humans who are infected with these organisms and who live in regions in which malaria is endemic. Bacteria that induce iron-deficiency anemia in humans also might confer resistance to malaria"

Bloodletting & Tea Drinking

Tea has been drunk for at least 5,000 years. The plant, *Camellia sinensis*, originated in southwestern China and north Burma and may have its roots in the Holocene 'Broad Spectrum Revolution' of increasing plant use as the temperature across the planet increased. Tea contains tannins, a type of polyphenolic compound which are remarkably good at binding to proteins. This property is especially acute when looking at iron absorption and excessive tea drinking is a major risk factor for anaemia due to the ability of tannins to sequester iron. One statistic has eliminating tea drinking producing a three-fold increase in non-heme iron uptake. But as with anaemia in general, it is possible that widespread tea consumption may be adaptive against the persistent threat of plague and malaria, decreasing free iron and improving survival rates at the cost of general overall health. Some researchers have linked the explosion of tea drinking in Europe with its beneficial effects against the 'White Plague' of 17th century tuberculosis. Similarly, although I haven't seen any research into this topic, the boom of nut consumption in places like Japan, California and Central Europe during the early Holocene may have had a similar effect against the increase of malaria and infections of sedentary lifestyles, due to the high tannin levels of certain nuts.

On the opposite end of the iron-spectrum, those suffering from haemochromatosis, particularly men, have no way to reduce their excess iron except through bleeding. There are hints in the literature that this may have been a selective mechanism for aggression and warfare amongst northern European populations, but certainly the 'quack' medical intervention of bloodletting may also have been an effective remedy in the same regions of the world. As Burke & Duffy note:

"In medicine, Armand Trousseau presented the first case description in 1865, and Friedrich Daniel von Recklinghausen applied the name "hemochromatosis" in 1889 (Geller & de Campos, 2015). Screening and early diagnosis of hereditary hemochromatosis can offset the potentially damaging effects of iron accumulation, and **regular phlebotomy provides "a simple, cheap and efficient therapeutic modality" to purge excessive iron from the body** (Girouard et al., 2002:185). Phlebotomy was first introduced clinically in 1950, an effective treatment because the blood loss stimulates erythropoiesis, helping to draw iron out of storage in peripheral tissues (Hollerer et al., 2017:812)."

Other review papers looking at bloodletting, or phlebotomy, come to the same conclusion. This suggests that our scornful view of mediaeval and early modern medicine needs some revising, since male populations in Britain, Ireland and Scandinavia at least would have gained some benefit from purging their blood on a semi-regular basis.

Ireland & Iron-Overload

Having set up the discussion so far, we can see that agriculture had a widespread effect globally on iron-metabolism and introduced both anaemia and some of the pathogenic conditions under which anaemia might be beneficial. Crowded and disease-ridden cities, booming tropical populations and the growth in malaria and other parasites may have been offset or at least managed by lower free iron in the body, despite the huge toll it takes on the individual's general health. Vegetarian diets low in iron and cultural phenomena like tea drinking may have helped people survive plagues and infections. So why then would an excess of iron be of any benefit to anyone?

An excess of iron in the context of an agricultural diet would in general promote greater health and well-being. An over reliance on cereals, dairy and eggs and a reduction in meat consumption causes lower iron absorption - therefore haemochromatosis offers an advantage to a farming-pastoralist population. But this doesn't explain why the C282Y mutation appears more frequently in Celtic and northern European peoples. One possibility is that anaemia causes a decrease in thyroid output and lowers overall body thermogenesis. A paper from 2016 suggests that C282Y is a climate-driven adaptation for Neolithic groups moving into a cold and damp climate, helping to maintain a higher body temperature:

> "The C282Y allele is the major cause of hemochromatosis as a result of excessive iron absorption. The mutation arose in continental Europe no earlier than 6,000 years ago, coinciding with the arrival of the Neolithic agricultural revolution. Here we hypothesize that this new Neolithic diet, which originated in the sunny warm and dry climates of the Middle East, was carried by migrating farmers into the chilly and damp environments of Europe where iron is a critical micronutrient for effective thermoregulation. We argue that the C282Y allele was an adaptation to this novel environment."

However, this has been challenged on the grounds that similar iron-overload mutations have appeared and spread in other parts of the world where temperature is not an issue, most notably during the Bantu Expansions in Sub-Saharan Africa, where the *Q248H* mutation performs similarly. Even today the condition known as *Bantu Siderosis* still affects many individuals, especially those who drink homemade beer brewed in traditional iron pots.

Ireland offers a particularly interesting case though for the confluence of culture and biology when looking at haemochromatosis. The traditional pre-Famine diet of Ireland was based around oat porridge, buttermilk and dairy, some beef and fish and then, infamously, potatoes. Potatoes are an absolute powerhouse of nutrition. As anyone interested in historical diets knows, a person can live perfectly healthily on potatoes, dairy and the occasional bowl of porridge for trace elements. The introduction of the potato to Ireland was a biological revelation. Boiling them, as per the traditional Irish method, helps preserve the majority of the vitamin C, a factor absolutely crucial to non-heme iron uptake. On average, adult Irish males ate 12 lbs, adult females 10 lbs, and children under 11 years of age 4 lbs of potatoes per day, which combined with some dairy, was a monotonous but healthy diet.

Unexpectedly, the Irish population is amongst the most gluten intolerant in Europe. Roughly 1% of Irish people and their descendants suffer from celiac disease, likely due to a combination of genetic and dietary factors. Wheat and other cereal grains fare poorly in the damp boggy conditions of the northwest Atlantic, but oats grow much better. Oats are significantly lower in gluten and were prepared as a fermented porridge with dairy, increasing their digestibility.

Combining these two facts together with the bottleneck of the Famine, we can piece together perhaps a major selection pressure for the persistence of C282Y in Ireland compared to elsewhere.

The Great Famine & Its Consequences

The potato blight which spread rapidly across Europe hit Ireland hardest of all, due to its over-reliance on this single crop. Potatoes, as we've seen, are exceptionally good crops for a poor farmer, plus they can be harvested twice, sometimes even three times a year. When *Phytophthora infestans* struck, it created an enormous and sweeping selection mechanism across the population.

The major substitute famine food introduced by the British was maize, a crop which was poorly understood. The phenomena of niacin-deficiency in those on a predominantly maize-based diet was not known to early European populations and it took major famines and pellagra outbreaks in Italy and in the southern United States to prompt extensive research into the topic. For Irish tenant farmers in the 1840's, the knowledge that maize had to be heat-treated with an alkaline material to be fully edible was a world away. Metabolically, the absence of niacin can be remedied through the conversion of the amino acid tryptophan. Tryptophan was available from the buttermilk and dairy in the traditional diet, and coincidentally, the more iron the body has available, the easier the conversion process. Anaemic people cannot convert tryptophan so readily, thus the C282Y 'enriched' Irish were at an advantage during the early years of the famine.

Famines also cause disease, often the greater killer than starvation. Stressed and malnourished people become easy prey for any number of infections, and in Ireland this was combined with widespread scurvy, since the potato was the major source of vitamin C in the diet. Curiously though, the C282Y mutation may have offered enough protection against many of these diseases to act as a selective mechanism for survival:

> "It is reasonable to infer that epidemic typhus bacteria would be disadvantaged by the iron withholding associated with C282Y, since work on Rickettsia rickettsia, a related species, confirms that limiting the bacterium's access to iron inhibits growth (Ellison et al., 2009). **In this instance, amidst the malnutrition, scurvy, and anemia apparent in emigrants boarding ships, high mortality caused by epidemic typhus would have offered strong selection for C282Y, and promoted the allele's distribution**, via gene flow, into territories such as Canada, the United States, and Australia that received waves of emigrants escaping the Famine."

The final major stressor here was the replacement food that Ireland came to rely on during and after the Famine, namely wheat bread and black tea. As mentioned, celiac disease is far more common in Ireland than elsewhere and the phytate levels in wheat are significantly higher than found in oats. Together the diarrhoea and loss of available non-heme iron would have favoured those who already possessed excess iron levels.

The introduction of black tea was equally devastating for the general health of the population. As we've seen, the tannins are exceptionally effective scavengers of non-heme iron, which combined with phytates, a lack of meat, widespread alcohol consumption and high infection rates, compounded the pressure on those with any extra iron stored in their system. Tea production was through day-long stewing on a stove, a method which simply increased the tannins in the final drink. The effects of tea became obviously deleterious, as stated in this quote from Miller (2013):

"Concerns about the impact of tea on mental health reached a crescendo when **tea drinking became implicated in an apparently dramatic increase in insanity in Ireland**, discussion of which reveals the extent to which medical opinion on the matter had begun to penetrate even official circles. Like other countries, Ireland had suffered during the agricultural depression of the late nineteenth century. Contemporaneously, Irish asylums reported dramatic rises in admissions, which were blamed in a special inquiry undertaken on the issue in 1894 upon a lack of nutritious food, increased vexation and worry and the gradual derangement of physical and mental functions. Tea was targeted repeatedly throughout this report. It was observed that Indian tea of inferior quality was commonly consumed by Ireland's poorer classes – stewed, rather than infused – and that this caused a peculiar form of dyspepsia which in turn debilitated nervous systems and generated psychological problems. **Inspectors observed that a general dietary change from oatmeal, porridge, potatoes and milk to bread and tea had occurred throughout the country**. This, combined with severe mental strain, had resulted in epileptic seizures and consequent mania, noted to rapidly pass away following a period of rest and nutritious food supplied in the asylum. One inspector noted that in districts including Ballinasloe, County Galway, alcohol usage had declined dramatically, **meaning that what was termed 'the insanity of malnutrition' seemed to have been a prime explanatory factor for rising incarceration levels**. Special prominence was also given to the excessive consumption of stewed tea by factory workers in the industrialized region of Belfast."

Doctors repeatedly noted that families traded away eggs and other nutritious foods for tea and that, on average, women were drinking 12 cups of strong black tea every day. The resulting ill-health was horrific, particularly on children, who became pale, anaemic and disease-ridden, raised on a diet of black tea and bread. Again from Miller:

"Over-indulgence in the substance, claimed the newspaper, was causing numerous housewives to seek solace in the outpatient departments of hospitals, where washerwomen, kitchen girls and mothers would arrive daily with symptoms including headaches, nausea, loss of appetite, physical distress after eating, and dizziness. The Belfast Newsletter depicted a cycle of events whereby the housewife would gradually lose her appetite due to excessive tea consumption, slowly coming to loathe food. She would then find solace in the tea-cup, although this ultimately intensified her condition. **Methods of tea preparation which entailed obtaining as much tannin (or tannic acid) from the tea as possible would then be fostered to quell her physical cravings**"

The decrease in potatoes and replacement with maize, bread and tea, plus the rise in infectious disease, combined to create a new cultural niche where C282Y carriers were more likely to survive childhood and reproduce. Although this scenario is exceptional in many ways, not least the global trade in foodstuffs, it does raise the question of whether haemochromatosis was generally adaptive during earlier periods of starvation, famine and widespread disease.

Conclusions

The story of how agriculture came to alter the human body is long and extensive, but iron surely ranks high on the list of problems it has brought. Almost every population on earth now suffers with iron-deficient anaemia in one form or another and, despite any benefits it might bring with regards to disease, it clearly creates a form of sickly life, hardly brimming with health and vitality. Haemochromatosis on the other hand is a strange disorder which on the face of it should be more widespread, given the advantages it offers agricultural peoples. And yet it remains confined to small pockets of the world and with no overarching reason as to why. Complicated histories of disease, diet, famine and maybe warfare seem to have mixed together to promote the C282Y variant in northern Europe and for Ireland specifically the Famine was a major selective pressure. The biological story of the Famine is a reminder of the power of basic metabolic facts like iron absorption and niacin availability. These facts underpin how a population tackles a catastrophe like a famine, or in our times, a global pandemic. We should always be cognizant of the hidden factors of ethnicity and genetics in such scenarios and do our best to understand how populations form, where they come from and what pressures they have been through.

An Elite Apart: The Biology of Hierarchy

A core principle of Western liberal politics, at least from the French Revolution, is the insistence that everyone is equal when our social roles are stripped away. The inherently horizontal nature of humanity is now the hegemonic view across most of the world and it's hard for someone born and raised in modernity to think anything else. However, this was not always the dominant view and it demands closer scrutiny in light of our increased knowledge of prehistory and genetics. There are lurking questions across the fields of hunter-gatherer and early farming studies - how did social stratification occur and when? How was it maintained and developed, and what do these inequalities mean for us today?

I want to explore some of these ideas here, whether such a thing as a 'biological hierarchy' existed and how it would have arisen amid the much lauded egalitarian nomadic societies of our earliest ancestors? I'll trace a winding path, from Voodoo priests to Polynesian chiefs, from Palaeolithic cannibal cults to Bronze Age island pyramids, all to show you how different conceptions of power and hierarchy function and to reveal the ancient roots of the enemy today.

A word of warning - this is not a scholarly dissertation, concerned with tedious referencing and hedging. I'm laying out a story, one that is surely wrong in its minutiae, but broadly correct I think from a wider vantage point.

Two Types of Foragers

To begin the search for a natural hierarchy, we have to start with the traditional image of the small-scale nomadic foraging band, which is assumed to be the norm for the Palaeolithic. This social structure is defined as 'simple'. This doesn't mean that the group can't have rich and complex traditions and stories and art, but it refers to the levels of social difference.

A small band like this would be basically egalitarian. This word is slightly misleading though, it doesn't refer to the modern liberal idea of free individuals doing whatever they want. Even in small bands, people are governed by norms, precedents, group control methods such as mocking, enforced sharing and punishments like banishment for offenders. There will be natural hierarchies, between men and women, adults and children, the competent and the dependent, the elderly and the young. These form the texture and fabric of life, but they aren't institutionalised or fixed, much like a group of boys at school, or a club of friends. Dynamics change and shift and some people will rise and fall as coalitions form and fracture. Economically, this egalitarian form of social structure tends to also be simple. Food is collected and hunted and usually eaten on the spot. Very little if any is preserved for long or even medium term storage. This economy is referred to as 'immediate return', in the sense that each person gets an immediate return on energy invested. The opposite to this is 'delayed return', which is associated with complex hunter-gatherers, groups which have a more formal system of hierarchy and power, sometimes hereditary.

It's not always obvious where the boundaries between these two start and stop, but what is clear is that highly complex hunter-gatherers mastered just about every technology typically associated with the Neolithic - ground stone tools, carpentry, astronomical maps and knowledge, pottery, early metalworking, warrior elites, slavery, monumental architecture and sacrificial rituals overseen by a shamanic or priestly class. We know less about these complex hunter-gatherers as they have been eradicated from history. We're left with anthropology, archaeology and surviving societies to bear witness to their achievements. In North America the two dominant examples are the fishing civilisations of the Pacific North-West and the Calusa people of Florida. Both were noted for their sedentary and stratified societies, based on aquatic resources, with rich traditions of boat building and a population of slaves. The interesting question is how did we get from egalitarian nomads to slave owning forager-fishers without agriculture?

Secret Societies

One of the more unknown social realities of hunter-gatherers all around the world, is the presence of secret societies within the tribe. Anthropologists have long documented their existence, but for some reason we prefer the simple nomad vision and it comes as a surprise to many that secret cults dedicated to sex, astronomy, cannibalism, music and art were a normal part of human life since our origins. Brian Hayden, a specialist in forager religious and ritual practices, defines hunter-gatherer secret societies as:

> "voluntary, ranked, ritual associations whose memberships, or at least the upper ranks of memberships, were exclusive and who typically claimed to possess ritual knowledge of great value to their own members or knowledge which could be used for the benefit of others, usually at a cost. This ritual knowledge constituted the 'secret' in these organizations. The existence of the societies and their memberships was typically public knowledge and was not part of the secret"

These secret societies often have similar characteristics, which Hayden lists as: 1) a body of esoteric knowledge, 2) the use of costumes and masks to transform into animals and spirits, 3) instruments such as flutes and bull-roarers to create spirit noises, 4) images and artwork of powerful animals, 5) an initiation ritual involving an ecstatic experience, 6) the presence of human sacrifice and cannibalism, 7) use of prestige objects such as shells, precious stones, rare feathers etc, 8) a secret iconography, 9) special locations and structures for rituals, 10) exclusive and unusual burial practices for members, 11) vast majority of secret societies were exclusively male and 12) children of members were usually initiated.

What we can take away from this is that, as hunter-gatherers develop in technological and social complexity, groups of men begin to form exclusive, hereditary organisations to enhance their wealth, power and prestige within the society. These rights and esoterica are jealously and violently defended from becoming common knowledge. Describing the fear Amazonian Mehinaku women have of accidentally seeing a secret ritual or even glimpsing the musical instruments, the anthropologist Thomas Gregor relays:

> "It has always been like that since our grandfathers' day. I don't want to see the sacred flutes. The men would rape me. I would die. Do you know what happened to the Waura woman who saw it? All the men raped her. She died later. Kauka had sex with her. I don't like it. But I would not get angry with the men if they did it to another woman."

Similar stories of rape and murder accompany the ethnographic record around the world when describing the relationship of women and girls to male secret societies. Sometimes women are violently initiated into the group, thus forcing her to guard the secret knowledge, but also trapping her somewhere between a biological female and a spiritual male; other times females are simply killed for having witnessed a ritual, sacred instruments or artwork or for contaminating a ritual space. In the wider context male cults often serve to separate young boys from their mothers and extended female kin, to teach them the secrets of hunting magic and warriorhood.

A useful outcome of this mechanism is to effectively recruit all kinship groups and their male leaders into one group, reducing competition and conflict and turning the society into a hereditary vehicle for power. In many cases there were strict rules around who could be admitted and even who could procreate. The Tahitian / Polynesian Arioi, a priestly secret society who worshipped the war god 'Oro, while admitting both men and women into their ranks, had severe control over their reproduction. While members of the Arioi had total sexual freedom before marriage, any child was killed at birth, to prevent contamination between the serf class and the nobility. Similarly the Hamatsa cannibal society of the British Columbian Kwakiutl people had clear rules about the lineage of any candidate boy, who had to be from a high ranking aristocratic family.

Palaeolithic Cults

Having seen some of the characteristics of documented secret societies, we can turn to the prehistoric evidence to look for patterns and commonalities which might point to the existence of similar organisations. One of the most dominant pieces of evidence comes from the spectacular and ornate burials in the Upper Palaeolithic.

At sites such as Sunghir, Arene Candide, Dolni Vestonice, Grotte des Enfants and La Madeleine, the rich burials and adults and children with mammoth beads, ivory spears, shell bead caps, large flint knives and other prestige objects, shows a likely class divide within Palaeolithic groups. The mammoth beads buried with the Sunghir children took thousands of hours to manufacture and the children themselves may have been ritually executed, all classic signs of a secret society. The cave art which adorns the walls of Lascaux and Chauvet, among other sites, likely shows a society which could afford to have dedicated artists and the time and resources to grind huge amounts of pigment and build scaffolding in the pitch dark of a cave to access roof spaces. Animal figurines such as the Lion Man of Hohlenstein-Stadel or the exploded clay animals of Dolni Vestonice also fit into the model of rare prestige magical objects. In the case of Dolni Vestonice, the animals were intentionally made with a wet clay called loess which was deliberately overloaded with water to make them explode when placed on the fire. The kiln itself was a small secretive structure away from the main campsite, all of which speaks to the trickery and deception used by secret societies to demonstrate their power over their people.

Caves are a perfect place for secret and exclusive rituals and many have offered up evidence of specialised cannibalistic rites, such as the 'skull caps' of Gough's Cave in Somerset, which are interpreted as drinking vessels. The heads were carefully defleshed and the skulls broken in a specific way to produce a vessel shape.

The Dysgenic Shaman

If we accept the premise that secret societies likely existed among Palaeolithic and later hunter-gatherers then we broadly have to accept the existence of some form of religious, priestly or elite class. Palaeolithic archaeology is comfortable with the presence of shamanism during this time period, meaning people who engage in specialised forms of ritual designed to alter their states of consciousness and travel through other realms or worlds to cure disease, find animals and other important social tasks. A common feature of shamans which often goes unrecognised is that they are typically ill, sick, deformed, diseased, neurologically atypical, epileptic or physically unusual in some other way.

Eliade and other specialists in shamanic studies often call them the 'Wounded Healer', an archetype of the doctor or medicine man. This leads to the curious phenomenon where a sickly and deformed person ends up with a huge amount of social power. Examples of potential shamans in the archaeological record often focus on physical impairments of the skeletal remains, such as the Romito Dwarf, Lady of Bad Durrenberg or the Sunghir children. Secret societies then, could end up being ruled by the least strong member. By any Nietzschean analysis, this could lead to the prioritisation of a resentful form of politics, characterised by spitefulness, petty disputes, cruelty, trickery, vengefulness and backstabbing. This is borne out in the literature - a study of Buryat shamans highlighted the importance of gossip, rivalry and constant magical attacks between shamans, vying for status. Among the Venezuelan Hoti, shamans are the main source of fear within a highly egalitarian and peaceful society. More disturbing are the 'dark shamans' of the Warao people, those who perform the horrific 'kanaima' revenge ritual, leaving their communities trapped in a constant cycle of feuding.

The Biology of Hunting Elites

Could we begin the search for a hierarchy within a foraging society based on biology? The first place to start would be diet, which traditionally is one of the most important factors in population differences. A poor diet leads to poor health, which in turn reduces the health of one's offspring and begins the epigenetic differentiation from the group which eats a good diet. While agricultural civilisations show a far more pronounced difference in diet quality, hunter-gatherers can still create significant differences in nutrition. A well documented example comes from the Comanche people, who divided up their tribe by the foods they ate - the Yamparika (root-eaters), Kotsoteka (buffalo eaters), Penateka (honey-eaters), Taykahpwai (no-meat) and the Tanima (liver-eaters), to name a few.

An interesting paper by Germonpré and colleagues investigated whether Palaeolithic dogs were a source of social inequality, by helping distribute wealth, food and prestige vertically as individuals and families gathered and bred more dogs. There is also a marked decline in bone robusticity, individual height and tooth health as the Palaeolithic gives way to the Holocene Mesolithic fisher-foragers, but it's unlikely that we have enough skeletal remains to pinpoint when and where biological differentiation began to occur as the Mesolithic communities became more sedentary and hierarchical.

What is more clear-cut is the case for biological difference as agriculture becomes the dominant mode of food production. In Levantine pre-pottery Neolithic cemeteries we begin to see dental caries being unequally distributed, similarly in later Portuguese Neolithic burials, the isotope markers for diet show social differentiation based on meat vs plant consumption. This shouldn't be a surprise, meat is the most highly valued food group across the world, regardless of economic system. The relegation of a lower class to a life of grain eating while an elite class consumes more meat is a trope which continues to the present day. An interesting exception to this trend are some highly mobile pastoralist cultures, such the Ligurian Neolithic. Skeletal analysis from this period show individuals with higher upper and lower limb density than Mesolithic hunter gatherers, most likely due to the rugged terrain and a high protein diet. To quote from the paper:

> "This provides further evidence to suggest that although domesticated animals and plants replaced gathered products, vegetable consumption was less important than for other Neolithic communities and a significant part of the diet was derived from meat and dairy products"

With this new system of stratification in place, with the rise and dominance of agriculture and domesticated livestock, we can weave the threads together so far and make the following arguments:

Hunter-gatherers often organised their systems of hierarchy through secret societies

Secret societies allowed for the hereditary maintenance of power

This social differentiation was likely marked by minor differences in nutrition

Agriculture hugely widened the differences between groups, particularly in diet

Warrior Aristocracies

"Between 1600 and 1500 BC in Bronze Age Europe, warrior aristocracies appeared along an axis from mainland Greece in the south to Norway in the north. In the archaeological record, the new warrior aristocracy is identified by graves under barrows containing valuable equipment, including bronze weapons. The personal equipment of this emerging group centred on four themes: warfare, horse riding and chariot driving, bodily decoration, and alcohol drinking"

This concise passage sums up the sweeping social change from the Neolithic to the Bronze Age across Europe and Eurasia. The emergence of a warrior elite, largely driven by the earlier expansion of mounted steppe warriors and Beaker people on boats, developed into a full hereditary aristocracy at the beginning of the Iron Age. This change, from a relatively egalitarian settled farming community to a highly stratified warrior society is best summed up by Joseph Campbell, who said it thus:

> "It is now perfectly clear that before the violent entry of the late Bronze Age … there had prevailed in that world an essentially organic, vegetal, non-heroic view of the nature and necessities of life that was completely repugnant to those lion hearts for whom not the patient toil of earth but the battle spear and its plunder were the source of both wealth and joy"

One of the most crucial changes here is the rise of a young male elite, tasked with expansion and conflict, which seems in direct conflict with the older shamanic elites that seem to have been in control for much of human history. As has been noted: "minding flocks against depredations of wild animals, or, above all, by other shepherds … constitutes a permanent training in violence". The move from a hunting economy, in which the hunt itself was managed by a potent spiritual animism, to a pastoral herding economy, in which the shepherds themselves were responsible for physically defending their charges, broke the original and ancient order of control, and liberated young men in particular to create new orders outside of the control of their elders.

We can see how these new cults took shape on the steppe by examining the 'midwinter wolf sacrifices' that appear around the late Bronze Age. At Krasnosamarskoe in Russia, the Srubnaya-era site revealed over 60 wolf and dog remains who had been systematically butchered and eaten. The interpretation is that it was a midwinter initiation site, where young men broke the food taboo on eating canids and transformed into wolves for the evening as they were welcomed into a youthful warband. Other similar sites have been found on the Lower Don and in the Rhine Valley.

It's not inconceivable that these youthful war bands were in direct conflict with older, more secretive forms of political and religious power. Prior to the Palace dominance of the Aegean and Minoan Bronze Age, there is evidence for more classic secret society rituals. In caves across Europe from the Grottes des Perrats to Nakavona Cave, evidence of cannibalism, bronze drinking cauldrons and smashed drinking cups suggests active cultic activity. On the Greek island of Keros, there is ample evidence of powerful rituals, including a pyramid made from hundreds of tons of marble, complete with underground drains and raised monuments. Similarly on Crete, many shrines and caves show the remains of drinking feasts and a possible human sacrifice. It has been argued that these pre-palace societies gained enough power to either become or be incorporated into the kingships that came to dominate the Late

Bronze Age in the Mediterranean. It could be that these sites represent a youthful, exuberant energy, unleashed to conquer islands and build statues. But it could equally be the continuation of a more secretive sclerotic form of power, which held down any aggressive energy with carefully managed displays of prestige.

Polynesian Caste Systems

One of the most profound examples of a biologically superior elite is from the Kingdom of Hawai'i. Despite the Disneyfication of the Polynesians in popular culture, in reality their societies were governed through a strict caste system, with a lower class of war captives and slaves who may be sacrificed at ritual events. Marriage between these captives, or Kauwā, and the higher ranks was forbidden. At the top of the caste hierarchy were the Ali'i, the hereditary nobility which governed over all, including the Kahuna priestly class. In a wonderful 1917 article, Professor Vaughan McCaughey outlines the 'Physique of the Ancient Hawaiians'. He notes that the aristocratic class was often mistaken by the earliest anthropologists and explorers for an entirely separate race. They regularly stood taller than 6 foot, possessed of enormous muscular stature and refused to engage in any drudgery or menial work, but busied themselves with sport, combat and lengthy massages. Vaughan notes with surprise:

> "The physical superiority of the chiefs is striking negative
> evidence against the popular belief in the bad effects of

inbreeding. The chieftain class married habitually within itself, very commonly within the same family ... There is absolutely no evidence of deterioration of any sort. On the contrary, all who saw the chiefly classes in the early days agree as to their striking bodily and mental superiority."

This is an interesting insight, since it has long been an archetype of early kingships that incest was a crucial mechanism for maintaining familial power. Anthropological and historical evidence, although contested, does point to Egypt, Peru, West Africa and Hawai'i, among others, as having royal families which engaged in incest to protect their privileges. Some potential confirmatory evidence for this came from Ireland, where an adult male was identified in the Newgrange passage tomb as being born from first-degree incest. This potentially confirms a traditional story about a builder-god-king who restarts the solar cycle by sleeping with his sister. The question of what biological effect this kind of incest has on the blood line of these royals is debatable, but a paper by Berghe & Mesher concluded that the strategy is viable, provided the king has access to a large harem to offset any potential biological problems with his children.

Vital Nobility vs Slave Cults

What I've tried to sketch out here, is a road map through early prehistory into the recent past and how the elites of those societies structured themselves, both politically and biologically. Elites can be both physically and spiritually healthy, or they can be sick and degraded. Both are possible and perhaps in reality, humans lean towards being ruled by the weak. Contrasting the Nietzschean vision of a carefree, beautiful, war-like and physically strong nobility against the sickly, ugly, weak and spiteful - this is the framework I want to work with.

In many cases, the shaman is a perfect representation of slave morality - often sick or crippled, diseased and wracked with headaches and afflictions, they look at power with a certain lust and can be incredibly cruel and vindictive in grasping it and defending it. Many kinds of secret societies also feel the same, full of old men, looking to control the behaviour and sexual lives of the young men, using trickery and theatre to deceive and maintain status. By contrast, the rise of pastoral and sea-borne life generated a new kind of elite, one concerned with movement and space, with violence, domination and colonisation. This noble class was primarily driven by younger men, fighting and travelling together in bands, exploring their worlds and gaining glory for themselves and their people.

While this is a highly simplified image, and many shamans do not comport themselves that way, it nevertheless captures something of the spirit of aristocracy which has moved through us since the beginning. Secret societies are ambiguous of course, there have been and hopefully still are societies where vital and noble traits are celebrated. However, they can of course go in the opposite direction, and this is the lesson of Haitain Voodoo.

Haitian Voodoo

In its origins, Voodoo is a syncretic blend of Catholicism and Yoruba / West African beliefs. The character of Voodoo has been determined by its necessity as a secretive, furtive, underground slave religion. Having developed in opposition to the plantation slave owners, Voodoo practitioners became experts in organising without leadership, in practicing their rites without attention and communicating without oversight. These qualities allowed it to become a dominant force during the Haitian Revolution - in 1791 a Voodoo priest named Boukman became possessed during a ritual and channelled the spirits' insistence that the slaves be freed and the French driven from the island. To quote Michel Laguerre:

> "After independence ... former slaves and maroons congregated in secret societies around influential Voodoo priests. Throughout the nineteenth century they participated in and organised peasant revolts against the appropriation of their land by influential politicians and army officers ... During the presidential elections of 1957, there were half a dozen secret societies that had almost complete control over the daily life of the Haitian peasantry and urban dwellers. As a kind of underground police force, judicial body and regional government, they issued their members with passports that have ever since been honoured"

Despite how intriguing and fascinating Voodoo is, it's hardly a paradigm of health and vitality. It's a phenomenon created under the greatest pressures, the need to survive at all costs and reproduce itself in the next generation. This yields a familiarity with secrecy, deception, trickery, forgery and resentment. For a peasant to join the Bizango society for example, he must give his money, spend time cleaning other people's toilets or similar base work, be subjected to daily oversight and spying to ensure he doesn't give away secrets, and all this just during the initiation phase.

When Voodoo did find itself with a measure of real political power, during the Duvalier regime, the imprint of this underground character came to the fore. As Laguerre notes - "it is less the Voodoo ritual that was retained than the political significance of the Voodoo church and the structure of relationships that it generates". The installation of Voodoo priests into government meant Duvalier could have a subterranean reach into the lives of every individual citizen, through spying, secret society control and fear. His creation of the Tonton Macoutes, named after a child snatching monster, was the logical result of this kind of politics. Their modus operandi involved kidnapping, murder, torture, intimidation and creating a regime of fear. Many leaders with the Macoutes were known Voodoo priests and their leader, Luckner Cambronne, was nicknamed the 'Vampire of the Caribbean' for forcing and extorting Haitians into donating plasma to his company. By 1972 Hemo-Caribbean was exporting over 1,500 gallons of plasma to the US every month, much of which was tainted and some potentially infected with HIV. The image of a mythical monster which sucks the blood from its victims, leaving them lifeless husks, could not be more terribly manifested in the world.

Conclusions

If you've followed me this far then hopefully this argument has made some kind of sense. It is impossible to precisely and thoroughly deal with the question of biology and hierarchy in a short essay, partly for space and partly because it isn't a subject that receives any scholarly attention. To sketch a path like this one needs to read between the lines, follow clues and bring together very different fields of study. If I haven't managed this then at the very least I've hopefully whetted your appetite to research further on your own.

The study of what kinds of society and what kinds of elite exist should be of central importance to us. Our world is not one driven by vitality, youth and health, but rather by the kinds of secret society I have talked about. Dominated by the old, the sclerotic, those with a pure lust for power. These societies are very old and they give preference and advantages to the enemy. The opposite of this is the military society, the brotherhoods of men, those who train to hunt, sail, ride, fight and move. These two are not always cleanly divided or even obvious within a society and some of the mechanisms by which elites maintain their hereditary rule, namely incest, should rightly be dismissed. Societies like the Polynesians display one of the crucial social divides, essential for preserving health and vitality

- keeping the priestly class subordinate to the warrior class. There's a rich history here to be tapped someday, from Henry II's murder of Thomas Becket to the modern Saudi regime, a constant tension and conflict between the priest and the soldier.

You may disagree with everything I've written here, and that's fine. What I hope to have brought to the fore, that elites matter, that the quality and character of those elites matter, is my goal. We can disagree on specifics, but on this I hope we are united. It's time to break the ancient order of the secret society and bring forth the cleansing nobility the world desperately needs.

Frenzied Like The Wolf

The Berserker Phenomenon and the Science of Aggression

On the night of March 10th, 2012, Staff Sergeant Robert Bales left his military base in Kandahar, Afghanistan, alone. He was armed to the teeth and out for blood. Barely 48 hours earlier he had watched impotently as an IED ripped the leg off a comrade in front of his eyes, now he was going to have his revenge. Amped up on Jack Daniels, sleeping pills and steroids, Bales murdered four Afghans in cold blood, including a three year old. He then came back to base to reload and tell his friends what he had done, then left and killed 12 more. **He shot an elderly woman in the chest and then stomped on her head until she was unrecognisable**. After pouring the family's kerosene over their mutilated bodies, he set the house on fire, wrapped himself in a blanket and waited to be arrested. Bales doesn't remember what he did, nor does he have a decent explanation. He says that he felt something inside him snap...

The story of Robert Bales is shocking to the modern ear. *How could he do something so utterly barbaric and cruel?* But were you to recount this tale to an ancient, you might get a very different response - for lurking within the human psyche is a beast of rage and blood. It has come down to us through the centuries as the *'berserker'*. There is at present no consensus among the psychological and medical world as to why and how a man can turn into something so dangerous and violent, seemingly without warning. I want to try and tie together what little research is available into a coherent hypothesis about how a berserker state may come about and how it works. Hopefully this approach will be illuminating rather than debunking, complementary rather than dismissive, for as we shall see, modernity has a shaky grip on a phenomenon like Robert Bales and the 'Kandahar Massacre'.

How To Go Berserk!

In John Protevi's work *'The Phenomenology of Blackout Rage',* he distinguishes between three types of aggressive behaviour:

> ***Reactive Aggression*** - the instinctive behaviour of an organism to defend itself and to override the tendency to freeze with fear when under attack. This can be an appropriate response, or it can be disproportionate, a *hyperbolic* response.

> ***Proactive Aggression*** - the controlled response to a threat, but combined with an emotional reaction, typically anger, in order to motivate oneself to use violence.

> ***Instrumental Aggression*** - the cold blooded and totally controlled use of violence for a specific end, not always self defence. Requires a long process of training to overcome the

113

emotional responses to using aggression. Typical of psychopaths and professional hitmen/assassins/special forces.

What we can see here is that aggression, or the use of force against another person, is usually part of a series of emotional responses to violence. Fear and anger are powerful motivators for action, one more associated with reactive than proactive violence, but both play a role. Jaak Panksepp's work on *Affective Neuroscience* shows that 'rage' is an archaic, modular system of the mammalian brain. In this view, the 'rage' system is akin to a piece of software, running automatically with no self-conscious direction or interference. Panksepp cites evidence that rage can be triggered in human subjects through chemical and electronic stimulation, but is likely to be part of a fear response rather than a predatory one. Its deep roots were confirmed for him when he showed that infants become highly enraged when their arms are pinned to their sides. As he states, rage is an adaptive action:

"It invigorates aggressive behaviors when animals are irritated or restrained, and also helps animals defend themselves by arousing FEAR in their opponents. Human anger may get much of its psychic energy from the arousal of this brain system; ESB of the above brain regions can evoke sudden, intense anger attacks, with no external provocation."

Many people today have little experience with repeated bouts of extreme personal violence. Nevertheless the emotional circuitry of rage is still triggered under a number of curious circumstances:

Air Rage - the state of anger and aggression that some passengers experience when onboard a long flight

Computer Rage - aggression towards computers and other technology. Can lead people to shoot or throw computers out of windows.

Wrap Rage - frustration and anger experienced when trying to unwrap an object from multiple layers of packaging.

Road Rage - violence and hostility from drivers towards cyclists, pedestrians and other drivers which can result in homicides.

'Roid Rage' - the possible increase in aggression and violence experienced by steroid users.

Narcissistic Rage - an extreme response from people diagnosed with various personality disorders towards perceived slights or small acts of aggression.

As trivial as some of these examples are compared to violently murdering whole families, it underscores that a rage response can be easily triggered by circumstances where people feel trapped, anxious, insecure, are frustrated when attempting to do something or have biochemical and neurological differences from the baseline person.

'Lifting the Car Off Grandma'

Just beyond the grasp and study of formal science is the realm of the anecdotal and the reported. Here we find the most useful information concerning the potential for humans to enter into states which are directly or tangentially related to the berserker phenomenon; in particular - *'hysterical strength',* or the capacity for people to momentarily perform feats far beyond their normal power; 'drug induced states', the use of PCP and other chemicals which profoundly affect the performance of the body and similar alternate states of consciousness, including delirium, psychosis, out of body dissociation, time dilation and similar atypical phenomena.

In 2013 in Oregon, two teenage girls lifted a 3,000 lb (1360 kg) tractor off their father, saving his life, to the astonishment of the fire crews. In 2006, Nunavit, Quebec, a tiny 41 year old woman successfully fought off an adult polar bear, saving several children's lives before the bear was shot. An informal diagnosis of *'excited delirium'* has sometimes been applied to unexplained deaths in police custody where (typically) young men become extremely aggressive, unresponsive, manic and display superhuman strength. It is strongly associated with cocaine toxicity and the use of police tasers. Cases such as these blur the boundaries between rage, aggression, fear, physical exertion, mania and other extreme forms of agitation. In a now infamous case, a young ex-high school wrestler Luke Haberman broke into the home of MMA champion Anthony Smith. Smith recounted a chilling five minute encounter with the tiny aggressor during which he simply could not stop Haberman, despite being a professional fighter and slamming his knees into the man's head:

""No normal human is able to fight like that," Smith said. "I'm by no means the baddest dude on the planet. But he's a regular Joe and I had a hard time dealing with him. And he took everything that I gave him—every punch, every knee, every elbow. He took every single one of them and kept fighting me."

In a brilliant Youtube video, the account '*Traditionalist Tolkienist*' breaks down the salient points of the fight and points out that, despite taking severe blows to the head, Smith was unable to knock out Haberman. Even using methods which have left other MMA fighters unconscious, something about the drug fuelled rage that Haberman was under, left him impervious to even the basic physiology of cranial trauma. Also of note to the student of military berserkers was the blood-curdling 'war cry' that Haberman performed on Smith's doorstep, caught on home camera.

In some research I did for this article, I requested from my twitter followers any accounts from their own lives which involved any of these unusual, adrenaline fuelled episodes. Here's a brief taste, the remainder I will publish separately:

"Once in middle school where I got into a fight with a kid because he spit on me after kneeing the back of my head during a football game. He was taller and stronger than I was, but I took three hits and a kick to the chest from him and didn't feel a thing. I had the singular thought of 'GO' in my head, and I just screamed and ran at him, tackled him, and started wailing on him. Took two male teachers to pull me off. Afterwards I felt incredibly tired and sore. Was afraid too that I'd get in trouble at home for fighting at school."

"One morning I am up before dawn with my son, waiting for our carpool to his basketball tournament. I realize that our car in the driveway, just 15 feet away from me is being rummaged by a thief.

Instant rage!

I immediately ran out the door with a berserker yell "HEY!!!!"

I must have scared him, he took off running *fast*

Had never experienced so much adrenaline energy in my life. I sprinted after him, still yelling, with some vague notion of raising the alarm.

Caught him before he got more than a block away, tackled the thief and put him into a choke-hold. Rage starts to subside once I have him submitted, enough to think "now what do I do?" That was when the police showed up so I didn't have to problem-solve. Got cuffed and stuffed into the cruiser while they figured out who was the perp and who was the crime victim. Unlike the berserker rages as a child, I didn't "go away" mentally and "find myself" in the middle of a fight. It was hyper-lucid and focused. While I stayed in a physically elevated state for a while (maybe another 20-30 minutes to come down?) with high heart rate and breathing hard, was able to mentally calm & speak to the police calmly, give them my story, then carry on with letting my wife know the (resolved) situation. Made it on time to the basketball tournament, too."

From southeast Asia, the phrase 'running amok' is the English loanword for a social phenomenon where a normally quiet and gentle person suddenly loses their mind and attempts to attack and kill anyone nearby, usually with a sword or knife. Since southeast Asian societies have a strong taboo against suicide, it has sometimes been understood as a way to kill oneself, but it also has long been interpreted as a possession by a tiger or other animal spirit and the offender usually cannot remember what happened. Similar terms like 'going postal' or 'suicide by cop' explain random outbursts of extreme violence following a long period of brooding or an outward calm demeaner.

In the medical literature describing *'excited delirium'*, a number of cross-over symptoms with the typical berserker mode are present, including - removing clothes, not being able to recognise friends or family, superhuman strength, unprovoked aggression, collapse or extreme lethargy after some time and the inability to feel pain. Taken alongside the fight-or-flight type hysterical strength episodes and the power of drugs to induce manic or psychotic states, it seems clear that humans can be moved from a state of rational calm to one of total dis-inhibited violence and rage simply through chemical and situational stimulation.

'Insania Zooanthropica'

The medical term for the belief that one can shape-shift into an animal is *therianthropy, lycanthropy* or *lycomania*. The name reflects the ancient connection in Eurasia between man and wolf and the terrifying capacity for certain individuals, under particular circumstances, to change into a ferocious and aggressive carnivore. Other animals are common in the literature, including bears, crocodiles, foxes, tigers, leopards and hyenas, depending on where one lives.

There appears to be no one causal reason why someone would believe themselves to be an animal, or possess the capacity to change. Medical diagnoses range from psychosexual disorders, head injuries, forms of psychosis, extreme depression, schizophrenia and other related pathologies. The vast majority can be traced to something of this type and can be treated with different medications. Some evolutionary theories have offered that it remains part of the human psyche as an 'archetypal' brain pattern from our earliest moments as *Homo sapiens*. A paper from T.A. Fahey (1989) offers these case studies:

"In two women the onset of the delusion followed sexual intercourse. In both there was a history of marital difficulties and the abnormal belief was seen by therapists as a vehicle for feelings of guilt and aggression. Jackson reports the case of a 56-year old woman who began to behave like a wild dog following an attempted reconciliation with her husband through sexual intercourse. A 49-year-old woman had chronically ruminated and dreamt about wolves, culminating in the delusion of wolf-like metamorphosis after sexual activity with her husband and on another occasion, coinciding with a full moon. In two young male cases lycanthropy was a symptom of schizophrenia. One also suffered from an organic brain syndrome of undetermined cause and the other abused hallucinogenic drugs and had a long standing interest in the occult.

One interesting tradition surrounding lycanthropy is the noted desire for raw meat or human flesh which seems to accompany some documented cases. The Greek stories of Parnassus include a grisly tale where shepherds disembowel a child and make a soup from his entrails, condemning one of their number to live as a wolf unless he refrains from eating humans for eight years. In 16th century France a young boy called Jean Grenier was hauled in front of a judge and condemned as a 'wolfman'. He confessed to eating more than 50 young girls and children, including a newborn. His appearance was typically described as bestial, with matted hair and fangs than protruded over his lips. Even as late as 1852 a man was admitted to the Asile d'Aliénés de Maréville in Nancy, France, describing himself as a 'werewolf' and demanded to eat rotten raw meat.

The relevance of this topic to the wider point of berserkers, especially historically, is the strong association between animal cults and ritualised violence. Warriors who felt themselves to be possessed by the spirit of an animal, or maybe to become an animal completely, would perhaps lose all voluntary self-control and engage in acts which they either may not remember or may feel to be beyond their control. What is striking today is that, even among military veterans, the need for rigorous *instrumental aggression* (as discussed above) seems to have largely eradicated the older, more visceral, forms of battle violence. Soldiers and veterans do snap, do engage in mass shootings or great violence towards civilians abroad, but accessing these mental states is severely discouraged by modern military training, making these the exception, rather than the *modus operandi* of warfare itself. We would need to look perhaps to more irregular warfare, in places like the Congo, Liberia or Sierra Leone, to find examples of institutionalised disinhibited aggression.

Sex, Drugs & Battle-Hymns

Several prominent characteristics of older berserker cults and modern appearances of similar phenomena are the uses of sex, music and chemicals to help break down the balanced, rational actor and push him into an aggressive and irrational state. The use of sexual violence, drugs and music are well documented among the military, dating back to the oldest Greek records of combat to the use of rock music and amphetamines in Vietnam and Iraq. To do justice to all three would take book length histories, so I shall merely cherry-pick some useful key points as they relate to entering into an aggressive state of mind.

Song and dance have their common root of expression in rhythm. The ability to coordinate groups of warriors, to make them move as a group, to dissolve the individual ego into the collective will was, and still is, a vital part of military training. Drums, beats, marching and coordinated drills are therefore a core component of combat training, whether bands of barbarians or modern infantrymen. In his fascinating book *Keeping Together in Time: Dance and Drill in Human History,* William McNeill provides dozens of examples of warrior cultures making use of dances and music to train and provide coherence and morale. Aztecs, Zulus, Maoris, Moros, Sumerians, Greeks, Scots, Germanic tribesmen and Chinese soldiers all made use of coordinated dances and music. Music itself can also shift the individual's state of mind from relaxed to agitated to aggressive. To quote from Speidel's excellent 2002 work on berserkers:

"to do deeds of berserk daring, one had to be raging mad…. Shouting and singing were ways to raise such rage. Early Greek and Roman warriors screeched like flocks of raucous birds—a mark of manhood. with a song of thunder and wind, the young Marut warriors of the Rig Veda awakened Indra's prowess. Husky Thracian, Celtic and Germanic war songs, like crashing waves, heartened warriors… Dance emboldened even more. Not only Tukulti-Ninurta's berserks danced on the battlefield: Vedic Indians did the same…. Dances, though done by all the early warriors, mattered particularly to berserks as they fanned their fury"

In modern settings the desire and requirement to both bond and agitate soldiers before they engage in combat still makes use of music. Jonathan Pieslak's descriptions in "Sound Targets: Music and the War in Iraq" highlight how rap and metal were both employed to create a unit coherence and to rouse the young men into a state of aggression:

"It was you and your head and your music. And for me I'd listen to some Jay-Z or something like that or some Wu-Tang that really just got you pumped up, that way when you went out there, you weren't as scared, I guess. A part of you is like, "Yeah, I'm a thug. I'm ready to go. I'm ready to fight.""

"War is so ugly and disgusting, and it's very inhuman. It's an inhuman thing. It's unnatural for people to kill people. It's something that no one should ever have to do, unfortunately, someone does. And we happen to be that someone sometimes. And so listening to music would artificially make you aggressive when you needed to be aggressive."

Drugs have played an equally vital role across time and culture for soldiers and warriors to push through their fear and inhibitions. Alcohol has been used (with the exception of Islamic forces) by every society that could manufacture or acquire it. From Greeks, Chinese and Aztecs to the annual 550,000 gallons of rum required for the 36,000 men of the British Imperial Army. Of interest to us for berserkers is the obvious link with the *Amanita muscaria* or 'fly agaric' mushroom. Traditionally dried to enhance its toxic effects since one of its compounds, ibotenic acid, is converted into muscimol, the alkaloid which is a sedative-hypnotic agonist of the GABA receptors. The effects include an overwhelming need to move, superhuman strength, resistance to fatigue and hallucinations. The 'mushroom warriors' of Siberia, including the Chukchi, Yakuts, Yukaghirs, Kamchadals, Koryaks, and Khanty, made great use of the fungi and used it to powerful effect in combat.

The potential use of *muscaria* by the Norse berserkers has been questioned, despite having many vocal advocates. One potential alternative is *Amanita pantherina,* the 'panther cap', which is also hallucinogenic but with the added properties of bodily dysmorphia, including the feeling of hair or feathers growing from the skin, and generalised mania. No doubt that either could have been used and many tales of later soldiers using fly agaric abound. In *Shooting Up:*

A Short History of Drugs and War, Lucasz Kamienski notes modern battles in which fly agaric was potentially used:

"The Tatars produced a special drink made of hemp and Amanita muscaria, which they drank before combat to induce trance-like fury and raise the spirits. During the war between Sweden and Norway in 1814, some Swedish soldiers of the Varmland regiment were reported to be fighting hopped-up, most likely on Amanita muscaria, "seized by a raging madness, foaming at the mouth." And in 1945 a group of Soviet infantrymen, perhaps Siberian, was intoxicated with the mushroom and performed equally fearlessly at the battle of Székesfehérvár in Hungary. They were said to be fighting in a wild frenzy like "rabid dogs" and then falling into a deep sleep"

Finally, sexual violence has also been one the major techniques that soldiers have used to remove themselves from their more steady rational instincts and allow themselves to enter a more bestial, primal state. Without dwelling on the history of rape in warfare, suffice to say that initiation rape and the use of gang rape in both ancient and modern warfare is a powerful tool for dehumanising the enemy and, especially in combination with drugs and alcohol, a potent way to mould outrageously violent warriors.

"Uncomfortably Numb"

The final piece of the berserker puzzle to explore is the regularity with which immunity or a disregard for physical pain appears in the literature and descriptions. Trying to group different cultural forms of fighting together as 'berserk-like' is fraught with difficulty, but if we consider fighters like the Zulu, the Moro and the Norse, then we see similarities in the records. Quoting Kamienski again on the Zulu:

"The Zulus fought with fanaticism, dedication, and fury… Even when injured they did not stop fighting because their bodies were rendered insensitive to pain through the use of powerful anesthetizing plant remedies. The Zulu warriors seemed immune to the enemy rifle fire, so they readily launched almost suicidal massed charges and incredibly easily retained their combat effectiveness"

Similarly on the Moro:

"what frightened the Westerners most was their resistance to bullets, as after being shot several times they still kept fighting, causing further death and terror. Killing them was not an easy task; they were like zombies. The bullets pierced their limbs and torsos, scratched their bodies, but astonishingly the Moro did not drop dead, just like the Zulus. Captain Cornelius C. Smith reported that "in hand-to-hand combat our soldiers are no match for the Moro. If our first shot misses the target, we rarely have time to get off another.""

The Moro famously did not use intoxicants or stimulants of any kind, but instead used a combination of religious ecstasy and self-inflicted pain to somehow 'shut out' the pain of being shot. Before combat they would tie ligaments around their arms and legs to minimise blood loss. They also bound up their testicles and penis with shrinking cords, resulting in an intense infuriating rage on the part of the fighters. These particular warriors were known as '*juramentado*' and were essentially frenzied suicidal swordsmen, dedicated to slaying as many enemies as possible before death.

We can see here two different 'routes' into accessing the raging state: the drug induced and the pain induced. The pain caused by deliberately binding the genitals likely activates the primal rage circuitry as discussed at the beginning; it also bears a strong resemblance to the '*excited delirium*' also previously mentioned. In particular the frequency with which tasering appears in those diagnoses looks similar to the Moro custom of binding - an intense, agitating pain, one that drives rational thought away by again activating the rage circuit.

The scientific study of pain perception is complex, since it crosses the difficult subjective boundary between experience and the biology of sense and response, the two bridged by the nervous system. The translation of the biomolecular mechanics of cells receiving signals from external stimuli to the internal experience of pain is poorly understood and may never be truly explained. But several things about pain relevant to our topic have been reported in the literature:

> People with mental pathologies, such as schizophrenia, are more likely to have an altered experience of pain sensitivity.

Persistent or chronic pain is strongly associated with anger and rage

What is lacking is any comprehensive study of how ordinary people can move in and out of states of consciousness which alter typical pain sensitivity. As far as I can tell, the only main area where this is explored is for practitioners of 'BDSM' or 'bondage/discipline/sadism/masochism' (unfortunately). Researchers interested in how pain can be interpreted as pleasure by the brain have studied those involved in BDSM activities and report the following:

Those who 'dominate' enter into a brain state called the *'Csikszentmihalyi Flow'*

Those who 'submit' enter into a brain state called *'transient hypofrontality'*

Obviously it goes without saying that BDSM is not in the same league as frenzied killings, *but*, if these two brain states bear any resemblance to the reported experience of a berserk frenzy, then they are worth exploring.

In The Zone

A mental state which most people have experienced and has been extensively studied is the idea of the *'flow state'*. That feeling when playing music or sport or even just washing up - the focus of consciousness into the present moment without any reflection or self-awareness. Athletes and musicians in particular are familiar with this feeling, sometimes called 'in the zone'.

Psychologist Mihaly Csikszentmihalyi has pioneered research into this area and MRI scans are now able to detect someone in this particular and transient mental state. Hence the term *'Csikszentmihalyi Flow'* to describe the sensation. Crucially people often forget what happened during the state and report it as an almost out-of-body experience or one of autopilot. The brain engaged in playing a piano recital or jazz improvisation doesn't actively remember the next sequence, but instead seems to become free and relaxed and the activity just *flows* from the person.

Alongside this brain state we have the idea of *'transient hypofrontality'*. This term was proposed by Arne Dietrich in 2003 as a hypothesis for explaining how the brain responds in altered states of consciousness. The key idea here is that consciousness is organised hierarchically and downward pressure can be exerted to essentially 'shut off' a number of external inputs. Hence when dreaming normal stimuli don't provoke a response. This control over consciousness explains how, in certain states, pain can be minimised or eliminated from conscious experience.

Linking these two ideas back into our berserker theory then - the brain can respond to a profound shift in consciousness by both engaging in the present moment and running on autopilot, as well as switching off certain external cues. This could help unlock what is happening in the berserker brain.

Putting It All Together

Looking back over the article we can identify several key points which are supported by the scientific literature:

Rage is likely an archaic neurological program, designed to help someone defend themselves when under attack or stress.

Rage can be provoked using drugs, chemicals, electric shocks, pain and scenarios where one's intentions are thwarted or where violence may be inflicted on oneself or loved ones.

Forms of mania, hysterical strength, dissociation and other phenomena can occur alongside a rage state and may interact in different ways.

Brain pathologies, such as schizophrenia, bipolar disorder, lycanthropy etc may also be related to the ability to enter a rage state very quickly and easily.

The use of aggression in warfare is complex, but tools such as music, drugs and sex can be employed to override fear and to dissolve the individual's ego in a collective will.

Two brain states in particular - flow and transient hypofrontality - may explain how berserkers are able to ignore pain, even without drugs, as well as forget their experience afterwards.

This all strongly suggests that the act of 'going berserk' is rooted in a deep evolutionary mechanism to defend and protect oneself, but can be induced in people through manipulating the brain and body through specific actions. It also suggests that some people may be more prone to the phenomenon than others, particularly young males. In this context it makes clear sense that early warfare would be a prime theatre for combining the different elements necessary to going berserk.

Visceral and highly interpersonal forms of combat, immense fear and stress, probable traumatic memories from previous fights, use of drugs to either calm or agitate, maybe drunk as well - add chants, music and dancing and the stage is set for someone with perhaps a particular disposition to lose control of their senses and 'snap'. Looking back at our initial story, of Robert Bales in Afghanistan, we see the tiredness and fatigue, the mounting frustration and anger, the use of drugs and alcohol, the loss of control, the autopilot flow state and the total loss of memory around the worst parts of the massacre.

What science we do have seems to confirm that all these are a nested series of biological capacities, leading to the chilling conclusion that perhaps most of us are capable of something similar if put under the same stresses and the same fear.

Part Three - History

The Origin of 'Two-Spirit' & The Gay Rights Movement

The Strange Story of Harry Hay and Will Roscoe

If you have encountered any academic discussion of LGBT topics in North America, you will almost certainly have heard the phrase 'Two-Spirit' - sometimes included in the acronym as 'LGBTQ2S', or some variant thereof. The most crude explanation for the term is something like 'a gay Native American', but it has a much more complex and subtle origin. Regardless, the implications and the cultural usage of the term amounts to a differentiation in the way Native and other indigenous peoples think about and describe homosexuality, gender and minority sexual identities. If you push on this terminology you'll be told that it was invented by Native Americans as a way to self-define and take control of their own culture. Push further still and you'll find a particular conference, held in Canada in 1990, which voted to adopt the term. You may also come across two names in particular: Harry Hay and Will Roscoe. As far as I can tell, no-one has looked much further into the murky origins of the term, beyond accepting this conference and its decision. This is my attempt then, in a single article, to dive into the weeds. We'll cover some truly bizarre and unsettling territory - the

Radical Faeries, mythical pederastic Pueblo rites, cross-dressing shamans, Jungian homosexuality and, at the centre of it all, Harry Hay and his obsession with discovering the secret, hidden history of gay spirituality. Let us commence.

What Means 'Two-Spirit'?

'Two-Spirit' is a slippery word to define, since it contains within it an explicit critique of the very thing it tries to explain. Post-colonial activists describe how the condition of colonisation doesn't just mean the physical loss of land and sovereignty, but also the mental and cultural colonisation which accompanies it. 'Two-Spirit' is meant to be a way of defining and describing the experience and identity of gay, lesbian, transgender and other sexual minorities from *within* the 'Native American community', but using the language of modern Anglo-America. If this sounds pedantic and tedious, you may have a point. The embrace of Native American concerns by that strata of academia which uses obfuscatory and confusing language has formed a sort of crust, preventing the wider public from directly listening to Native Americans themselves without this impenetrable terminology.

As I see it, 'Two-Spirit' is a simplistic and simple term to describe how Native Americans apparently thought about homosexuality and transgenderism, I say 'apparently' because I'm deeply sceptical of the proposition. Almost all Native cultures have terms and ethnographic descriptions of gay men, men and women who cross-dressed and performed tasks meant for the opposite sex. How they understood these aberrations is unique to each culture and language-group, but the term 'Two-Spirit' is meant to capture what is *different* about the 'Native perspective' versus the Western. The phrase refers to the dual nature of the person, perhaps containing both a male and female essence. Modern Western culture is brutally materialistic about sexual identities, interested in genes, twin studies and summed up in the slogan 'Born This Way'. This differs from other parts of the world where homosexuality, like all parts of the human condition, is governed by the spiritual world.

The famous conference, held in Winnipeg in 1990, was the third meeting of the "Annual Inter-Tribal Native American, First Nations, Gay and Lesbian American Conference". Here the delegates designated an Ojibwe term, *niizh manidoowag,* to be the official descriptor of indigenous sexualities. This word literally translates as 'two-spirit', but crucially, both terms were invented at or around the time of the conference, they have no history within Ojibwe culture or their language. Herein for me was the opening part of the mystery - where did this term come from if it had to be retrospectively created in a Native American language? We will turn to that shortly, but first we have to introduce the main character in our story.

Introducing Harry Hay

Harry Hay is one of the gay liberation movement's legendary figures. Born in 1912 in Britain and raised across the world, he came from an illustrious and religiously devout family line. His maternal great-grandfather, General James Allen Hardie, was appointed by President Martin Van Buren to West Point Military Academy where he studied alongside Ulysses S. Grant. General Hardie fought in the 1857 war against the Spokane Indians and his son, Francis, served at Wounded Knee, carrying the Third Cavalry flag. He was also distantly related to Oliver Wendell Holmes through a woman called Anna Wendell. This legacy of conflict with the Native Americans would prove crucial to Hay's later interests and affiliations.

Compared in temperament to General Hardie, Hay was equally a sensitive, emotional and scholarly man. His father, 'Big Harry, passed down to him a streak of total self-reliance and a fierce inner discipline and work ethic. Hay's relationship with his parents, in particular his father, was tense and difficult. When he finally admitted to his mother in 1951 that he was gay, her response was terse: "Your father knew Cecil Rhodes", and that was the end of the matter. The family left for Chile at the outbreak of World War One, his father to work overseeing the mining industry, an employment which cost him his leg in an accident. After this the family relocated to California. Hay was an intellectually gifted boy with a photographic memory, studying with children three years older than him in school. By the time he was nine Hay was effortlessly quoting the history of Egypt and listening to Wagner, but in his biography he recalls that this was the period of his sexual awakening with boys.

An older boy called Calvin introduced him to oral sex, and they learnt to practice on one another until Calvin was sent away to another school. An incident with his father where Hay contradicted something he said is noted as a fundamental moment in his biography. His father whipped him with a leather cat-o-nine-tails until he recanted, which he did not do. At once Hay realised that not only was his father wrong, but that every authority in his life, from the priest to the police, could be wrong as well.

At age 11, Hay knew he found boys attractive. A reference in a book entitled *The Intermediate Sex*, by Edward Carpenter, introduced the term 'homosexual' into his vocabulary and mental map of the world. Carpenter's unique and risky book described a class of men he called 'Uranian', gifted scholars and artists like Michelangelo, Shakespeare and Whitman. He called them 'homogenic' and lit a fire in Hay that such a breed of men were set aside and destined for some special task in society. He was hooked. As Carpenter wrote:

> The instinctive artistic nature of the male of this class, his sensitive spirit, his wave-like emotional temperament, combined with hardihood of intellect and body; and the frank, free nature of the female, her masculine independence and strength wedded so thoroughly to feminine grace of form and manner; may be said to give them both, through their double nature, command of life in all its phases, and a certain freemasonry of the secrets of the two sexes which may well favor their function of reconcilers and interpreters.

We must note in this passage the emphasis on the double nature of the homosexual, it was this idea that grabbed Hay and forever kept him under its sway - a gay man is someone who unites both the male and female spirit, to become a creative and artistic soul.

When Hay was 13 his father sent him to Nevada to work on a ranch, possibly he sensed in his son some affliction which could be cured by hard, physical work and the company of tough men. Unfortunately for him this proved to be the final seditious nail in the coffin. Hay was introduced and integrated into the network of socialist and communist labourers who worked seasonally on the ranch. They gave him pamphlets of Marx, taught him union songs and captivated his mind with tales of the Haymarket Massacre, the 1887 Railroad Strike and the martyrdom of Joe Hill - Harry Hay left that summer a Wobbly in his heart. Just as importantly perhaps, Hay was also introduced to a legendary Native American figure, although he didn't know it at the time. The Paiute prophet Wovoka, known as Jack Wilson in later years, was the 'Ghost Dance Messiah' of 1889. The Ghost Dance movement which swept across the Plains, led directly to Wounded Knee. He would learn of this connection later in life and felt it to be fateful, given his family history.

Not long afterwards Hay had his first full sexual experience with an older sailor called Matt, who told him that 'people like him' existed in secret all around the world, as a kind of brotherhood. Hay described this experience later in life:

When in later years he told this favorite coming-out story, he referred to it ironically as his "child molestation speech," to make the point of how sharply gay life differs from heterosexual norms. "As a child," he explained, "I molested an adult until I found out what I needed to know." He recalled that Matt's promise of a new world and a future served as a life raft during the isolated period of high school. Far from being an experience of "molestation," Harry always described it as "the most beautiful gift that a fourteen-year-old ever got from his first love!"

After graduation Hay's father pushed him into a career in law, working for an LA firm for a year. During this time he discovered the 'cruising scene' and was mentored in the art of gay pick-up culture. In 1930 he enrolled at Stanford University to read International Relations. Informally he discovered acting and the stage life, meeting cross-dressers, openly gay actors and he immersed himself in the lifestyle of rebellion against his strict upbringing. A sinus infection in 1932 led Hay to drop out from university, never to return, but he continued with his acting career, much to the disgust of his father. It was through performing that he met a famous actor of the era, Will Geer. Geer was the man to fully lead Hay away from his Edwardian life into the world of serious political activism. Strikes, union conflicts, anti-racist and anti-fascism demonstrations, eventually being hidden by friends when he threw a brick at a policeman's head. Geer led Hay to join the Communist Party and the two became lovers. For Hay, Geer's boundless optimism and fundamental belief that human nature could be changed for the better was a heady brew, but he came up against reality when he realised that the Communist Party was strictly and institutionally homophobic. Out of desperation and fear, and on the advice of friends and a psychiatrist, Hay decided to marry a woman, to show his commitment to the Party. He chose Anna Platky, a Party member from a working-class Jewish family. He failed to find happiness and solace in this arrangement however, and after many years of drifting through jobs and activism he decided in 1948 to found his own, explicitly homosexual political group - The Mattachine Society.

The Mattachine Society & the Great Project

Hay's inner world was consumed with ideas and visions of this secret, spiritual brotherhood, and he was forever reading and making notes about pagan ceremonies, mediaeval folk festivals, fools, jesters, lepers - anyone and any affair which turned the normal order on its head. He discovered the term 'mattachine', which refers to a 16th century phenomenon of secret societies in Europe, dedicated to dance, satire and clownish rebellion. The Mattachine Society became a fixture in Hay's mind:

> "the Mattachine troupes conveyed vital information to the oppressed in the countryside of Thirteenth to Fifteenth century France and perhaps I hoped that such a society of modern

homosexual men, living in disguise in Twentieth century America, could do similarly for us oppressed Queers."

The Mattachine Society was born out of Hay's belief that homosexuals in America were an oppressed class, but one which should naturally ally with the Left and be capable of determining and lobbying for their own political agenda and future. For a group of people accustomed to living in secret, Hay's provocative and public approach was radical and some found it threatening. He wrote a manifesto, 'Androgynous Minority', which he shared with his lover at the time, a man called Gernreich. Gernreich warned him with the story of the Magnus Hirschfeld, and his Institute for Sexual Research, which had been obliterated by the Nazis. Determined anyway, Hay pushed forward and founded the Mattachine Society, a group modelled on Alcoholics Anonymous and enthused by the recent Kinsey Reports books. The Society ran like a kind of Leninist Freemasonry, with oaths of loyalty, secrecy, cells and five layers of membership.

For Hay this changed everything - he divorced his wife, cut off ties with his respectable friends and advised the Communist Party to expel him for his homosexuality - which they did. The Society grew rapidly, with 100 people comfortably attending each meeting. But the legacy of Hay's communist beliefs and activities attracted considerable public attention and the leadership of the Mattachines pushed for a patriotic and loyal vision of American homosexuality, eventually pressurising Hay to step down from his position. The Society adopted an official stance of non-confrontation, causing Hay to have an emotional breakdown. Dismayed and upset, Hay turned to his intellectual life, looking for inspiration and ideas from the past, continuing his lifelong search for the history of gay people in human societies.

Hay had always maintained his academic and scholarly pursuit of this subject, building boxes of notes with tens of thousands of comments, margin scribbles, reference cards and indexes. This was to turn into something more concrete, or at least that was the goal - "The Homophile in History: A Provocation to Research," sketched out from 1953 to 1955. The project was described:

> "Divided into fourteen periodic sections, it traces homosexual prototypes from the Stone Age through the European Middle Ages up to the "Berdache and the American Scene," where Hay cited Johnny Appleseed as one example of an "American Fool Hero." Much of the study for this was expanded from the syllabus of his music classes at the Labor School. The model Harry used for his study was the berdache. A French term applied to cross-dressing Indians found by the European colonists in the New World, berdache sometimes referred simply to an Indian who committed "the abominable vice" of homosexuality. But to Harry, it meant a cultural role."

We will come on to the subject of the 'berdache' shortly.

Academically, Hay was decades ahead of the zeitgeist. His study ranged across the entire span of human prehistory and written history, attempting to link together primitive matriarchies, goddess worship, druidism, social deviancy, folk festivals and carnivals, peasant religions, banned calendars, societies of jugglers, clowns, glee-men, itinerant nomads and colonies of paupers, trickster figures, folk-heroes and anything else esoteric and unorthodox which he could weave into his narrative of 'gay anthropology'. As we've seen, Hay was convinced that gay people exist in order to fulfil certain, special social functions, but that these had been suppressed, particularly by Christianity. He wrote several papers on Biblical homosexuality - *The Moral Climate of Canaan in the Time of Judges* and *Christianity's First Closet Case* (unpublished). One particular interest for him was the role of the 'craft-specialist' in earlier societies. He was convinced that these were usually gay men, adopting woman's work but excelling and mastering the craft, elevating it to a civilisational level.

But his core mania was for locating specific references to 'us', gay people, and the rites and rituals which were specifically reserved for them. Patient readers may have been wondering at what point does 'two-spirit' emerge in this story? The answer is in Hay's perseverance in tracking down every last reference to gay people in every field of study he could lay his hands on:

"Harry unearthed a forgotten document written in 1882 by a former United States Surgeon General Dr. William A. Hammond, while in the field, observed Indians called *mujerados*, a Spanish term meaning "made women." This tantalized Harry as a possible type of berdache. Hammond described the *mujerados* he had found among Pueblo Indians in Northern New Mexico, who were the "**chief passive agent in the pederastic ceremonies.**" Hay offered a lengthy commentary and roundly protested this paper's "burial by omission" for nearly one hundred years."

"Harry's long search for the report was not an easy one. He had read references to Hammond's paper in several turn-of-the-century books. But in 1962 when he decided to look up the original text he ran into trouble. He started at the U.C.L.A. Research Library, which listed in its holdings Volume I of the American Journal of Neurology and Psychiatry, the first publication to print Hammond's findings. **But when Harry requested a copy he found, to his and the librarian's surprise that the Hammond article had been cut out**."

"Four more copies of the journal that Harry ordered from other libraries had been similarly mutilated. He surmised that Hammond's findings may have been repudiated by some government official and censored. After many months, Harry found a copy of the report in a later text by Hammond titled *Sexual Impotence in the Male and Female*, published in 1887. **Over the years, Hay continued to find many other such cases of obliteration of historical references to homosexuality**."

At this point it is worth taking a break in our story and turning to the question of the 'berdache'.

The Berdache in Native American Culture

The term 'berdache' is strongly out of fashion today; you won't find any references to it in modern literature from the late '80's /early '90's onward. The word is French in origin, meaning 'catamite' or 'boy kept for unnatural purposes', and emerged during the early years of Native anthropology to describe a particular phenomenon observed in some cultures. Typically a berdache describes a man, or less frequently a woman, who breaks with their social expectations and chooses to adopt female clothes and activities. Like all human societies, Native Americans had a binary division of labour, some tasks and roles were for men, others for women. People who intentionally crossed that division were known to anthropologists as berdaches. Confusingly to modern ears, raised on a bewilderingly complex system of parsing out sex, gender, sexuality etc, the berdache was also associated with homosexuality, transgenderism and prostitution. Thus the 'female man' was a gay man.

Berdache as a term is certainly outdated, and even without political sensitivities in the academy it is too broad a description. Each culture had its own understandings of sexuality and gender roles and its own cosmology to explain how some people came to act like the opposite sex. Where the crossover between the European gay rights movement and Native American anthropology occurred was

146

precisely in the confused descriptions of the berdache as having a special *spiritual* role and position within Native cultures. We'll see more of this as we continue, but it is worth establishing here that this belief *cannot* be justified in the light of rigorous anthropology.

Hay & the Radical Faeries

At this point in his life Hay was all in on the search for the historical homosexual. He began corresponding with a number of academic and scholarly figures, including Robert Graves, the writer, critic and translator of historical myths. Hay was convinced that Graves knew a great deal about Greek homosexuality, but was reticent to divulge it. He wrote to him, hoping to gain some insight and information. Graves responded with a diplomatic take on the subject:

> Homophilia as a natural phenomenon is respected in most societies—and by me ... Homophilic careerism and Homophilia indulged in for kicks are what I hate... An alliance of Goddess worshipping Heterophiles with natural Homophiles makes sense to me. The literary and art world is so full of irreligious and perverted messiness. You should purge your ranks! Yours v.s. Robert Graves.

He also attended an extremely strange private lecture series by the English savant, mystic and historian, Gerald Heard. Heard gave a number of talks about homosexuals (he called them 'isophyls') and how they were the next stage in human evolution, due to their prolonged youthful nature and historical ability to organise into secret brotherhoods. According to Hay's biography, Heard remarked to Hay that such an organisation still existed:

> Heard kept hinting at a sort of hidden 'Illuminati,' or secret, Sufi-type brotherhood with initiates in each generation down through the centuries. At our fourth session, he asked if our group was willing to make a commitment to study this brotherhood and hinted at our joining it." Harry was fascinated with the idea of studying with the great scholar, but felt extremely reluctant to re-involve himself in a secret, gay group. "I did not think it was historically correct to go back underground. What Heard wanted were adepts"

Frustrated with this and other dead ends, Hay took to the road, aiming to track down for himself some of the Native American rituals and rites he believed had been forced underground. His experience with the Pueblo people and his studies on the enigmatic *mujerados* made them an obvious choice. Managing to befriend a local Pueblo man by the name of Enki, Hay finally thought he had stumbled upon the evidence he was missing. Enki took him out to a number of ruins, one in particular called Tsankwe, where he told Hay that 'this is where your people lived'. Hay learnt from Enki the term *kwidó*, which Hay believed to be the word for berdache or homosexuals. Elated at the prospect of finding some 'authentic' evidence, he would repeatedly return to Tsankwe with friends and lovers, proudly pointing to the place he believed linked them to some ancestral past.

In point of fact, the term *kwidó* is not a well understood term. In her article *Is the "North American Berdache" Merely a Phantom in the Imagination of Western Social Scientists?,* gender scholar and anthropologist Sue-Ellen Jacobs refers to her arguments with Hay over the correct spelling of *kwidó*, but also her inability to confirm its existence among the Tewa Pueblo. She laments that *"I was told on several occasions that I had misunderstood. They had "never had any people like that here". I was also told that people "like that" had learnt such ways from white people.".* It seems obvious in retrospect that Hay was simply confirming his own beliefs. Convinced that homosexuality had been suppressed, any ambiguous evidence merely supported his convictions.

Hay moved to San Juan Pueblo in 1971, committing himself to a number of projects, including Albuquerque's first Pride parade and a fight to prevent a dam being built over the Rio Grande. Here his deepest desire for a brotherhood of men imbued with 'gay consciousness' finally came into being, for a short while. The Radical Faeries was established in 1979, the aim being to create 'Faerie circles' of gay men who could live a certain way. It was a mish-mash of New Age ideas, hippy aesthetics, western style shamanism, Jungian psychology, drugs, the carnival and riotous dance atmosphere of Hay's dreams. He implored people to *"throw off the ugly green frogskin of hetero-imitation to find the shining Faerie prince beneath"*.

Some 200 men turned up to the first circle:

> The workshops were on such varied subjects as massage, nutrition, local botany, healing energy, the politics of gay enspiritment, English country dancing, and auto-fellatio. Those assembled took part in spontaneous rituals, providing invocations to spirits and performing blessings and chants, with most participants discarding the majority of their clothes, instead wearing feathers, beads, and bells, and decorating themselves in rainbow makeup. Many reported feeling a change of consciousness during the event, which one person there described as "a four day acid trip – without the acid!".

The Dionysian frenzy which took hold of the participants at the first gathering would be savagely condemned today as denigrating Native culture and role-playing of the highest order. They rolled in mud, built a giant earth phallus, crowned one another in laurel leaves, howled at the moon and experienced a group vision when a huge black bull entered a drum circle at the moment of greatest crescendo. The testimonies afterwards are full of ecstatic language, allusions to baptism, renewal, spiritual cleansing and a heightened sense of gay consciousness. Many would come to adopt pseudo-native monikers, like Crazy Owl and Morning Star.

Crucially for our story, this gathering was the first time a man called Will Roscoe met Harry Hay. In tracing the origins of 'two-spirit', this encounter between the young Roscoe and the veteran Hay is central. Roscoe would go on to turn Hay's jumbled and eccentric boxes of research into fully fledged books and scholarly works, infused with the Faerie-spiritually gay ethos. Roscoe stayed close to Hay after the gathering, becoming involved with a possible land purchase for the Faeries and keeping his friendship with Hay after the Faeries splintered and collapsed in the early 1980's.

During this visit Harry's gay historical research had the dust shaken off it. "One night after dinner," Roscoe recalled, "while making some point about gay people in the history of civilization, Harry made a sweeping gesture toward a dark corner of the room and said, 'Of course, if you really want to know about this you'll have to get into that: He was referring to a haphazard pile of cardboard file boxes crammed with thousands of pages of notes from the Fifties." When Roscoe returned to San Francisco the next Autumn, he took four boxes of the notes with him to index and copy. He found Harry's notes impressive in their scope and detail... Roscoe was intrigued by the fact that Hay had started with the North American Indian berdache, and then researched the history of civilization as he looked for specific manifestations of that role. Roscoe decided to take up where Harry had left off and develop full empirical studies

Roscoe, Jung & Gay Indians

With the Faeries collapsing and splintering, a new group was founded in 1982 - Treeroots. This was led by two 'gay pyschologists', Mitch Walker and Don Kilhefner. Both were interested in using Jungian theory and ritualistic practice to explore gay consciousness. This particular technique rests on Jung's belief that men possessed an 'anima' - an unconscious feminine aspect which can be explored through therapy. In one sense gay men being attracted to Jung has an obvious logic, with his emphasis on duality and the a female aspect to man, as well as the negative consequences of this, self-hatred and projection. But we can trace here an explicit connection between Jung's archetypal 'two-spirit' and the later development of a Native American spiritual category of 'two-spirit'.

There is a much larger critique to be made one day about how Jung himself, who visited Native Americans in Taos, made use of 'primitive' religious thinking in his work and how this ultimately contributed to the appropriation and development of his philosophy by 'gay psychology'. But this article is long enough already. Suffice to say that the tributaries of ideas which fed into this psychological movement already included severe mischaracterisations of Native American religion by both Jung and Hay. A modern example of this phenomena can be found in the 'work' of Aaran Mason, the author of such papers as *The Gay Male Goddess and the Myth of Binaries: A Queer Archetypal Meandering*. A recent discussion of his work explores this muddled cross-over of 'Native' and Jungian thought:

While at Pacifica, research led Mason to the work of Will Roscoe, who writes about Native American "two-spirits"—a term used to describe "non-binary gender roles among Native American tribes." Roscoe's writings also introduced Aaron to research on the "Galli" cult: ancient groups of men who worshiped the Great Mother Earth Goddess, Cybele...

Armed with these kinds of ideas to provide context and understanding, Mason realized that drag is a "trickster type of process," that it relies on the trickster energy. In some Native American tales, for example, Coyote would dress like a woman to get what he wanted. In other tales, he would do other outlandish things such as removing his own genitals, getting caught in traps, or enacting outlandish or bawdy schemes...

On that note, Mason told me about a documentary film he discovered called "Two Spirits" in which a Navajo man, Wesley Thomas (who identifies as a two-spirit himself), relates a Navajo origin myth about four genders... Instead of "black and white thinking" where one thing is pitted against the other, when the binary is enlarged to four, an individual might identify as a feminine female, a masculine male, a feminine male, or a masculine female.

Aaron recognized that this concept might also be symbolized by a quaternal mandala, which has a place in Jungian psychology as a sacred circle, encompassing a whole with four equally contributing parts. It also offers the opportunity for the feminine to enter into the Trinity, and for us to view the feminine through two pairs of two binary figures (potentially reunited): Mary mother of Jesus paired with Mary Magdalene and Eve paired with Lilith (the temptress), Aaron suggests.

For Roscoe, Walker, Kilhefner and others involved in the genesis of 'gay psychology', the intellectual and emotional power of the Faerie circles and gatherings was the raw material to be fashioned into more serious and institutional products. Roscoe was both the conduit and sculptor of Hay's decades long project into the history of gay personhood. He did not disappoint.

In the years following the Stonewall riots (1969), a small but significant exodus began to take place. A number of Native Americans, attracted by the gay liberation movement, travelled to San Francisco and started identifying with the Anglo-European scene of gays, lesbians, bisexuals, transgenders and cross-dressers. It has proved extremely difficult to track down exactly how this happened, but in 1975, two Native Americans - Randy Burns, a Paiute, and Barbara Cameron, a Lakota - founded the Gay American Indians (GAI). The relationship between this group and Will Roscoe is murky, but somehow he ended up becoming the Project

Coordinator for the Gay American Indians History Project (1984) and editor for the *Living the Spirit: A Gay American Indian Anthology*. The records and papers related to this time period are held by the GLBT Historical Society in San Francisco (the Will Roscoe papers and Gay American Indians records). These have yet to be digitised and surely contain the story of how Roscoe, a non-Native, came to be embraced and placed in a leadership position by the GAI.

The dynamics here are exceptionally complicated. For Roscoe, Hay and many gay-identifying Native Americans, the anger and aggression shown towards gay Native Americans by other Natives has its origin in the Christianisation of their culture. Roscoe became the 'expert' who could claim and 'prove' that previous generations of Native Americans were not only tolerant of gays, third-genders and transgender people, but that these people were celebrated and even worshipped for their spiritual powers. However, and this gets to the heart of the problem, much of this research, and the claims that flow from it, are *simplified, distorted and propagandised* images of pre-Columbian American life. Roscoe went on to write dozens of books and articles about the existence and reverence for homosexuals and third-gender people in numerous indigenous and traditional societies - including Islam, Christianity, African and Native American groups.

"Why Was the Berdache Ridiculed"

So if patient readers have followed along, they might be asking what exactly is wrong with this definition of two-spirit if Native Americans themselves have adopted it? Native history and control over it has become an essential part of the progressive cosmology since the 1960's, in particular making use of it to fortify a vision of a world where a patriarchal, dominant Christian colonial state wiped out a peaceful, matriarchal, ecologically-friendly and egalitarian society of hunters and farmers. Almost everyone has seen this form of propaganda, the Noble Savage doomed to extinction, and with it the earth suffers. The specific question of the 'berdache' and how Hay's acolytes and companions managed to distort history certainly deserves to be told, and hopefully I have provided the reader with some background here which explains how this new image of the 'two-spirit' came into being. But let us turn to the problem of what exactly was distorted.

Scholarship on the historical 'berdache' is overwhelmingly biased in one direction or another. Progressive activists and scholars are correct that earlier anthropologists were horrified by some Native culture's acceptance of what they saw as deviance and perversion, which created a false picture of reality. But equally the push-back from Roscoe and co is overrun with mistakes. I want to point to several key criticisms:

> In converting 'the berdache' to the 'two-spirit', Roscoe and
> co are guilty of exactly the same offence as earlier

156

anthropologists, of homogenising Native cultures, many of which had *no such thing* as a 'berdache'.

The foisting of the modern gay movement's notion of 'queer' onto Native cultures is both anachronistic and degrading.

Roscoe and co minimise historical evidence for ridicule, dislike and hostility towards 'berdaches' and overstate the case of their sacred and divine nature.

The first of these is the least controversial and most commonly discussed. Internet articles such as "what were the five Native American genders?" are guilty of straight up falsehoods. Even within the enormous 'culture zones' of North America, such as the Pacific Northwest, there is a vast amount of cultural differentiation and each people dealt with the topic of gender, cross-dressing and sexuality differently. For many groups, most famously the Iroquois, there is no evidence at all for a 'berdache' phenomenon. From the detailed 1983 paper, *The North American Berdache:*

We might add that Loskiel's (1794:11) report of homosexuality among the Delaware and apparently the Iroquois (Katz 1976:290) did not describe berdache behavior. **The case for the absence of berdaches among Iroquois cultures is strong.** Kehoe points out that Miller (1974) reached a similar conclusion

In a pretty damning comment by Carolyn Epple, on her work with the Navajo *'nadleehi'* :

> It appears that Roscoe, Williams, and others have frequented the shrine of The Perpetual Homosexual and, in so doing, not only have overlooked the cultural boundedness of sexuality as a concept but also subsume nadleehi (and possibly others with similar characteristics) under the principles of present-day sexuality classification—an unfounded inclusion... thus they attempt to "*demonstrate that preindustrial societies are more 'tolerant' ... or'accommodating' of erotic diversity and gender variation than 'the West'*". The benefits of identifying with "preindustrial" societies are many, thus, for example, Williams looks to "the American Indian concept of spirituality to break out of the deviancy model to reunite families and to offer special benefits to society as a whole" (1986:207). And Roscoe adds, "*I have no difficulty imagining the rationale and rewards of specializing in a work otherwise considered female. My own consciousness has thus absorbed the berdache*"

Although both authors acknowledge differences between Euro-American and Native American meanings of gay, they clearly conflate the meanings for their political and personal purposes. It is little wonder that Jaimes, a Native American woman, objects to such perspectives: "*Particularly offensive have been non-Indian efforts to convert the indigenous custom of treating homosexuals (often termed 'berdache'by anthropologists) as persons endowed with special spiritual powers into a polemic for mass organizing within the dominant society"*

Epple's remarks on how Roscoe and Williams have made use of Native culture to help fight their own struggles - "an unfounded conclusion" - have been echoed by many others over the years. Attacks on the concept of 'two-spirit' often emphasise how radically different Native conceptions of sexuality, kinship and spiritually were, and still are. Some, like the Dene, believe a child can be born with the soul of a dead relative, but this in no way affects their sexuality. Many now question how this terminology was pushed onto them, such as the Mohawk poet James Thomas Stevens in his paper *Poetry and Sexuality: Running Twin Rails:*

> Speaking of constructed identities —enter the Twin-Spirit. Since the mid-1970s, and the founding of GAI (Gay American Indians), those interested in sociosexual and anthropological/cultural research have taken up terms such as *berdache, Winkte, double-sex, Nadle, Hwame,* and *Twin-Spirit… Twin-Spirit* is too often used as a pan-Indian term for queer-identified Native peoples, even where no such terms existed before.

Queer is an especially grating term to use to describe Native sexualities. As a word which arose in the Anglo-European context of a 'liberation' movement, queer is specifically defined as 'deviant', 'non-normative' and 'perverse'. Conceptually this is nothing like the documented 'berdache' of Native anthropology, and whilst they can be disliked, marginalised and mocked, the 'berdache' existed within an accepted social framework, often with explicit rules of who they could and could not have sex with. In a paper entitled *Dance to the Two-Spirit: Mythologizations of the Queer Native,* Marianne Kongerslev takes aim at Roscoe's depiction of North America as "the queerest continent on the planet". She notes:

Two-Spirit does not signify queerness, as many tribal cultures did not conceive of their non-binary members as outsiders or contrary to traditions. The western notion of queerness here is inaccurate and insufficient for understanding the term. **Two-Spirit people served central purposes within their nations and cultures, and are thus not 'queer'.**

Whilst I disagree with the use of the phrase 'two-spirit' to describe all Native cultures, something she discusses herself in the paper, the point is clear. Likewise in her article, Epple insists that the Navajo view gender as the primary cleavage of nature, everything can be divided into male and female categories. Thus even the *'nadleehi'* third-gender cannot 'queer' or deviate from this.

Everything, as any Navajo will tell you, can be divided into male and female.... Kluckhohn points out that chants, rivers, plants, and other items are arranged as male and female... Matthews makes a similar observation: "There are many instances in

Navaho language and legend where, when two things somewhat resemble each other, but one is the coarser, the stronger, or the more violent it is spoken of as male or associated with male; while the finer, weaker, or more gentle is spoken of as female, or associated with the female"

I don't want to bombard the reader with an endless series of quotes, so I shall end this critique section with just one more. Although the 'berdache' is often institutionalised in Native cultures, what Roscoe and co have done in presenting their existence as both 'queer' and spiritual is to invert the documented dynamic. It is true that some tribes viewed them as possessing spiritual powers, it is also the case that they were routinely shunned, mocked and taunted, sometimes even exiled. There is no paradox here to my mind, the existence of a category of person which has a certain status but is nonetheless disliked is commonplace, a blacksmith being a classic example. To round this section out I will present a definitive quotation from David Greenberg's 1998 work *The Construction of Homosexuality:*

Alongside the sources that refer to berdaches as honored or accepted, there are others that describe negative responses. The Papago "scorned" berdaches; the Cocopa "apparently disliked" them. The Choctaws held them "in great contempt," the Seven Nations "in the most sovereign contempt." The Klamath subjected berdaches to "scorn and taunting;" the Sioux "derided" them. Pima berdaches were ridiculed, though not otherwise sanctioned, as were Mohave berdaches who claimed to possess the genitals of the opposite sex. The Apache treated berdaches respectfully when they were present, but ridiculed them behind their backs. Although the Zuni accepted their berdache, "there was some joking and laughing about his ability to attract the young men to his home." In some groups, berdaches' partners were also ridiculed or despised.

She describes the process by which, over a period of years, a young Santee man became a winkta. As a boy, he had preferred headwork and housework to boys' sports. With approval for his transformation coming through his dreams, he adopted female attire and forms of speech. The winkta's transvestism elicited no special response until he began to flirt with and attempt to seduce many of the men in his village. At this point the villagers held a formal ceremony exiling the winkta for life. This was a very severe penalty, greater than that imposed for homicide. Following his exile, the winkta took up residence in a neighboring village. There he was welcomed by the women, who were grateful for his contribution to women's work (male berdaches often excelled in performing traditionally female tasks), and by the men, who were happy to partake of his "hospitality" (not described further, but presumably the reference is to sexual hospitality). Despite this seemingly positive reception, the winkta was persistently subjected to flirtatious teasing

There are many explanations for this behaviour, but one obvious source of tension was the ability for a 'berdache' male to avoid going to war by identifying with the occupations of a female. Interested readers can track down the book for a more in-depth discussion of that argument.

The 1990 Conference

Throughout the 1980's, Roscoe and others worked tirelessly on the topic of the 'berdache', rehabilitating the image of a maligned deviant into a powerful and beloved figure which had been suppressed by the colonial state. Roscoe drew on Hay's work to create a global narrative of where the homosexual fit into numerous cultures, how they were revered and helped the current generation of gay activists feel connected to a deeper and even 'primitive' vision of their place in human history. All this work was to lead to the formal adoption of the term 'two-spirit' by the delegates in Winnipeg. The details of the conference and the following 'Two-Spirit' Movement have been archived at the University of Winnipeg, curated by Albert McLeod. Without these details I can't present the intricacies of the conference debates and discussions, but it seems almost certain, given the nature of Roscoe's work, that the term and its implications came from Hay's and Roscoe's philosophy. This isn't to ignore the contributions of the Native delegates and activists, who obviously welcomed and accepted the term, but as we've seen, the interpretation of the historical record is paramount.

The links between the Gay American Indian movement and its successors with the academic world matters, for it was the patina of legitimacy that activist scholarship supplied which propelled the term 'Two-Spirit' into general use. The term appears in academic journals in the late 1980's and then explodes after the conference, being picked up by advocacy groups, AIDS charities, NGOs, local governments and then the wider media and culture. Today it has become accepted vocabulary, along with its attendant beliefs, such as "Native people had four genders" or "Native cultures worshipped queer and transgender people", a trope which has become embedded and seems unlikely to disappear.

In Closing

Hopefully this has been an interesting and illuminating read. Researching this topic led me down many strange rabbit holes and the character of Harry Hay in particular I found both fascinating and repulsive. His obvious intelligence, organisational skills and talents have to, in my mind, be put into the context of his desires and temperament. For instance, Hay was doggedly determined to have the North American Man/Boy Love Association (NAMBLA) included in the general gay rights movement and be allowed to march at Pride with a flag and banner. His views on homosexual love and age-of-consent reveal his consistent belief that homosexuality was not only a distinct biological phenomenon, but brought with it a distinct spiritual nature as well, one which should not confine itself to the views, customs, habits and morals of the

164

heterosexual world. He went to his grave holding out that a boy of 14 should be allowed to 'molest', in his words, an older man, to get the information and knowledge he needed. It is this belief in the radical separateness and incompatible moral codes of the gay and straight worlds which I believe fuelled his philosophical and scholarly pursuits. He wanted gay men in particular to have their own cosmos and their own unique place in history.

I have no doubt that his commitment to the Native Americans he lived amongst was sincere, but his obsession with locating the 'primitive origins' of homosexuality taints these associations. A most revealing quote from his biography displays this in full:

> Despite Harry's frustrations with his berdache investigation at San Juan, he suspected that a berdache tradition—at least in part —remained beyond the observation of whites. This suspicion was bolstered one afternoon as he watched San Juan schoolchildren debarking from their bus in front of the trading post. "A small boy of about eight was weeping and hiding behind a girl of the same age. I heard her shout at some other boys who were taunting this poor scared kid, 'Leave him alone! He has every right to act however he wants to, and you know it!' It was clear she was defending a little sissy." Harry never got the chance to catch a clearer glimpse of this possibility, but felt that any such tradition would be carefully guarded from outsiders.

He had created a world for himself where, behind every door, was a secret gay rite and ritual. Even in the bullying of a small boy he saw a missed opportunity to prise open the secrets of a culture that was not his.

Ultimately I think that Roscoe and Hay are responsible for creating a mythical Homosexual, what others call the Perpetual Homosexual, and for pushing this into the new activist-led academia and into that crossroads where gay Indians and gay Westerners met. 'Two-Spirit' encapsulates Hay's and Roscoe's belief in a matriarchal worshipping divine gay man, one who integrates some archetypal binary male/female essence and who is destined for a special role in society and history. Not only do I think this is obviously the fantasy of an introverted and precocious boy, but it is one which has profoundly influenced the modern gay rights movement, in particular the philosophy of transgenderism. But that is perhaps another story, someone else's to tell. If contemporary Native Americans are happy with the term 'Two-Spirit', that is up to them. But my conversations with Native friends suggest otherwise, and so I offer this piece to anyone interested in finding out the origins of these terms and ideas which feel foisted upon them.

Bibliography (not already in text)

The Trouble with Harry Hay: Founder of the Modern Gay Movement. Stuart Timmons. 1992.

Becoming two-spirit: Gay identity and social acceptance in Indian country. Gilley BJ. University of Nebraska Press. 2006.

Two-spirit people: Native American gender identity, sexuality, and spirituality. Jacobs SE, Thomas W, Lang S, editors. University of Illinois Press. 1997.

Indian Blood: HIV and Colonial Trauma in San Francisco's Two-Spirit Community. Jolivette AJ. University of Washington Press; 2016.

The Zuni man-woman. UNM Press. Roscoe W. 1991.

Islamic homosexualities: Culture, history, and literature. Roscoe W, Murray SO, editors. NYU Press; 1997.

Cannibalism With Chinese Characteristics

Exploring China's Long and Unique History Of Cannibalism

"The flesh was consumed not simply out of "class hatred" or "revolutionary revenge." Livers and hearts were taken for other reasons: to "embolden the eater" or to cure the eater's ailments... Some old men took the brain of a dead victim while an old woman suffering from an eye ailment sought the eyeballs. Filial piety and parental duty motivated some young individuals, who took pieces of flesh home for their parents, and some mothers brought their sick children to the site of the butchery for a piece of liver. Various culinary procedures adopted seem to suggest the presence of "gourmet cannibalism" as well... This does not cohere with any "system" of classification."

This disturbing paragraph, taken from Gang Yue's book '*The Mouth That Begs: Hunger, Cannibalism and the Politics of Eating in Modern China',* manages to capture exactly why the Chinese experience with cannibalism is so odd, so unusual and so unique. The context, which we will explore more thoroughly later on, is the so-called *'Guangxi Massacre'* of 1966-76. We see encapsulated here all the reasons why academics and researchers struggle to explain the

Chinese anomaly in this area of the human experience. I want to try and break down this description and look at what sources and works we have to make sense of the following: Do episodes of Chinese cannibalism follow an older historical script? Why do we see medical, nutritional and revenge cannibalism occurring in the same time and place, and why does China seem to be almost alone in practising 'filial' and 'gourmet' cannibalism? This combination is what I will dub 'Cannibalism with Chinese Characteristics'.

The Nuances of Eating People

Cannibalism seems a straightforward topic to describe: the act of eating a human body. But as soon as we start to look more closely, we find that cannibalism, far from a blind act performed by unthinking creatures, is typically a socially taboo subject with specific rules and episodes determining where it takes place. The most basic distinction, credited to Dutch ethnographer Rudolf Steinmetz, is between *endocannibalism* and *exocannibalism*. Endocannibalism is where only the bodies of those related to you as part of your kin network or larger social tribe are eaten. Exocannibalism is the opposite - only the bodies of those unrelated and far distant from your group are consumed. The standard definitions of these come from anthropological and archaeological work studying groups such as the Maori, who eat the bodies of their enemies, or the Amazonian Amahuaca, who eat the pulverised bones of their relatives to banish malevolent spirits.

Other classification schemes have explored *medical cannibalism*, consuming body parts for health reasons; *mortuary cannibalism*, related to endocannibalism - where consumption takes place during funeral rites; *dietary cannibalism*, eating human flesh for sustenance or to fend off starvation and *non-normative* or *deviant cannibalism* - modern serial killers or internet cannibals who do not reflect their social norms.

Chinese Medicine

In the 1919 short story '*Medicine*', written by Chinese author Lu Xun, an old man and his wife go out to purchase a folk remedy to help cure their son from tuberculosis. They invest their savings in this medicine, but it fails to work and their little boy dies. The remedy in question turns out to be a warm bread roll soaked in the blood of an executed revolutionary. After the sick boy dies and is buried, the mothers of them both - revolutionary and citizen - meet at the graveside and Xun draws our attention to the metaphor of the old literally feeding off the blood of the young and dynamic.

China is not alone in having a history and medical tradition which called for the use of human body parts and substances. The consumption of blood, ground up bone and all sorts of grisly products has a long pedigree, likely stretching back into the archaic past. The European penchant for eating dried and powdered mummified corpses was well documented, right into the 18th century. Recipes for human blood marmalade, skull bones in alcohol, moss grown on the heads of executed men - these all fill the excitable columns of journalists quick to point out that Europeans had gruesome tastes at exactly the time they were demonising Native Americans and others for cannibalism. This may be a fair point, but China presents its own unique set of historical phenomena surrounding the medico-religious use of the human body.

Chinese civilisation is often touted as the world's oldest and most continuous, particularly by the modern Chinese state, who wish to emphasise the extended lineage of writing, education and even human evolution through time from at least the Neolithic onward. This is a debatable claim, but at the very least it has more merit than attempting to derive European civilisation from an equally early time period, so let us withhold scepticism and engage on their terms. With the religious traditions of Taoism drawing on the Neolithic Hongshun Wuist cultures of shamanism and Confucianism tapping into ideas dating back to the Xia Dynasty (2070-1600 BC), we can therefore argue that the medical traditions and prohibitions of both belong to the deepest wellsprings of what it means to be Chinese.

The oldest written medical text in China is the *Wushi'er Bingfang* - Recipes for 52 Ailments - dating to 168 BC in the Han Dynasty. Among magical incantations and snake bite cures is the mention of several human body parts: hair, fingernails and menstrual cloth, to be used as remedies. In 1597, Li Shizhen published the *Bengcao Gangmu*, his most important work and the best preserved source of Chinese medicine. In it, Shizhen details the extensive and meticulous use of human body parts for a wide range of conditions. These can be as crude as a whole human head, or as particular as the white sediment from a child's urine, the first faeces of a newborn baby, placental fluid, the earth from underneath a hanged man, ground gallstones, human tears and saliva, or the 'bregma' - the point at which the sutures on the skull meet. Detailed instructions exist for processing human urine or the collection of copious quantities of semen, and even female vaginal secretions. (Shizhen warns against using such secretions, saying "They consider this a treasured drug and indulge in sex excessively, eating such a foul thing. This practice will shorten their lifespans greatly. What a stupid thing!").

What is crucial here is that this use of the human body for medicine is deeply rooted, forms part of a continuous tradition and has yet to be properly stamped out. Claims and cases of herbal folk healers using body parts continue to be reported in modern China; as late as 2005 a Chinese cosmetics company was investigated by the UK House of Commons select committee on health for apparently using human skin, harvested from executed prisoners, in their beauty products. The company's agents defended the practice as "traditional".

Warlords & Warriors - Cases of Cannibalism

One of the oldest literary references to cannibalism in the Chinese canon is during the *War of the Three Kingdoms*, set between AD 169-280. The warlord Liu Bei, who founded the state of Shu Han, is recorded as engaging in and permitting cannibalism as his men went hungry. Surrounded by the forces of Yuan Shu, he and his troops ate dead bodies to stay alive. More interestingly, the tale of the criminal hunter Liu An reveals what will be a theme in this essay - the uniquely Chinese concept of *filial cannibalism*. Liu An has nothing to serve Liu Bei, which is embarrassing and degrading, so he kills his own wife and serves her flesh up to the warlord. Despite Liu Bei discovering this the next day, Liu An is rewarded later by the Emperor as a faithful servant.

In a similar story, the Tang general Zhang Xun and his men experience severe hunger during the Battle of Suiyang. Zhang repels attack after attack from Yin Ziqi, and the city is at first well stocked with supplies. Eventually the men resort to eating their horses, then birds and rodents. Finally Zhang kills his favourite concubine and divides her among his men. This prompts an explosion of cannibalism as first the servants, then all the women of the city, then all the non military men are killed and eaten. A point worth mentioning is that none of the victims are recorded as putting up any resistance to their fate. The death and consumption of the concubine has been a source of literary creativity ever since - Yao Maoliang's southern drama *Shuangzhong ji* provides agency to the concubine so that she willingly volunteers her body for the greater cause. In doing so the author leans on the Confucian line of thinking that links the macrocosm of the state with the microcosm of the family, her sacrifice and total absorption into the political unity of the body politic, in other words - the state is a natural organic entity which rests on the *filial love* of its subjects.

The historian Key Rey Chong documents a number of similar sieges and moments of military peril where opposing sides agree to swap children as food. He provides evidence for 177 instances of cannibalism, either from starvation or some other cultural imperative. The numbers between dynasties stay roughly the same. In a paper by Harry F Lee, published in 2019, a meta-analysis of Chinese literature, archaeology and history revealed a huge number of incidents of cannibalism over the period 1470-1911. Lee reports that 1194 cases of cannibalism can be positively identified, and that the majority of them match the time periods for both drought and war. This is unsurprising, given that the majority of cannibalism cases stem from the need to eat. But the number is high and certainly Lee could not have captured every episode.

Confucianism & Filial Cannibalism

By now it might be clear that Chinese cannibalism does have certain characteristics which set it apart - there aren't a great number of military sieges where the defending army resorts to eating the people it is trying to protect. Central to these unique elements is the Confucian notion of *filial piety*.

"Among the various forms of virtuous conduct, xiao comes first (baixing xiao weixian !")," declares a well known Chinese proverb. In the Shuoyuan , Confucius is quoted as saying, "Among human practices, none is greater than xiao." Xiao is commonly rendered as "filial piety… Some scholars contend that the character xiao appears in the oracle bones; most agree that it occurs in Western Zhou (1045–771 BCE) sources, frequently as a verb in texts about the performance of sacrifices… probably at the very earliest stages in their history, the Chinese gave filial piety an extremely exalted position – treated it as something one might almost call an absolute, a metaphysical entity"

"Holzman's study describes "the peculiar passion [for filial piety] that took hold of the country at the beginning of the Later Han dynasty (25–220 CE)," and explains how "the excesses to which filial piety was carried at that time illustrate an aspect of Chinese psychology that, once understood, will help us appreciate much that usually remains incomprehensible in Chinese history." According to Holzman, the centrality of the homage children rendered to their parents and ancestor worship in Chinese culture, which create a strong tie binding succeeding generations one to another, explain both its enduring character and the difficulty of adapting it to the modern world"

The concept of filial cannibalism comes from the zoological study of cannibalism. A wide range of animals, fish and insects engage in the practice of eating all or part of their offspring. In fish it is particularly associated with paternal care species, and in insects it serves to limit parasites, to fend off starvation and improve reproductive fitness for the survivors. In general there is no consensus as to how and why the practice emerged in evolutionary history.

Why this is important for our subject is that China has been noted by various historians as essentially the only place where filial cannibalism became a standard human practice (Confucian practices in Korea led to children finger chopping for their parents). At its deepest most spiritual level, the filial act of a child offering up their own body to their parents is a reversal of the natural order of biology, for the next generation to feed the old with their very flesh. In a story by the early Qing philologist Mao Qiling, a young man called Yang engages in both *gegu*, the act of slicing off a body part (usually a portion of thigh, upper arm or finger) to feed to a parent, and coprophagy. He tastes his ill father's faeces, and is upset that their sweetness indicates his coming death, he then slices off a portion of his arm to feed and cure his mother. Tina Lu, in her work *Accidental Incest, Filial Cannibalism, & Other Peculiar Encounters in Late Imperial Chinese Literature,* describes this incident:

> "Parenthood's essence is to create new bodies; when Yang chooses coprophagy and cannibalism to express devotion to his parents, he seems to suggest that filiality's point is to defy—or at least undo — the heart of parenthood. If biology makes three where there were two, this filial son, through both eating and feeding, attempts to make one of three."

Gegu has a long documented history as an accepted social practice. Noted in the tenth century, by the sixteenth it was a staple feature of stories, dramas and debates. The physician Li Shizhen, who we met earlier, railed against gegu:

> "How could any parent, even if seriously ill, possibly desire their offspring to harm their bodies and limbs, and consume their own flesh and bones? Such [practices] stem from the views of the foolish".

As we saw, his criticism falls flat as he begins listing all the medical uses of human body parts. His disgust is in line with a basic reading of Confucian ethics, that children should not harm their own bodies, but this prescription has never stopped serious acts of filial devotion where children look to feed starving parents. Religious scholar Jimmy Yu notes that filial cannibalism perhaps has a political parallel wherein earlier Chinese rulers would eat the body of a previous claimant. The Yellow Emperor claimed victory over the monstrous Chi You and had him quartered, simmered and served to his soldiers. Dynastic succession, from the Xia to the Shang and then to the Zhou often involved stories of one leader being fed to another, such as the Zhou inheritors eating King Zhou of Shang's body raw, or drinking his blood. Yu tentatively makes the case that gegu fits into a Chinese concern with regeneration and renewal through sacrifice.

The Emotions of Eating

A number of Chinese writers and thinkers, such as Lu Xun, Zheng Yi and Mo Yan, have discussed the interesting theme of hunger and of eating which runs through much of Chinese literature and thought. Two ancient idioms exemplify the primal emotion to not only kill your enemy, but to fully abolish them through ingestion - *shirou qinpi* (eating your flesh and sleeping on your hide) and *henbude bani chile* (I really want to eat you - said as an expression of rage).

The first comes from the *Zuozhuan*, the oldest work of narrative history detailing the period 722 - 468 BC. The warrior Zhou Chuo resents that his Duke praises two adversaries which he had just beaten, and declares to him that he will eat them and sleep on their hides. While this isn't a formal declaration of intent, it underscores the emotional resonance of eating one's enemies, just as the second popular saying also reinforces. Historian Edward Schafer describes this kind of impulse writ large during the Tang Dynasty:

> "A very special kind of ritual food was human flesh. It was by no means an uncommon occurrence for outraged Tang citizenry to chop up the body of a corrupt or tyrannical official and eat him .... In 739 an officer of the court, who enjoyed the monarch's favor, accepted a bribe to cover up the crime of a colleague; the affair came to light, and the ruler had the offender beaten severely, after which the official supervising the punishment cut out the culprit's heart and ate a piece of his flesh. Again, in 767 a man murdered his rival, who had accused him of misdeeds, and having sliced his body into gobbets, he partook of them. In 803 a military officer

led a mutiny against his commander, killed him, and devoured him, presumably with the help of his associates"

This kind of cannibalism has been described as 'revenge cannibalism', springing not from the pangs of starvation and hunger, nor from the filial excesses of Confucian piety, but rather from the primal urge to absorb and obliterate an offender, a criminal, a heretic or a rival.

China's long agrarian history has fostered a near obsession with eating as a central metaphor for existence. Adages such as 'people revere food as if it were Heaven' or the more recent 'anything with two legs is edible except your parents; so is anything with four legs, except the bed' exemplify the importance of food and eating almost without cultural constraint. The Maoist Revolution and the language of Revolution pitched itself intentionally against an old-world order of human flesh and feasting, focusing on the belt tightening and iron bowl sacrifices the people would need to make to renew the world. We saw earlier in Lu Xun's parable of traditional medicine how the revolutionary impulse was itself cannibalistic, but the luxury and decadence of the former epoch was often described through the notion of 'gourmet cannibalism'.

The idea of gourmet cannibalism is a disturbing one, that people would consume human flesh not out of necessity or even ritual proscription, but for its taste and properties as a form of food, like any other high value victual. It is hard to evaluate any serious claim that China at any point institutionalised the practice of making feasting foods from human bodies, but hints do exist. In the fictional story *The Republic of Wine* by Mo Yan, gourmet cannibalism becomes a major theme; in the apocryphal story of Yi Yan, a chef to the Duke Huan, he cooks up his own son's head to serve to his superior, not only out of filial loyalty, but because the Duke enjoys the taste and flavour. Most sensationally, in his potted history of cannibalism, the writer Bill Schutt claimed to have seen Yuan Dynasty era documents detailing numerous ways to cook and eat children, including recipes and complex cooking and roasting methods. Again, such stories are almost impossible to corroborate, but it appears that at the very least, whispered rumours of such practices pepper Chinese history, to be drawn upon by writers and thinkers in later generations. To quote Yun-Chu Tsai, author of a dissertation on Chinese cannibalism in literature and reality:

"Chinese gourmandism and gourmet cannibalism share the same discourse in which the existence of "the other" is meaningful only for the desire and satisfaction of the self. Both Chinese gourmandism and gourmet cannibalism share the logic of eating animals or human beings for one's own immoderate physical need and pleasure"

A Spasm of Violence - The Revolution

Turning to one of the most disturbing outbreaks of cannibalism in the modern world - the Cultural Revolution - we see all the major themes discussed so far appear in the same place at the same time. The quote at the beginning of the article can now finally be put into context - the emphasis on a widespread, shared belief in the medicinal powers of human flesh, the author's insistence that *not only* was revenge cannibalism at play, but also undertones of gourmet and filial cannibalism, and finally the simple reality that unrelated people engaged in a spasm of violence, culminating in shamelessly carving up corpses to take home for their relatives. So what exactly happened in the Guangxi Massacre?

For a full and truly devastating account of the massacre one must turn to Zheng Yi's *Scarlet Memorial: Tales of Cannibalism in Modern China.* Here the darkest episodes of the Revolution played out and the mildest descriptions contain off-handed remarks such as: *"Strolling down the street, the director of the local Bureau of Commerce carried a human leg on his shoulder, which he was taking home to boil and consume".* In a nutshell then - Guangxi is an autonomous region in the south of China. During the Cultural Revolution two factions of communists emerged, allied to different powerful leaders. This turned into a violent struggle during which the 'reactionary' faction lost ground and was defeated. The scale is tragic, anywhere between 100 and 150,000 people were killed, and in the most savage fashion. Researchers list: beaten to death, stoning, drowning, electrocution, buried alive, boiling, beheading, disembowelment, lynching (hanging) and gang rape to the point of death. At least one person had dynamite strapped to their back and blown up for amusement. On top of this came the even more shocking revelation that over 400 of these people were eaten -

"A geography instructor named Wu Shufang was beaten to death by students at Wuxuan Middle School. Her body was carried to the flat stones of the Qian River where another teacher was forced at gunpoint to rip out the heart and liver. Back at the school the pupils barbecued and consumed the organs."

Everything we have talked about so far came to the fore. Revenge was in the air and in the stomach. According to the Chinese historian Song Yongyi:

"There were reports of cannibalism across 27 counties in Guangxi; that's two-thirds of all the counties in Guangxi. There was one man who was beaten to death where he stood. He had two kids, one of 11 and one of 14. The local officials and armed militia said that it was important to eradicate such people, and so they not only killed those two children: they ate them too. This took place in Pubei county, Guangxi, where 35 people were killed and eaten in total. Most of them were rich landowners and their families. There was one landowner called Liu Zhengjian whose entire family was wiped out. He had a 17-year-old daughter, Liu Xiulan, who was gang-raped by nine people [for 19 times] who then ripped open her belly, and ate her liver and breasts. There were so many incidents like this."

The Scarlet Memorial and other works on the massacre are truly gruesome reading, in part for the outrageously normalised attitude that militia and faction leaders had towards killing people for crimes such as crying over a dead relative or collecting a loved one's mutilated body for burial, but also for the passivity of the victims and the quiet toleration and harvesting of bodies by the local populace. In the forward to the book, historian Ross Terrill laments the total acceptance of death by the accused: *"as the sticks and knives were wielded, the innocent just knelt down silently, no begging, no cursing, no arguing, and not the slightest show of a willingness to resist.... Not one act of direct physical heroism is recorded by Zheng Yi... no-one died in a physical attack on a murderer"*. The most heartbreaking reading was of children made to lie on top of their parents as they were buried alive, and yet, there was no protest. This is a motif we have seen before, in the Battle of Suiyang - one wonders whether Confucian piety and deference had been so inculcated into the civilisation that people simply could not halt what was happening.

The tales of cannibalism in Guangxi between 1966-76 are too numerous to cover, but they range from emboldened thugs who kept tallies of the number of livers they ate, to students who cooked their teacher in a bout of revolutionary fervour; a militia woman who enjoyed severing male genitalia, storing them in alcohol to drink for their power; a killing committee, held at Pingshan Square, in Shangsi County, ended with 10 people being beaten to death and a committee member (Li Hao) removing their hearts and frying them for the remaining members. The mind boggles and protests that surely this must be exaggeration and slander, someone must have known this was happening further up the Communist Party hierarchy? The massacre ended in 1976, the first official investigation began in 1981, and more followed. Historians know of at least one petition to Beijing, from a former veteran and rightist, Wang Zujian, imploring that the central authorities step in and halt the bloodshed and cannibalism across Guangxi. The consensus is that, even if Mao himself was not aware, some close to him certainly were.

Concluding Thoughts

This has been a long essay, so my conclusions shall be brief. We've traced a narrative across the entirety of Chinese civilisation, from the earliest sieges and battles, to popular literature, medicinal textbooks, religious duties and well documented modern events. We can say with some confidence that China has had a unique relationship with this taboo. The longevity of agriculture has exposed the historical population to lengthy periods of starvation and famine, the early codification of religious morality, in particular Confucianism, created a distinctly Chinese approach to the relationship between ancestor worship, the family and the state. One's filial duties go so far as to serve up yourself, both for your parents, and for your emperor. The cultural focus on food, on eating, combined with the vampiric ancestor cult and vision of the human body as mere meat created a potent brew, topped off with traditional medicine. If I had time I would explore the psychology of bureaucracy as a petty and spiteful motivator of revenge, but that can't be here.

Overall I have hopefully shown that, while cannibalism is a part of the human story in general, in China it very much comes with distinct Chinese characteristics.

Was Mozart a Shaman?

Orpheus and the Cult of Genius in the 18th Century

"Gradually, Mozart became known all over the globe as "the living Orpheus", the mythological figure that the eighteenth century had come to consider the shaman par excellence. The seven-year-old Wolfgang Amadeus was already believed to be the reincarnated enchanter of all nature who successfully cast his spell over its innumerable creatures. He was further described with other words from the realm of magic and bewitchment. Even the emperor referred to him as the little magician… Mozart was not only a child-wonder, a singular phenomenon, a miracle, but one who publicly performed the kind of wonders that captivated audiences and left them spellbound. Some went on to surmise that Mozart had curative powers."

Shamanism and the Eighteenth Century - Gloria Flaherty

This remarkable paragraph highlights part of the intoxicating and creative brew that was the eighteenth century in Europe. It was a time where vitalising currents from outside the continent electrified and transformed the zeitgeist; the enchantment and mystery of anthropology in turn summoning and breathing fresh life into the Classical world. Wordsmiths and poets, musicians and sculptors suddenly had broad new vistas of inspiration, from cannibals to cannabis, savages to Scipio. One of these intellectual tributaries ran

186

from Siberia into central Europe, the beating pulse of shamanism. When this concept began to take root in the imagination of eager listeners, it found its home among the older stories and myths, but it also helped animate the passion for 'genius', that intangible but fascinating quality of the rarest of men. A quasi-spiritual understanding of human creativity. Among the many figures of the age, Mozart was declared to be one such genius. But it also seemed that his contemporaries went further and saw in him some attribute or property which fully transcended the material realm. He had been reincarnated, he was a living Orpheus. I want to ask why his friends and enemies thought of him in this way, did they genuinely believe him to be a shaman of sorts? Answering this question will require a dive into the history and nature of shamanism, the Greek religious mysteries of Orpheus and the intellectual climate of Europe in Mozart's lifetime. I hope to convey to you that shamanism needn't be some exotic and remote barbarism, fit only for New Agers and peripheral tribal peoples, I want instead to recast and re-enchant our household names and reinvigorate history with its vital and powerful energies. Our musicians can once again be our medicine-men.

To the ends of the Earth

The mediaeval imagination had long been suckled on a rich mixture of travel literature and the knowledge that the world surrounding Christendom contained horrors and wonders beyond comprehension. The literal and mental marginalia of a society raised on Mandeville and Marco Polo accepted that, on wild and distant shores, lived races of giants, pygmies, men with the heads of dogs, no heads at all or with feet large enough to block the sun. Renaissance knowledge of Sami witches, the magic of Tartars, Cathayans and New World sorcerers was combined with the dual paranoia of witchcraft within Protestantism and the intellectual curiosity of alchemy, astrology, medicine and divination. Texts such as Robert Burton's *The Anatomy of Melancholy* and Samuel Purchas' travel compilation were carefully compared with Marsilio Ficino, Pico de Mirandola, Agrippa von Nettesheym and Paracelsus. Burton noted the reports on 'ecstatic trances', of witches' mania after flying all night, agrarian cults and bouts of madness and dancing. Jean de Nynauld's medical work on lycanthropy and the different substances such as belladonna, aconite and opium were mixed with readings of Pythagoras, Simon Magus and the newly discovered savage witches of North America, Lithuania and China. This curiosity was tempered with a Christian fear and an empirical scepticism of the powers of these new '*schamans*' (the word appearing in Europe for the first time in 1692). Robert Burton, like other observers, noted ventriloquism, prestidigitation and theatrical showmanship as part of the shamanic toolkit. Louis Hennepin (1640-1701), a friar who travelled in the upper Mississippi valley, protested that:

"These imposters would be counted as prophets, who foretel things to come: they would be look'd upon as having almost an infinite power: they boast that they make rain or fair weather, calms or storms, fruitfulness or barrenness of the ground, hunting lucky or unlucky. They serve for physicians too, and frequently apply such remedies, as have no manner of virtue to cure the distemper. Nothing can be imagin'd more horrible than the cries and yellings, and the strange contorsions of these rascals, when they fall to juggling or conjuring; at the same time they do it very cleverly."

One part of the world that lay beyond the reach of Europeans for a while was the frozen north, particularly towards the east. Even the Baltic coast was a place of great heathen activity. Explorers and missionaries such as Paul Einhorn reported on superstitious practices and rituals among the locals, who apparently worshipped the god Comus and engaged in carnal deeds. Others stated: *"they are by nature obtuse and dull, inclined to necromancy and sorcery, but in the service of an exorcism, so palpably ridiculous, that I wonder how they have obtained that repute they have in the world among those, who ought to be wiser than to believe such groundless fictions"*. Further afield than the Baltic were the expanding domains of imperial Russia. The earliest explorers and visitors to Siberia and Kamchatka included: Nicolas Witsen (1640-1717), who wrote the earliest descriptions of a shaman and sketched the top image (sans Mozart); John Bell (1691-1780), a Scottish surgeon; Daniel Messerschmidt (1685-1735), one of the earliest to be commissioned by Peter the Great to chart Siberia and Philipp von Strahlenberg (1676-1747), a Swedish officer who was imprisoned in Siberia for 13 years. Between them they wrote extensively about shamanism. Their accounts were largely rigorous, honest and fair, but devoid of any sympathy for the shamanic practice and its purported benefits, medicinal or otherwise. In general then, an attitude of Baconian scepticism was rife amongst the early reporters of trances, sorcerers and shamans. Rationalist 'debunkers' quickly filled up books with explanations for the power of oracles and magic. Bernard Fontenelle's 1686 book *Histoire des oracles* provided staple accounts for mystical events, such as breathing toxic fumes, the psychology of being in deep caves and the trickery of magicians. The English language translation of the work in 1688 re-titled it *The History of Oracles, and the Cheats of the Pagan Priests*. However, in trying to explain to their audiences how and why these oracles fell into degeneracy and disuse, they began to stumble towards a powerful, unsettling conclusion.

Poetry as Primal Magic

In 1724 Joseph Lafitau, a Jesuit missionary, published two volumes of studies on native American societies, including detailed accounts of their religious and medicinal practices. Lafitau was not the first to draw direct comparisons between shamanism and ancient Greek religion, but he was among the first observers to take seriously the question of what quality or attribute in the human psyche generates a phenomenon like shamanism. What he began to conclude was that shamans tap into the creative power of the human imagination and harness it to full effect. Even if they were tricksters and liars, the practice had persisted from archaic times and was clearly meaningful to those people the shamans helped and cured. Further observations noted the extraordinary power that shamans had over their people; the power to terrify, to terrorise, to calm, to soothe and to cure. By listening to their dreams and their complaints they could provoke paroxysms of fear or render them comatosed. Medical researchers regularly described native Siberian peoples as hypersensitive and neurotic, becoming excessively alarmed by the smallest of noises:

"Each unexpected contact, for example, on the sides or on the other sensitive parts, sudden shouts and whistling, or other frightful and quick manifestations bring these people beside themselves and almost into a kind of fury. Others, much like the beserkers of Norse mythology, would fall into uncontrollable rages, get hold of knives, axes or other lethal instruments, and go after the people who had disturbed their tranquillity... If they cannot give vent to their rage, they beat about themselves, scream, shake violently, and are completely like madmen"

Whilst this frightening capacity to become irrational and hostile was diagnosed as both a product of the harsh Arctic environment and the native's 'childlike' constitution, it also yielded great gifts of story, myth and most importantly, poetry.

The intellectual discussion about prose versus poetry had already been raging in European circles for some time, and with the continual input of observations from all over the world, including Australia and Polynesia, the mood had become favourable to the idea that poetry was a primal part of the human mind. Shamans were respected, even by hardened empiricists, for their effusive powers of speech. Since these people used no alphabets, read no books or literature, their entire medium of communication was designed to bring about changes within the body. Rhythm, tone, pitch, volume, speed - all gave the poet nearly direct access to the corporeal, rather than the higher faculties of reason. This is crucial: *by appealing directly to the body, the shaman is a conduit for a highly creative imagination to powerfully impact upon another person.* Bypassing the rational altogether gave near unmediated power to the shaman and they knew well how to use it.

These insights into the power of imagination and creativity to affect the human body, along with the positioning of shamanism as potentially the most archaic or ancient of man's religions, sparked an intellectual turn towards the 'folk arts' of Europe. Suddenly the old fables, superstitious tales, village plays, pantomimes, masked festivals and other folk practices were recast as surviving relics of Europe's primaeval spirituality and of the capacity for creativity to arise from these simple origins. Along with poetry came the obsession with collecting and gathering folk songs from all around the world, from Scotland to the Caribbean. The German polymath Johann Gottfried Herder (1744-1803) devoted tremendous energy to hunting down and compiling songs, which he argued were foundational to the social order. Herder argued that shamans were the founding inspiration for mathematics, art, music, law and writing, weaving a creation out of pure chaos. For him the songs were nothing less than a doorway into the soul of Man. He compared all the works he had gathered with those of the Celts, the Norse and, most importantly, the Greeks. In particular he focused his attention on the character of Orpheus, who he held to be a shaman:

"Do you believe that Orpheus, the great Orpheus, eternally worthy of mankind, the poet in whose inferior remnants the soul of nature lives, that he was originally something other than the noblest shaman that Thrace... could have seen?"

It's at this point in our story that we pause for breath and turn towards this other foundational stream of myth which so animated our European chroniclers. It's time to turn to Greece and her Mysteries.

Mycenaean Cults & Orphic Shamans

In 1962 in Macedonia, the excavated grave of a nobleman revealed an astonishing find. The charred, but still legible fragments of a papyrus script, dated to around 340 BC, during the reign of Philip II of Macedon, now known to be the oldest surviving manuscript of European history. But more astonishingly than this, the fragments revealed (in painstakingly difficult detail) itself to be a treatise, a text written about an Orphic poem from the time of Anaxagoras composed at the end of the 5th century BC. This rocked the classical world and has been a burning source of interest to scholars and autodidacts for decades. The final text was published in 2006, nearly 40 years after its discovery. The 'Derveni Papyrus', as it came to be known, was a miracle. What it actually means will be the subject of infinite discussion, but the Orphic poem in question was a theogony, a story of the birth of the gods, used during Dionysian Mystery initiation ceremonies. The commentary mentions Zoroastrian Magi, quotes from Heraclitus and Parmenides and debates whether the composer meant the theogony literally or allegorically. All heady stuff for scholars of ancient Greek religious practices.

But let us take a step back. Orphic poems are among the most esoteric and arcane of Greece's mysterious spiritual history. They refer to poems attributed to the mythical poet Orpheus. Sadly only two poems survive - the *Orphic Hymns* and *Argonautica,* remembered today for the tale of Jason and the Argonauts. Orphism is the academic term for the cult and spiritual practices which developed in Greece, Thrace and Asia Minor, all focused around the Orphic 'way of life', which included vegetarianism and abstention from sex. Orphism is a difficult term to define, let alone explore, and much ink has been spilled on the subject without providing many meaningful answers. One confusion is that Orphism has become associated with both Dionysus and Apollo. Readers of Nietzsche will know that these gods, while complimentary in their opposition, represent both the rational and irrational, earth and sky, order and chaos. Orphic beliefs overlap with both gods - Orpheus in one story is said to have spurned all the gods but Apollo (Orpheus famously also plays a golden lyre) and is torn to shreds in revenge. His journey to Hades and rebirth mirrors an older tale of Dionysus, who is a reincarnation of Zagreus, daughter of Persephone, who is likewise torn to shreds by the Titans. These and similar stories present

Orphism as potentially possessing a cosmology of reincarnation and a return of the soul to the 'Oneness' of the cosmos. The connection to Dionysus runs especially deep in the Orphic traditions; some held Orpheus to be a follower of Dionysus, others that he was a reincarnation of the god. One story has him being ripped apart in an orgiastic rage by female followers of Dionysus for spurning their advances. Beyond being interesting in its own right, the motifs of the Dionysian (or Bacchic) rituals and myths share a striking similarity to a number of core elements of shamanism, something we will return to shortly.

One reason why Greek religion can be tricky to fully grasp is the accreted layers of myth, culture, deities, oracles, heroes and sacred landscapes, built over time from the earliest traces of Hellenic memory. The murky origins of the Mycenaeans and the civilisation they built in the eastern Mediterranean, beginning circa 1700 BC, is the wellspring for the earliest gods and their cultic activities. Strong archetypal concerns such as the harvest, trees, hunting, thunder, the underworld, horses and water were reflected in the characters of the deities. Oracles such as Dodona and Delphi were already important sites in the landscape. The introduction of Apollo came late in the development of the pantheon and he was originally a far more chthonic and menacing character. He was the son of Leto, rumoured to have arrived from the far frozen land of Hyperborea in the north, accompanied by a pack of wolves. The wolf became a symbol of Apollo, with one nickname - *Lyceus* - directly attesting to his wolfish character (although *leukos* could refer instead to the sunlight). The

Spartan festival of *Karneia* reflects how their original deity *Carnus* was replaced with Apollo, both concerned with protecting the flock, but also through the Spartan *krypteia* demonstrating their lupine ferocity. In the words of Classics Professor Carl Ruck:

"In the reorienting of Delphi's shamanic axis, Apollo's lycanthropic persona was displaced and reinterpreted as related not to the 'wolf' (lykos), but to the 'light' (lux) of his solar manifestation. The deadly twanging of his toxic bow was transmuted into the harmonious, but equally entrancing, spell cast by the music from the plucked strings of his lyre. Apollo is paired with Dionysus as inspiring antithetical modes of human mentality, with Apollo presiding over the separation from Gaia and rational control over nature, and his half-brother finding the source of inspiration in the mediated encounter with the irrationality of the natural wilderness"

Both gods - Apollo and Dionysus - display elements and indicators of classical shamanism. From the divine madness, suffering, the transformation into an animal, the playing of music, communication with plants and beasts, dying and rebirth, the journey to the underworld to retrieve a soul and so on; these are all potential markers that Orpheus and his progenitor gods were shamans of some description or another. Many academics who study shamanism feel that anything outside of true Siberian shamanism is either a misattribution or a stretch. But, for our purposes here what matters is that, when shamanism was being received into Europe as a set of concepts and ideas, it was fused with the Classical tradition, partly in order for it to be contextualised and absorbed. The visions of Orpheus as a divine poet, a psychopomp, a mediator between worlds, was enhanced and strengthened by the knowledge of real, existing shamans out there on the edges of the world. As Herder reinforced:

"Also the Greeks were once primitives, and even in the flowering of their most beautiful era there is much more nature than the blinking eye of the scholiast and classicist finds... Tyrtaeus's war songs are Greek ballads, and when Arion, Orpheus and Amphion lived, they were noble Greek shamans"

Mozart - the "Living Orpheus"

We finally return to the original question, having travelled through several centuries and traditions, to tackle the problem - why did so many of Mozart's contemporaries write about him as a shaman, a living Orpheus? Consider again the opening quotation with all its connotations:

"Gradually, Mozart became known all over the globe as "the living Orpheus", the mythological figure that the eighteenth century had come to consider the shaman par excellence. The seven-year-old Wolfgang Amadeus was already believed to be the reincarnated enchanter of all nature who successfully cast his spell over its innumerable creatures. He was further described with other words from the realm of magic and bewitchment. Even the emperor referred to him as the little magician... Mozart was not only a child-

197

wonder, a singular phenomenon, a miracle, but one who publicly performed the kind of wonders that captivated audiences and left them spellbound. Some went on to surmise that Mozart had curative powers."

Having seen the arguments and motivations that went into that fusion of Enlightenment thinking, Hellenism and Romanticism which electrified the decades and centuries of European colonialism, we can see it fully expressed here in the creation of Mozart as a genius, a shaman, a renewal of the Greek spirit. In part, the emerging medicalisation of human temperament began to build a picture of the 'genius'. Leaning on the reports and descriptions of Siberian shamans, a sketch of a type of nervous and hypersensitive disposition took hold in the Continental imagination. These people, whose fibres were 'highly strung', were acutely sensitive to music, noise, poetry, the spoken and written word and were likened to conduits of spirit. The character of genius was also often feminine, but in a masculine body, which struck many observers as parallel to the shaman, who often seemed to channel a female energy. These androgynous and eccentric people seemed to create their own worlds through the force of madness and divine inspiration. The young Mozart, born in 1756, seemed immediately to embody these characteristics. As an adult he was often described as a kind of child - "irritable, melancholic, immoderate, mercurial and careless" in the words of Jean Baptise-Antoine Suard. His music was so enrapturing and powerful that only the descriptions of Orpheus and Apollo would suffice to capture its effect on the listener:

"When Orpheus' magic lute out-rings, Amphion to his lyre sings, the lion tames, the rivers quiet grow, the tigers listen, rocks a-walking go. When Mozart masterly music plays and gathers undivided praise, the quire of Muses stays to hear, Apollo is himself all ear"

The physician Simon Tissot (1728-98) was utterly convinced of Mozart's internal force of genius. As a doctor of the nervous system he was fascinated by Mozart's apparent intolerance of harsh, discordant or loud noises and sounds. He saw in the musician a compulsion, from beyond his own self, to create and birth new music. Mozart would be "driven to his harpsichord, as by a hidden force, and he drew from it sounds that were the living expression of the idea that had just seized him". At his most fever pitch, Tissot described Mozart as an immortal who was ultimately possessed by a spirit of heaven itself. Nor was Tissot alone in these almost crazed outpourings for the composer. A Berlin periodical in 1790 confessed:

"Mozart is among those extraordinary men whose reputations will endure for centuries. His great genius embraces, so to speak, the whole extent of the art of music… None before him have surpassed him, and posterity will never deny this great man its profound reverence and admiration. To judge him one must be more than a mere connoisseur. What a masterpiece is the music of today!"

Just as the shaman flirted and travelled alongside and with ecstatic madness and total loss of the self, so Mozart was himself reported to go far beyond mere showmanship or even the heights of human skill. He was animated with the glowing light of the sun and his countenance changed and violent mood swings often accompanied his best performances. Caroline Pichler, a writer in the Viennese cultural milieu, described how Mozart performed the most exquisite improvisations for an audience and then without warning leapt over the nearest table and began screaming like a cat, performing somersaults and overturning furniture. These reports chime with the fury and loss of inhibitions, so vividly reported by earlier explorers into the Arctic wilderness.

Final Thoughts

If you've read this far, then perhaps you'll be wondering whether this will have a satisfactory conclusion - was Mozart a shaman? The answer to this lies in resurrecting the now dormant enthusiasm and power of Western creativity and imagination. The traditional shaman, enmeshed in his duties in a small foraging tribe, seems a strange figure to cast such a spell over such a powerful culture as Western modernity. But it is precisely in the re-awakening of the senses, of madness, of sleeping and forgotten knowledge of the human spirit, that the humble sorcerer was able to re-enchant a world of sterile finance and utilitarian thought. Mozart was, in the broadest and most expansive sense of the word, a shaman. His birth was blessed and he was more than a mere man, but became a lightning rod for the subterranean and solar energies which began to pulse through Europe in his century. All who heard him recognised that they were in the presence of something more than just skill, more than just talent. They were witnessing one of nature's miracles. It is precisely in these stories of rapture and enchantment that I find the energy to confront our stagnant and exhausted world. May a thousand new Mozart's come forth and humble us again, may we be still able to recognise that magic when we see it!

On The Origin Of Writing - Part One

Proto-writing - From Lascaux to Rongorongo

This mini-series, on the origins of writing, was guest written by a good friend. His anonymous nom de plume is Pygmy Glottochronologist, and he can be found musing on languages most arcane at @GreatValueArhat on Twitter.

If any common thread can be said to weave our corner of the internet together, it's a keen interest in prehistory. The desire to peer into the time before time is strong in all of us, though we indulge it in the way that best suits our own form- archaeology, genetics, linguistics, even artistic expression. Those of you who know me will know me as a linguistics sperg, an appellation I suppose I began to bring upon myself in early childhood when my curiosity was first piqued by my family's sojourns across North America, coming across Spanish, French, Cherokee, Yiddish, Amharic, among others. Thus, when it came time to plunge into the sands of time in which we all swim in my own idiom, language was my diving-board. My search for the voices of our forebears have led me down many winding paths-scattered in files on my desktop are dissertations on hypothetical Saami subrates, PDFs of Ainu dictionaries, and memes bemoaning the public's lack of interest in the honey-gathering vocabulary of the Baka pygmies.

Of course, what separates the murky realm of prehistory we strangely sort of explore for recreation and the proper history of our grade-school social studies textbooks is inextricably related to language- specifically, to writing. It's quite a strange concept, writing, and perhaps we'd be more inclined to realize this were our modern lives not so dependent upon it. You're certainly too far away for me to speak with, and yet here you are, perhaps thousands of miles away and years after I write these words, and yet I am talking to you. The writings of those who came long before us and who are now long gone enable them to speak to us, if not with us, still today. It's in this way that history begins- we know of Egypt, China, and Rome because we were written of Egypt, China, and Rome- we know little of the Independence I culture of northern Greenland for this exact inverse reason.

But what differentiates the wealth of information that we've been able to glean from the corpus of Egyptian or Akkadian writing from the petroglyphs of the American Southwest or the famous cave art of Lascaux? These latter two are also markings on a physical medium-why do they not yield the same information as the former? The answer is that they are not writing- not "proper" writing- and not for the considerations of cultural or historical merit. No, they aren't writing for a very simple reason- they encode ideas and concepts, but not language.

Carvings, drawings, or other such markings are known in linguistics and archaeology as *proto-writing*. Rather than serving as a visual (or tactile, in the case of Braille) representation of spoken utterances, proto-writing such as this represents ideas and concepts for much the same reason that we use writing- for permanence, availability, and the transmission of information. Proto-writing is not capable of representing the same breadth of information as writing and its utility is limited in this way, but despite this our modern world is no stranger to the use of symbols to convey information. Consider the figures of men and women on bathroom doors, the snowflake on your phone's weather app, or the red octagonal sign on the side of the road. There are benefits to this means of communication as well- since these signs represent concepts, and not language, they are broadly understood irrespective of tongue. The meaning of the sign below is familiar to billions of people irrespective of culture and language, the writing on it is not.

As one may well expect from the name of the term, proto-writing is widely considered to have preceded writing itself. Though it's impossible to give an exact date of its earliest appearance, and there are various candidates for the laurels of the first example, the Kish tablet from the Sumerian city of the same name and dated to the Uruk IV period (ca. 3300-3200 BC) is an unambiguous example of proto-cuneiform writing. Though less certain and significantly more fragmentary in nature, the Jiahu symbols recovered from a site of the Peiligang culture of central China have been dated to around the year 6000 BC. Though the extreme paucity of the symbols (only sixteen have yet been noted) greatly inhibits both our understanding of the symbols themselves and their connection to any potential information that they convey, their similarity to the much later oracle bone script is difficult to ignore. If you're familiar with Chinese, take a gander and see if you can't make some of them out- even if you're not, I think you'll recognize the first.

As the above examples illustrate, societies are either exposed to the idea of proto-writing or originate it themselves at different times- meaning that one culture can have no concept of physical symbolic representation of ideas at the same time another does. Similarly, one culture can still use proto-writing at the same time another is using writing- and this is very clearly evidenced in history. The development of writing in Mesopotamia and Egypt spread outward and pushed aside most use of proto-writing in much of the ancient world- both in their own regions and beyond, as in Europe and India. These innovations however did not reach to the distant shores of the Pacific, and thus writing in China was able to develop independently, as was the case with writing in Mesoamerica. The cessation of the use of Mesoamerican and Mesopotamian writing has created an odd scenario- beyond a few strange examples like Canadian Aboriginal Syllabics - all writing today descends from the ancient scripts of the Nile or Yellow Rivers.

Because of the principle outlined above, we needn't reach into the far-distant past to find examples of proto-writing- many are quite recent, even into the 20th century. An example of this can be found in the calendar sticks of the Pima people of southern Arizona. Fashioned from the ribs of the saguaro cactus, calendar sticks are a way to record the events of the elapsing years for posterity- each year coinciding with the summer harvest of the saguaro itself- indicated by a complete horizontal line. One of the earliest examples we have dates from around the year 1850 (remember, as the Pima year corresponds with the summer cactus harvest, it includes portions of two years tracked with the Western calendar.) In this year, an illness known as the Black Vomiting is said to have spread through Pima communities, an event which is corroborated in the accounts of early European explorers and settlers. Numerous such events are recorded, Apache raids- both as attackers and defenders, the arrival of the first white man in a given area, meteor showers, earthquakes, floods, and the results of sports competitions.

There are also examples of glyphs found in the world that cannot be neatly categorized into writing or proto-writing. This is generally the result of extremely fragmentary findings in the context of a culture that either no longer exists or has lost the knowledge of the glyphs- sometimes even down to their origin and purpose, let alone their meaning. A good example of this category would be the Rongorongo of Easter Island, a place that seems time and time again to vex the scholarly world's attempts to understand it. Rongorongo- whose name means "to recite" or "to chant" is a system of glyphs that was first identified by outside scholarship in the 19th century, by which time knowledge of the system had long been lost by the Rapa Nui who inhabited the island before the arrival of Europeans, and who still do so today. Dating is tricky- the Rapa Nui held that it was brought to the island by either Hotu Matu'a or Tu'u ko Iho, the legendary first settlers of the island, though some interpret one glyph to represent the extinct Easter Island Palm, which disappears from the island's pollen record around the year 1650 and thus, should this identification be correct, Rongorongo must precede this date.

What is certain about Rongorongo, and very little is, is that only a small fraction of the island's population was able to make sense of the signs- if indeed it is writing, then literacy was a jealously guarded privilege of the nobility and the priesthood of Rapa Nui society. Disease and slave raiding reduced the Rapa Nui population to under two hundred individuals at its lowest

point, and in so doing eliminated any knowledge of the meaning of the glyphs from the remaining islanders. Yet, as I mentioned before, this strange, remote island continues to fascinate. Traditional Rapa Nui knowledge holds that the glyphs were brought from the outside, but where? Neither Polynesia nor distant South America have a tradition of writing, leading to the conclusion that it must be an *in situ* innovation. Similarly, if Rongorongo were found to be true writing it would be only the fifth independent invention of writing in the history of the world.

Since a proposal by the Russian linguists Nikolai Butinov and Yuri Knorozov, the latter famous for his contributions to the decipherment of the Maya script, suggesting that the highly repetitive nature of the glyphs is indicative of genealogical records, Rongorongo is most commonly considered to be proto-writing- in this instance a mnemonic aid for remembering the ancestries of rulers or other important families. Still others have suggested a use as a navigational aid, or as a calendar. This last proposal, by the late German ethnographer Thomas Barthel, represents the sole example of a Rongorongo text that has an accepted purpose, here, the insertion of an intercalary night required to keep the Rapa Nui calendar month synchronized with the phases of the moon. Even still though, the glyphs in this text cannot be read precisely, only their general function understood.

Perhaps the interested reader might be interested in taking a stab at Rongorongo themselves? The questions of form and function still remain nearly entirely open, and in many instances, most guesses are as good as any other. The ground on which archaeology and historical linguistics sit is sandy and shifting, and still today there are opportunities for interested parties to make their marks on our understanding of the world of the past. By all means, download reams of PDFs and drive yourself mad attempting to understand arcane symbols, or perhaps give them an inquisitive glance for an evening over coffee and never look at them again. But whatever you decide to do, reader, stay curious- in this I implore you.

On The Origin Of Writing - Part Two

Proto-writing: Kaidā, Adinkra and Ersu Shaba

It's believed that writing was invented independently only four times in our history: in Mesopotamia, in Egypt, in China, and in Mesoamerica. Proto-writing, however, appears far more often and in many more places. The context in which proto-writing arises mirrors that of writing itself- the need for the recording of information by illiterate people, though for more practical purposes than prose or shitposting. By examining the origins of far more recent systems of proto-writing, some even within the past centuries, we can perhaps better understand the context in which writing itself arose millenia in the distant past, the great chasms of time between our era and the dawn of cuneiform reduced to much more manageable interstices.

We'll begin with looking at the most recently developed of the three systems of proto-writing I'll be discussing today, the Kaidā glyphs of the most remote and southerly place in Japan- the Yaeyama Islands- far closer to Taiwan than Tokyo. Ryukyu, the southern islands of Japan of which Okinawa is the largest and best known, has only been subject to central Japanese government authority as a prefecture since 1879. Before then the islands, once an independent kingdom, had been beholden to the Satsuma Domain following their invasion and occupation in 1609. The Satsuma administration, based in the city of Kagoshima, was thus met with the ancient question of how to effectively tax its new, distant, and illiterate subjects.

Much like The Conqueror's survey of England following his successful invasion, the Satsuma Domain surveyed the southern islands for the purpose of determining the amount of tribute to be yielded on an annual basis. Though the Satsuma administration was naturally literate in Japanese, the islanders were virtually all illiterate, and the language spoken by the inhabitants of Yaeyama, at such tremendous remove from the center of Japanese culture and power, differs so significantly from the standard language as to be mutually unintelligible with it (a topic for another time). To solve this issue, the yearly quotas for each household were written on a small wooden board called an *itafuda* or *hansatsu*. This information was conveyed to the islanders using a system of proto-writing known as Kaidā glyphs- taken from the word *kariya*, a kind of government office.

The corpus of the Kaidā glyphs is largely pictographic- as can be seen in the image above- fish and horses are immediately identifiable, and the different markings on the squares indicate various forms of crops (if I had to guess, perhaps derivations from the character 田, meaning "rice paddy"). More opaque are pictograms indicating quantities and weights or those signifying names of places or households, which comprise the entirety of the repertoire beyond the numerals, which, as on the nearby island of Okinawa, appear to have been adapted from the Chinese Suzhou numerals, perfectly likely considering that Chinese merchants had visited Ryukyu for centuries and prior to their integration into the Japanese state the islands had long been a tributary of Imperial China.

The cessation of the usage of the glyphs is no mystery whatsoever- with compulsory education, mass literacy obviated the need for their use likely before about 1930- today, they are used nearly exclusively on tourist *tchotchkes* like t-shirts and coffee mugs. Much less certain is their origin- the Satsuma are recorded as having created "perfected" glyphs for the purposes of taxation in the 19th century, suggesting that these were perhaps adapted from earlier, "unperfected" glyphs. The Yaeyama Islanders record in oral tradition that they were created by an ancestor known as Mase perhaps in the latter half of the 17th century- coinciding with the period after the Satsuma invasion. Whatever their origin, their genesis closely resembles that of Mesopotamian writing- an accounting tool that, were it not obsolesced by written language, could perhaps have developed into a system of writing itself as it did in the fertile crescent thousands of years ago.

Our next system of proto-writing takes us far from the islands of the East China Sea to the interior of the West African country of Ghana. Here we find the Adinkra symbols- signs representing parables, sigils, as well as glyphs for more mundane concepts- carved into dried calabash gourd and stamped onto cloth of the same name most commonly, though also used in jewelry, pottery, and furniture. They were created by the Bono, an Akan-speaking people of western Ghana, of the Kingdom of Gyaman, certainly no later than the end of the 18th century or beginning of the 19th. Bono oral tradition credits their invention to the Gyaman king Nana Kwado Agymang Adinkra, who gave his own name to the symbols. Following the conquest of the Kingdom of Gyaman by the Ashanti, the usage of Adinkra symbols was more widely disseminated, and today they are found throughout Ghana.

While Kaidā glyphs were essentially exclusively pictographic, that is to say glyphs representing tangible, physical objects like eggs, fish, and rice, Adinkra symbols are nearly all logograms- they represent concepts and ideas, like kingship, prayers, and fearlessness. In this way, they are similar to other such "volitional symbology" found in the world- the Chinese double-happiness character, the Icelandic *Ægishjálmur*, or perhaps even the barnstars of the American Mid-Atlantic states. A variety of concepts are encoded in the Adinkra symbols- wards against jealousy, exhortations to bravery, indication of royal favor, and praise for the virtue of being a faithful confidant. Individually, these symbols can be found carved into wooden stools or printed above doorways, but the primary medium of their expression, and in which we find our oldest surviving example, is in textile.

Adinkra cloth was once the sole prerogative of the royalty and nobility of Gyaman- it was used in ritual clothing, royal regalia, and to line the bed in which the king of Gyaman slept. A glyph bearing the name *Musuyidie* was printed on a cloth placed beside the king's bed- every morning when he woke he placed his left foot on it three times to remove curses or other evils. Hung above the doorway lintel was a piece of paper bearing a sign that conveyed a prayer whose English meaning is given as "Oh God, everything which is above, permit my hand to touch it", which the king would touch before his forehead and breast and recite thricely. On his pillow was the sign of the *Nsoroma*, symbolizing an Akan saying- "Like the star- the child of the Supreme Being, I rest with God and do not depend upon myself."

Such symbolism and usage is perhaps most recognizable to Westerners in the form of a sigil- a word whose meaning is more deeply illustrated via its etymology, being taken from the Latin word for "seal". This type of proto-writing did not develop into true writing anywhere in the world, as far as we know. Perhaps the encoding of parables and aphorisms into glyphs inhibits the development of such signs into writing whereas a pictographic script would not, but it is altogether certain that the Kingdom of Gyaman had little use for writing as we use it today, and as occurred with the Kaidā glyphs any potential further development was made unnecessary by the imposition of written language from an outside power, in this instance the British and the French.

That is not to say, however, that writing never developed from systems used for magical purposes. It very certainly did, and moreover one of the only two independent inventions of writing

214

from which virtually all modern scripts descend originated in this way. Modern Chinese characters descend from the Oracle bone script- so called because of its use in the practice of divination, in which questions were posed to the gods by writing them on bone or turtle shell, heating them, and then interpreting the resulting cracks. This practice is first recorded as having taken place in the Shang dynasty, over three thousand years ago. However, one needn't look far to discover a form of magical pictographic writing developed closer to our own time.

In the mountains of western Sichuan dwell the Ersu, a Qiangic-speaking people whose origins are poorly understood- perhaps arriving from Tibet in the distant past. Few people speak the Ersu language, around 13,000, and still yet in a locale of great remove from major population centers. The reason that this obscure tongue has caught the attention of academics is due to a very peculiar system of writing developed by the Ersu. Known as Ersu Shaba, this script does not represent the Ersu language, but is used solely by Ersu priests (Shaba) in their religious texts- recited in the practice of divination or the curing of the ill. The restriction of knowledge of this script to the shamanic priests (always male) of a small, remote ethnic group has naturally led to the present situation- likely fewer than ten people are able to read the Ersu Shaba script, and yet today there are many unclear meanings and unanswered questions surrounding its interpretation. As to why this script is regarded as especially peculiar, one need only examine a sample:

The "comic-book style" panels of this writing system are integral to its function- each contains a discrete thought. You might recognize the animals depicted as being those of the Chinese zodiac- this is due to each day of the Chinese lunar calendar being represented by one of the same twelve animals used in the more familiar yearly zodiac known outside of China. Thus, we can recognize this text as representing a sort of calendar. The other elements in the squares have myriad meanings, but it is not simply the presence of these elements that conveys meaning, but their position within the square- for example, the left represents the morning and the right the evening- as well as the color- red corresponds to the element of fire, and, I believe, the moon and star sign present in the second square from the left on the middle row signifies that the day will be bright. Were this sign black instead of white however, it would carry the meaning of "dim."

Much like the Ersu themselves, the origins of this script are poorly understood. It is perhaps related to the Dongba symbols of the Naxi- used for a similar religious purpose- and has been in use for maybe between five hundred and one thousand years. Though extremely unlikely that this system will evolve into one capable of rendering the Ersu language (that is, true writing), we can learn from the context of its use how the need to record important information relating to astrology, divination, and magic can serve as the impetus toward the development of writing just as easily as a system of account.

The ubiquity of writing around us has blinded us to its existence just as fish aren't cognizant of the water in which they swim. Few people consider how one of the most important tools developed by man, perhaps the most important beyond pointed sticks and fire, came into being, and fewer still ask the question of why. I hope this series has given you the smallest insight into these questions, and if not I'd be more than content to know it's at least piqued your interest. My heartfelt thanks to the good herbalist for allowing me the use of his platform, and to you, reader, for lending an ear- or eye, in the context of our topic and medium. Stay curious. Pygmy

Part Four - Anthropology

The Vikings of the Pacific

Origins and Culture of the Haida People

Nestled into the misty coastline of the northern Pacific, just off the edge of British Columbia, is a small archipelago of islands known as *Xaadala Gwayee* - 'the islands at the boundary of the world'. Known previously as the Queen Charlotte Islands and now as Haida Gwaii, this small remote place is home to one of the most enigmatic cultures in Native American history - the Haida. The Haida are one of those people who, if you are of an anthropological persuasion, become something of an obsession. Like the Dogon or the Calusa, they have acquired a legendary status, in no small part due to their mysterious and fearsome reputation among their friends and enemies. The wonderful retort mentioned on their Wikipedia page entry sets the tone for how the Haida conceive of themselves:

"The Haida are known for their craftsmanship, trading skills, and seamanship. They are thought to have been warlike and to practise slavery. Anthropologist Diamond Jenness has compared the Haida to Vikings while Haida have replied saying that Vikings are like Haida."

That defiant response suggests something quite different in their national character, compared to what is typically offered about the supposedly peaceful and harmonious nature of tribal peoples. That they are happy and willing to be associated with aggressive sea raiding is refreshing and adds to their martial aura. I want here to be able to draw on the texts available for this culture, concerning their homeland, ancestry, way of life and history, to sketch a portrait but also to act as a set of resources and a narrative. Too often a student of world cultures will find themselves lost in the weeds of obscure scholarly citations, when all they want is a simple overview complete with more references. Why not Wikipedia I hear you ask? Sadly their page doesn't do them justice, with only five lines dedicated to their history before European contact.

I hope then to present to the reader a window onto a unique and ancient people which the world has largely forgotten. Part One will cover the pre-history and culture of the Haida and a later Part Two will cover their struggles and decline in the colonial era.

In the Beginning - Part One

The world was dark. Total blackness.

Raven (Yáahl) was tired of bumping into things. He longed for the light.

Raven learnt that an old man and his daughter lived in a small hut at the edge of the water. He learnt that the old man had a small box within which was all the light of the universe.

Raven waited until the girl went to the water to drink and transformed himself into a hemlock needle and the girl drank him down into her belly where he transformed again into a tiny human.

He grew and eventually the girl gave birth to him and the old man loved and treasured this strange child.

The boy begged to see the light inside the box and eventually the old man gave in. He opened the lid and tossed the glowing orb at the child.

The boy transformed in an instant and caught the light in his beak. Raven then stretched his wings and flew out of the chimney hole in the roof, carrying with him the orb of light which he shared with the world.

In the Beginning - Part Two

In the beginning there was ice, lots of thick ice. Glaciers that covered the continent of North America, pushing all life into the most remote pockets of existence. These refugia, as they are known, were the tiny points of survival from which recolonisation of the land could occur once the ice melted. The land of Haida Gwaii was one of these remnants, the sea being substantially lower than in other places and with an active volcano just over 100 miles west of the archipelago. Bowie Seamount as it is called, or *SGaan Kinghlas* in the Haida language - The Supernatural One Looking Outwards - was still active around 18,000 years ago and supports a vast host of marine life today. It may well have been visible, should you have been standing on the land all those millennia ago. The extent of ice cover on Haida Gwaii is still debated, but it seems to have formed part of a series of coastal refugia allowing bears, martens, multiple species of plants, trees and fish to survive the glacial maximum and to repopulate the landscape as it became available.

Despite the presence of these forbidding glaciers, recent evidence for early human presence in the Americas has been uncovered, pushing the confirmed date for habitation back to between 23 -21 thousands years ago. The relationship between these people and the later migrants is not fully understood and it may be that they died off before the advent of the Holocene and the raising of the sea levels. Whilst it is tempting here to divert into a full analysis of the current evidence for the peopling of the Americas, it is better to stick to the Haida Gwaii and what possible role it played in these migrations.

Water and Ice

To take Haida oral history seriously we have to entertain some fascinating possibilities: firstly that they have preserved memories and testimonies of the earliest migrants reaching the archipelago *before* it was disconnected from the mainland; secondly that the original Haida populated a landscape *without trees,* and thirdly that these voyages used forms of seafaring technology that we have yet to properly understand. According to Swanton, the most comprehensive ethnographer of the Haida, these early stories are the 'Period of the Supernatural Beings'. A time of Raven, a child cast adrift in a skin boat, Eagle and Stone-Ribs; when the four races of men were summoned from the earth - the Tlingit, Haida, Kwakiutl and Tsimishian; when the Great Flood cut off the 'reef' from the mainland.

In 1969 the Canadian Broadcasting Service interviewed Haida Chief William Matthews, a conversation covering all sorts of topics, of history and culture. In this discussion he mentions the original migration of the Haida people, the crossing to Alaska, as occurring *before* they could make 'good canoes'. Instead he references the earliest sea crossings as using inflated seal stomachs as rafts or pontoons. This extraordinary claim was bolstered in a similar interview with Henry Geddes - the greatest storyteller of his generation - he confirmed that in the earliest memories of the migrations, the Haida were not using canoes.

We know that sometime in the distant past, a movement of peoples from Asia must have crossed across Beringia and were potentially stranded. Further overland migrations have been demonstrated using genetics and scatters of archaeological excavations. Alongside these terrestrial paths have been hypothesised a number of other ways that humans could have reached North America, prominent among them is the 'Coastal Route' and the 'Kelp Highway Hypothesis'. These proposals suggest that, alongside the mainland path, other humans could have traversed the Beringian gap and migrated into the Americas down the coastlines, following the highly productive marine habitats. One of the main places that these migrants would have encountered would be the Haida Gwaii archipelago, then still part of the mainland. Studies of seal populations and carbon dating of osteological remains along the potential coastal path have confirmed that the route would have been open at least 16 thousand years ago.

Assuming that both the oral history and the hypothetical route suggested by the data are correct, this leaves us with the possibility that a secondary migration route was utilised by at least one wave of migrants out of Asia and most likely made use of the open land on the Haida Gwaii. We are hampered for early dates by the relative lack of underwater excavations in the area, since most of the archipelago was later submerged as the ice melted. Most likely the oldest site dates to 13 thousand years ago, which strongly suggests that the coastal migration routes were being made use of as soon as the climate permitted. Fragments of charcoal, tiny deposits of food, scatters of lithics - these are so often the only clues that archaeologists have when dealing with early colonisation phenomena, and the Haida are no exception.

The Eagle and the Raven

Having established that the Haida people had arrived as the warming temperatures of the Holocene was rapidly changing the landscape, we can turn to the question of who the Haida are. What kind of society are they? Why are they so distinct and what made them so unique?

To understand the Haida it is worth setting the scene in terms of their extraordinary homeland, the archipelago itself. Haida Gwaii consists of two main islands - *Kiis Gwaay,* or Graham Island in the north and *Gwaay Haanas* (Islands of Beauty) or Moresby Island in the south. Complimenting these are around 400 smaller islands, adding up to around 4,000 square miles of territory, roughly the size of the 'Big Island' of Hawaii. Rain soaked but blessed with a moderate temperature, the islands are a foggy, misty paradise for trees, famously red and yellow cedar, sitka spruce and hemlock. Everything is blanketed in a layer of moss and lichens.

Unsurprisingly the Haida are ruled by the waves, the rhythms of the sea and the tides, patterns of cloud and rain, the two winds which sweep in from both the north and south and the seasonal shifts. They use a lunar cycle calendar and split the year into two six month periods with October/November referred to as the 'in-between month'. These have wonderfully descriptive names like 'killer whale month' and 'month when the laughing geese fly north'. The interior forests were rarely explored and the Haida feared the 'wild men' of the woods, at most exploring for large cedar trees to make canoes. The ocean was also populated with 'sea people', as anyone who drowned came back as a killer whale. In between the forest and the ocean lived the Haida themselves, in plank longhouses, doors facing the waves since no-one ever visited from the woods. The back of the house was always associated with witchcraft, malice and sorcery. The woods were populated by bears, martens and otters, the sea itself teeming with seals, whales, sea lions, five types of salmon and abundant shellfish and seaweed. The fresh water streams which led into the islands were central to the salmon harvest every year and they shared the bounty with the eagles and ravens, the totemic birds so foundational to Haida identity.

The Eagle and Raven are symbolically the most important system of social division within the Haida. Everything, from the mountains to the dolphins, belongs to either the Eagle or Raven moiety. People are no exception and every Haida is born into one or the other. The other crucial component to their social system is matrilineality. Men marry across the divide, while the women maintain their birth membership. The importance of this has been underlined by genetic studies on the Haida showing deep and visible differences between the mitochondrial DNA of the two groups:

"When mtDNA data were sorted according to the descent groups of Tlingit and Haida individuals, we noted a strong correspondence between mitochondrial haplotype and maternal moiety affiliation… Haida mtDNA data showed a clear distinction between the Eagle and Raven moiety members. Aside from those persons adopted into an Eagle clan, all but one of its members had only the A2 founder

HVS1 haplotype #1. The remaining mtDNA haplotypes belonged to Raven clan members"

Intriguingly the origins of the two moieties have an 'indigenous/foreign' distinction. The Raven clan claim descent from a mythical being known as 'Foam-Woman' who was present on the 'reef' when the Haida arrived. The Eagles, who have a reputation for a more foreign influence, claim descent from multiple origins - some from Tlingit and Tsimshian sources; the majority from an ancestress called 'Djilaqons', brought to the islands by another deity - 'He-Whose-Voice-Is-Obeyed'. Swanton argued that the cognitive structure of the two totems reflected the founding of the Haida themselves, with a much larger number of ancient villages belonging to Raven and the mythical descriptors of Raven as connected to the sea and Eagle as a latecomer from the land. Within these moieties a number of lineages exist, each connected with a particular land or sea based resource - cliffs, river mouths, beaches and so on.

With these structures dominating Haida society there was a fissioning downwards from the lineages towards status and caste. There was never any formal class system among the Haida, with each lineage having heads and chiefs. Some observers of the Haida found them frustratingly flexible in their attitudes towards hierarchy, with many responses echoing the idea that *we are all chiefs here'*. However, while the politics of reciprocity and prestige ebbed and flowed among between the vague 'noble' and 'commoner' classes of Haida, there was a small group of slaves at the very bottom who served as the ultimate outsiders to support their social structure. Slaves were often captured in war and raids or traded with other peoples. They performed menial tasks and could be scapegoated for disease and sickness for bringing bad luck or evil spirits down on the people. Rumours that sometimes slaves were cast into totem pole holes while still alive before the pole was erected have been strenuously denied by the modern Haida, who insist only the Tlingit could have been so barbarous.

Potlatch - the bedrock of governance

The Pacific North-West peoples are famous for the elaborate and ostentatious social ceremony known as 'potlatch', the practice of rich and high status people distributing their wealth and goods outwards and downwards among others. These events, often conducted in special buildings, involved a high degree of ritual artwork, announcements of names, clans, kinship ties and were also the basis for discussing and agreeing to treaties and negotiating rights to resources and other necessities of governance. While the practice was made illegal in Canada in 1884, it has nevertheless persisted and since the repealment of the law in 1952, has been fundamental for the modern system of Haida government.

Westerners are often told that they are an individualistic people and that this tendency comes with industrialisation and modernity. In truth many indigenous and tribal peoples are just as oriented toward the individual and the Haida foremost among them. Their mythologies and stories regularly focus on the plight of a banished young noble who must court the supernatural and make use of plant medicine in order to regain and grow their wealth and status. The metaphysical description of hierarchy is pronounced, with no inference that in some 'golden era' was there equality, even between animals. In fact, in their cosmological ordering, there has been and always will be a hierarchy of species and beings, its existence a prior reality. With this in mind we can see how the potlatch becomes a key institution within a system that actively rewards the individual, even against their own clan or lineage.

The traditional potlatch ceremony amongst the Haida occurs for a number of reasons: on the completion of a new cedar longhouse, for a new totem pole, as a face-saving exercise, for a funeral and as part of an act of vengeance. It is difficult to assess, and indeed entire books have been written on the subject, whether the potlatch functioned as means of social mobility or whether it legitimised those with an already high status of birth. If a child of a high status family hosts a potlatch, how does it compare to an up-and-coming family who have built several new houses and have held potlatches for the first time? The flexible and complex politics of kinship, status, prestige and potlatching means that the social system was always in a constant flux of change, but anchored through the permanent institutions of moiety and lineage.

Warfare and Raiding

"A large ship supposed to be English and to belong to London put into a Sound at the south end of the Queen Charlotte Islands, some time last winter with the loss of some of her masts: the natives for several days traded very peaceably with them, but from the distressful situation of the ship they took their opportunity and cut off the vessel, killing the whole crew. (Howay 1925, 297)"

This capture of an English vessel occurred in 1794, the same year as the Haida also captured the *Eleanora*, another English ship, and killed the crew to a man, suffering no casualties in return. Again in 1799 the Haida attacked two more ships, the *Dragon* and the *Caroline* and in 1803 captured the *Boston*, along with several noted assaults on other foreign merchant vessels. This snapshot of recorded history should indicate the boldness and skill of the Haida in their own waters. Attacking ships many times their size, against crews armed with muskets and cannon, they thought nothing of aggressively defending their territory, where others might have shrunk from the challenge. This, more than any other part of Haida culture, has fascinated historians and readers of North American history. How could such a small and bounded people, armed with stone age technology, become so feared at sea?

The context of the Haida's success and notoriety is the general culture of maritime belligerence and organised violence that permeated the peoples of the Pacific North-West.

Each of these tribes - the Tlingit, Tsimshian, Haida, Bella Coola, Chinook, Coast Salish, Kwakiutl and the Nuu-Chah-Nulth - became proficient at littoral warfare, ambushes and raids from canoes, the capture of slaves and war prisoners, the highly aggressive but ritualised combat between professional warriors and each developed an astonishingly striking aesthetic in armour and war vessels. A few choice quotes from *Native North American Armor, Shields, and Fortifications* by David E. Jones provides a good overview:

"Boys who showed the right personality traits (surliness, aggressiveness, hostility, insensitivity, violence) were educated as warriors. Trained in the martial arts, these young men practiced running, swimming, and diving and were taught to be cruel and treacherous and to ignore all rules of decent social behavior. Their people disliked and feared them because of their violent outbursts, which could come at any time and for the slightest provocation. They carried rocks to attack people who irritated them. Never smiling or laughing, they walked with stiff, jerky motions—which to the Kwakwaka'wakw indicated tension and anger—and never wore a shirt or robe over their right shoulder, so that they would always be ready to fight. These martial specialists were sprinkled throughout the ranks of raiders to stiffen them for the displays of ferocity that Kwakwaka'wakw warfare demanded"

"The military organization of the Snoqualmie, a Puget Sound chiefdom, included Fall City, a town devoted to military training, and Tolt, the administrative center. Young boys who at the age of twelve or thirteen exhibited warrior traits were sent to Fall City for martial arts training. The best of them became the elite force of the chief, and these semi professional soldiers conducted raids and ambushes at his direction"

"Northwest Coast Indians warred for a variety of reasons. They sought revenge for affronts against their populations by other groups (murder, rape, assault, theft) and for what they felt to be insults against their honor, status, and the prerequisites of such ranked positions; they raided for slaves; they fought over women; they struggled to acquire, as well as defend, valuable food sources; they battled to defend territory and also to win it; and they fought for control of trade and trading routes"

From their cedar wood canoes the raiders would come, armed with bows, atlatls, spears, clubs, daggers, knives and lances, made from wood, bone, shell, stone and, later, copper. As well as these aggressive tools, there was also a culture of personal armour, by far the most elaborate and specialised on the continent of North America. The Haida, along with the Tlingit, manufactured rod and slat armour chest protection, solid wood greaves for the arms and legs and wooden helmets, described by the Spanish as 'hard as iron'. Along with elk-hide garments underneath, this combination prevented arrows and even musket balls from causing severe injury. As metals and currencies began to flow into Canada, these were found to be useful for further protection and ethnographers noted the presence of Chinese coins, sewn into armour plates, as well as sheets of copper and iron used for chest defence.

The final piece of the Haida warfare puzzle are their canoes, the powerful cedar wood vessels which are reported to have reached 60 feet in length.

The canoes were carved from red cedar in the manner of a dug-out canoe, hollowing the centre using fire and stone or bone tools. The walls were carved to the thinnest extent possible before the centre was filled with water. Hot rocks were placed in the water until it reached boiling point, whereupon the craft was covered with material and the wood allowed to steam. As it did so, long sticks and planks were forced between the sides, bending and extending the width and forcing the ends to curl upwards. The end result was a versatile, lightweight and fast boat which served the needs of the Haida perfectly, with their vast array of inlets, coves, shores, sounds and bays. When going into battle, the warriors would be armed on the ships and often fought hand to hand with their enemies from the boats themselves. This dance of rowing, managing tides and winds, avoiding being hit by arrows and rocks and standing up while attempting to hit an opponent or drag him into the boat, meant the Haida and their neighbours were some of the most skilled seafarers on the continent. Often they would try to sink an enemy vessel by launching small boulders to crack the hulls or capsize the boats.

Reading Materials:

Boelscher 2011. *The curtain within: Haida social and mythical discourse.*

Swanton, J.R., 1905. *Haida texts and myths.*

Leer, J. 2000. *A Story as Sharp as a Knife: The Classic Haida Mythtellers and Their World.*

Jones, D.E., 2010. *Native North American armor, shields, and fortifications.*

White, F., 2014. *Emerging from out of the margins: Essays on Haida language, culture, and history.*

Fedje, D.W. and Mathewes, R. eds., 2011. *Haida Gwaii: human history and environment from the time of loon to the time of the iron people.*

Exploring Madagascar

Interview with Malagasy anthropology student Lolo

Thanks for agreeing to a discussion, I'm a big fan of your twitter account. You're definitely unusual for being an anthropological poster focused on and hailing from Madagascar. How did you end up on twitter?

I've been on twitter for a long time now, maybe five years? I originally had a very personal account just for friends and family. But once I started studying anthropology last year, I made a separate account for posting about it. I deleted that account a few months ago and then restarted fresh with this one.

Madagascar is one of those parts of the world which most people know very little about. Give us a very quick history of the island?

Some thousands of years ago the first Malagasy arrived in Madagascar from multiple waves of migrations out of the Sunda Islands. According to some archaeologists and geneticists, it could have happened at the beginning of our era or hundreds of years prior, specifically between 500 and 200 BCE. In around 600 CE they started to move inland and became the Vazimba.

From the 7th century, contact with Omani Arabs occurred and trade between Omani and Malagasy people began. The spread of Islam happened in the northern part of the Island and many Sakalava sub-tribes and the Antakarana tribe today still practice a syncretic form of Islam and traditional beliefs.

In the 8th century, another wave of Austronesians arrived and also moved inland, where they came across the Vazimba, intermarried with them and formed the Merina. These new arrivals also went on to form the Andriana of other tribes, mainly the Zafiraminia, Zafikazimambo, Antaisaka, Antaimoro and Antambahoaka and Maroserana kingdoms.

There is some evidence of Bantu or Swahili sailors arriving in the 7th century, but most evidence suggests the bulk of them arrived during the Muslim Period of the Indian Ocean Slave Trade. Specifically between the 9th and 11th centuries.

European contact started in the 1500's, when the Portuguese started trade with the Malagasy and pirates also settled. This was all centered on the eastern part of Madagascar, where the Betsimisaraka reside, and this allowed a lot of European cultural diffusion and intermarriage to occur. The zana-malata are the result of these intermarriages and mainly live on St. Marie island.

After the Portuguese and the pirates, the French arrived, then the English, and then the

Norwegians. At this time, slavery was still being practiced in Madagascar and was headed by the Sakalava and the Betsimisaraka. And when they noticed how interested the European slavers were in them, a new period of slave trade began, but this time with Malagasy people being enslaved. They were mainly sent to other Indian Ocean islands, but a few hundred thousand were sent to Latin America, and around 3000-4000 were sent to the US.

After this, a lot continued to develop in Madagascar. The Sakalava and Merina continued to spread across the island, with the Merina eventually taking over. The Sakalava retaliated by allying with the French, which led to the colonization of the island and the eventual fall of the Merina kingdom. Multiple revolts led by Merina Andriana were organized which eventually worked and granted us independence, only for the French to set up a proxy government with the cotiers as the leaders. And now here we are.

On our strange corner of twitter there is a fascination with the Austronesian Expansion and the maritime travel between the East African coastline and the Indian ocean archipelagos and islands. It still blows my mind thinking about how people with Neolithic level technology sailed across the Indian Ocean.

I've always mainly wondered what inspired them to expand so far and for so long when there wasn't any obvious need to.

Is there any sign that the Austronesians may have coast hopped across the sub-continent and the Middle East down towards Madagascar?

As far as I know, there is none. But it is believed that the Austronesians used the coast of East Africa as a base for their trade in the Maritime Silk Road before eventually settling the island permanently.

What effect did that expansion have on the demographics of the country? There seems to be a bewildering number of ethnic groups in Madagascar?

The Malagasy viewed ethnicity very differently than we do today, which resulted in many different tribal affiliations. Many 'ethnic' groups in Madagascar are, more or less, the result of different political, cultural and religious differences. And sometimes, are the result of simply living in a certain place or working a certain occupation. For example, you are Vezo if you know how to freedive, Mahafaly if you are a farmer, and Merina if you live in Imerina.

After colonization a focus on ancestral descent was placed, but even then some people of a certain tribe will still avoid moving to certain areas or joining certain occupations so they don't "lose their ancestors" and accidentally join another tribe.

What has been the legacy of European colonialism for the country?

I would say the legacy of colonization can still be seen by our use of French. It's the language of business and education here, and the government bounces between Malagasy and French spots to ally. This makes it really hard for anyone who does not know French, which is around 96-98% of Malagasy, to receive an education and work.

The government also had deep ties to France post-independence, and at one point nearly every minister in the government was French.

Like lots of remote parts of the world, there are a number of legends of pygmies or little people in Madagascar, specifically the Vazimba and the apparently extant Beosi. What's your view of these stories?

I believe the Vazimba are the descendants of the first group(s) of Austronesian migrants to the island, who later on assimilated into the Merina.

The Beosi myth is most likely the result of invented ancestries though. After slavery ended, the Mikea (as well as European anthropologists at the time) were constructing their own ideas of indigeneity that revolved around the Vazimba myth. Since they were both described as foragers, it was fairly easy for them to assume descent from them and become the Beosi, or inheritors of the land.

One thing you rail against on twitter is the appropriation of Malagasy and other Madagascan groups by African-Americans,

who maybe see skin colour as creating a connection. What's your feeling about this phenomenon?

It annoys me. Mainly because it completely ignores Malagasy ideas of belonging and our own history. In Madagascar anyone that was not born in the *tanindrazana* (ancestor's land), is not considered Malagasy, no matter what tribe they descend from. So it is exasperating seeing people with 1-3% Gasy ancestry claim my identity as their own, when even people with 100% Malagasy ancestry are not even considered Gasy sometimes.

The Problems of Australia's Deep Past - Part One

The Lake Mungo Fossils and their Consequences

Australian prehistory has remained a constant enigma since it was first contacted by European explorers in the early 17th century. Confusing physical descriptions and lack of familiarity with the region led to many speculations about who, when and how the people of Australia ended up so far away from the rest of humanity. Ever since the debate has raged about how many times Australia was colonised - once, twice, three times, multiple times from many different routes? Since the mid 2000's the consensus has been reached that Australia was settled once, by the ancestors of the modern Aboriginal peoples. But this cosy vision is a paper-thin veneer, plastered over centuries of foment. Let us turn then to the problem of Australia.

The Victorian Imagination

Synthesising and compressing all the debates since 1642 left the Victorians with several burning questions about Australian prehistory, but none was so pressing as the issue of the Tasmanians. Put simply the accounts and descriptions of the people of Tasmania, as compared to the mainland Aboriginals, supported one major hypothesis:

The Tasmanians and the Aboriginal Australians were different populations from two different migration events.

The famous comparative anatomist Thomas Huxley had concluded that the Tasmanians were a Negrito people - short in stature, with the distinctive tight curly hair of other Southeast Asian Negrito peoples. Huxley proposed they had sailed to Australia from New Caledonia; in 1879 Francis Allen suggested they had arrived from Africa via a now sunken Indian Ocean land bridge; by 1938 the speculations had become wilder still - that the Tasmanians had come from South America across the Antarctic shoreline; that they had evolved on their island; that they were a Melanesian people who had island hopped around the Australian coast. James Wunderly cautioned that basing a theory of racial difference purely on the grounds of one or two features was inadvisable (but he suggested that crossing a 'Mongoloid' and a 'Negroid' would provide a 'practical enquiry' to solve the matter).

A number of anatomists and anthropologists were highlighting the continuity of Tasmanian and Aboriginal skull morphologies and their common material culture, indicating that the Tasmanians had arisen from the same founding group but differentiated through isolation. Still, scholars such as Ling-Roth and Meston were convinced the Tasmanians were an Asiatic Negrito people, who had been pushed to the margins of the landmass by an incoming group. This narrative was taken up with gusto by Keith Windschuttle, who argued that the Queensland Negritos (Barrineans) had been

241

deliberately forgotten by a generation of politically correct archaeologists. We'll return to this question of Australian Negritos later on.

Java Man & His Kin?

In 1891 the most remarkable discovery of its time came from the Dutch East Indian island of Java. The scholar and explorer Eugene Dubois, convinced he was correct that humanity evolved in Asia, had set out to prove himself right. He uncovered the first evidence of pre-human man - what we now call *Homo erectus*. Dated to between 700k and 1 million years old, his fossils are among the most important in scientific history, not until the 1920's were older fossils recovered.

Earlier than this, in 1886, fossils began to be uncovered in Australia that would eventually prove the antiquity of colonisation. The 'Talgai' skull came first, followed by numerous others: Cohuna (1925), Keilor (1940), Nacurrie (1949), Coobool Creek (1950), Kow Swamp (1968-72), Lake Mungo (1968), Willandra Lakes (1982) and so forth. Many of these were ignored and placed into storage or sold to collectors and the full impact of their importance took nearly a century in some cases to be properly realised.

The Java fossils however became a sensation, catapulting both the researchers and the implications into the public eye. The hominin population presumed to live on the island became known as

Pithecanthropus, later changed to *Homo erectus.* More remains started to appear as European academies poured money into expeditions - Wajak Man (1888), Solo Man (1931), Mojokerto Child (1936). The village of Ngandong (along with the other important sites Sangiran and Sambungmachan) produced many cranial fossils. These were classified as a new intermediary species *Homo soloensis* in 1932.

The integration of Darwinian thought into palaeoanthropology by Huxley relied heavily on the interpretation of both the Javanese fossils and living Aboriginal peoples. Many argued that the Aboriginal phenotype was a remnant of an ancient robust hominin form, linking Neanderthals to Australians. In the 1930's the anthropologist W.F.F Oppenoorth combined the analysis of the Javanese skulls and the worldwide collection of fossils, in particular the Rhodesian Man, into a single overarching racial category - the *Pithecanthropoid-Australoids.*

This idea, that Aboriginals were ancestors of a regional clade from Southeast Asia-Oceania, remained central to the anthropological understanding of Australian prehistory for decades. Detailed work on the Java collections showed that a variety of sub-forms existed, but frustration with the endless proliferation of taxa led the evolutionary biologist Ernst Mayr to group everything in Java under the name *H.erectus* in the 1950's, a move which has largely been retained. Nonetheless, the idea of a regional evolutionary morphology persisted and underpinned everything that happened when archaeologists finally began to study the fossils from Australia itself.

Enter Australia

In 1918 the first major publication to discuss Pleistocene expansion into Australia came from Stewart Smith. He had examined the Talgai skull and decided it was Australoid with primitive ape-like features. This was refuted in the 1930's with better comparative data; scepticism will forever remain given the tragically damaged state of the skull itself. The Keilor cranium from 1940 was assessed by Wunderly who reported a mixture of Tasmanian and Aboriginal features, a fact which suits everyone, regardless if you believe the Tasmanians were a separate or derivative population.

Kow Swamp finally introduced some radiocarbon dates into the mixture (> 20 individuals dated to between 13k - 9k BP) and cranial analysis showed the population to be of robust Pithecanthropoid/erectus origin. Thorne and Macumber (1972) argued that the frontal bones of the Kow Swamp fossils showed:

"an almost unmodified eastern erectus form, specifically that of Javan pithecanthropines"

But probably the most important discoveries came from Lake Mungo. The findings were a revelation at the time and remain the most enigmatic Australian fossils. The site in New South Wales was excavated at the end of the 1960's and turned up three sets of human remains:

Lake Mungo One (Mungo Woman) - LM1

Lake Mungo Two - LM2

Lake Mungo Three (Mungo Man) - LM3

LM1 is one of the oldest, if not the oldest cremation burial on earth. The bones themselves were dated to between 24,700 and 19,030 BP, and the charcoal at 26,250 ±1120 BP. LM1 was burnt, the bones smashed and then burnt again a second time. In a move that will become frustratingly common as this article goes on - LM1 was repatriated in 1992 to the Three Traditional Tribal Groups (3TTG), consisting of the Paakantji, the Muthi Muthi, and the Ngiyampaa who have essentially denied all research requests. As of 2022 all the Lake Mungo remains, including LM1, are set to be *secretly buried in unknown locations*, to prevent any future access.

LM3 is probably a contender for the most important set of human remains in Australia. A well preserved ritualised burial with red ochre and the remains of a fire, LM3's bones tell a fascinating story. Very tall at 6ft 5 inches (196cm), LM3 is decidedly gracile in build, with an almost feminine skull - a very different build and phenotype to the robust Kow fossils. The dating has proved controversial, with multiple tests and methods used reaching conclusions between 30 and 50 thousand years old. We'll return to LM3 when we look at DNA evidence.

Depressingly, Lake Mungo has only become more difficult to access. All the excavated remains are set to be secretly buried and any new discoveries, from erosion, are left where they lie. The skeleton of a child was spotted in 1989. From the book *The Bone Readers: Atoms, Genes and the Politics of Australia's Deep Past:*

> "The 3TTGs have blocked research on Mungo Child, probably a contemporary of Mungo Man and Mungo Lady, and discovered at Joulni in the late 1980s… The bones have remained in the dune, first covered with a sheet of corrugated iron and later protected with shade cloth and sand. There was talk of a salvage excavation, but it came to nothing."

Even worse, in 2005 an entire adult skeleton appeared but was left open to the elements. By 2006 it had been destroyed by the wind and the rain. An inconceivable loss for archaeology.

A final crucial, but by no means solitary, find was dubbed Willandra Lakes Human 50 (WLH50). This was identified as a robust cranium with dates between 20-30kya.

How Many Times?

By now the reader might have spotted that the Australian fossil record is not consistent - a number of remains are classified as robust and some as gracile. Two solutions to this problem was put forward in the 1960's:

> *Dual Origin:* A robust Pithecanthropoid-Australoid population emerged as a separate branch of the family tree from the Javanese *erectus* peoples. These colonised Australia and were met by a gracile *Homo sapien* population descended from East Asians.

> *Single Origin:* Alternatively, Australia was colonised once during the Pleistocene and remained extremely isolated, allowing great internal differentiation of morphologies.

A third minor theory was also developed in the 1960's which we'll discuss later but is worth introducing here.

> *Triple Origin:* A robust Javanese population colonised Australia around 150kya. These were followed by Pleistocene Negrito humans around 50kya (in some versions these are swapped around), and finally one or more waves of Holocene humans, introducing fresh genes.

The *Dual-Origin* hypothesis, based on the distinction between the robust fossils (WLH50, Kow Swamp, Cohuna and Coohol Creek) and the gracile (Lake Mungo, Keilor and King Island) has always remained popular, but it has struggled to establish which way around. The dating for all the fossils has been distressingly erratic and limited, with most remains inaccessible to researchers. As the decades went on, the narrative of who arrived first - the robust population or the gracile - flipped with each new dating publication.

Head-Binding - An Answer To The Problem?

Artificial cranial deformation - the deliberate alteration of an infant's skull shape when their bones are not fused and very soft - has a long and widespread history, including among the Arawe people of New Britain in the Bismarck Archipelago. Several anthropologists had noted that the unusual shape of many Australian fossils could be explained by either head binding or manual shaping of the skull during infancy. For those interested in making connections between these fossils and the Javanese population, the notion that the skulls could have been modified added extra pressure to demonstrate the validity of their claims.

DNA: Mitochondrial Eve & Her Children

In 1987 a landmark paper was published in *Nature* showing that mitochondrial DNA (mtDNA), extracted from modern human populations, could be combined with knowledge of genetic mutation rates to compute when the last common female ancestor of all humans lived. This turned out to be around 140 - 290 kya.

Unsurprisingly this was a paradigm shift within archaeology, using genetics to confirm the 'Out Of Africa' theory of human evolution.

What this meant for Australian archaeology was profound:

> That all humans, including modern and prehistoric Aboriginals, came from Africa within the last 200,000 years.

> That they had managed to migrate across the world and colonise Australia *without interbreeding with other human species.*

> That the Javanese *erectus* population had died out or was replaced by incoming humans.

So was the matter settled?

In the decade after the publication, a number of studies began to take seriously mtDNA in existing Aboriginal and Papuan populations, producing some confusing and contradictory results. But the real jaw-drop came in 2001, when a paper by Adcock *et al* threw this hand grenade into the archaeological fray:

> "Lake Mungo 3 is the oldest (Pleistocene) "anatomically modern" human from whom DNA has been recovered. His mtDNA belonged to a lineage that only survives as a segment inserted into chromosome 11 of the nuclear genome, which is now widespread

among human populations. **This lineage probably diverged before the most recent common ancestor of contemporary human mitochondrial genomes**. This timing of divergence implies that the deepest known mtDNA lineage from an anatomically modern human occurred in Australia; analysis restricted to living humans places the deepest branches in East Africa"

To paraphrase a Discover Magazine article from 2002 - the results showed he was not a match for anyone, alive or dead, on earth. **He was not related to any African individual.**

The lead researcher, Alan Thorne, was convinced that these results settled the dispute. Aboriginals were descendants of two populations, one unrelated to the modern movement of *sapiens*, the other a direct descendant. In his mind, *Homo erectus* was a fiction, and humans had in fact been living in Eurasia for over a million years, the gracile offspring of whom made their way to Australia and were eventually met by a more robust Papuan-like group of newcomers.

The response to these findings was explosive, responses in journals attacked the genetic mechanism, their methodology and insisted they must have contaminated the results. The researchers fired back, defending their workflow protocols, insisting they followed the strictest of procedures. But they would wait another 15 years for the rebuttal.

In 2016, a paper published by Tim Heupink and colleagues finally returned a proper genetic rebuke. Using different and more modern methods, they concluded that Adcock and his team had contaminated the samples, and that the genetic grouping to which Lake Mungo 3 belonged was consistent with Out of Africa. They also identified a novel haplogroup, S2, which was proof of deep Aboriginal separation once they arrived in Australia. They found no differences between the gracile and robust bodies, supporting the older idea that Aboriginal phenotypic difference was indigenous to the continent.

The 'Pygmy Problem'

As discussed in the opening section, the question and possibility of a Negrito or Pygmy population in Australia has deep roots and never truly went away. An anthropologist and researcher, Joseph Birdsell, had conducted fieldwork in south Queensland during the 1940's and published on his discovery of a 'Negritoid' race of Aboriginals. In 1967 he revealed to the world his 'trihybrid' model of Aboriginal descent.

The question of the Aboriginal Negrito was re-opened in 2002 by historians Keith Windschuttle and Tim Gillin. Despite being criticised for right-wing political bias, they raised the question of what had happened to the academic study of this population after the 1960's. Birdsell's research was effectively excluded from incorporation into the mainstream consensus. Parallel to this of course was the rise in indigenous movements across the world, a feature of which was homogeneity or 'pan-aboriginalism/indianism', to counter the mainstream colonial narrative.

In this zeal for unity, it appears that research into pygmoid or Negrito populations came across as crass, racialist and Victorian, a 'white man's' fantasy of finding lost races. Thus it was abandoned, forgotten, dismissed. Birdsell's work with another anthropologist, Norman Tindale, detailed extensive contact with a tribe which they named 'Barrineans', after a nearby lake. As Tindale wrote in his 1963 book, *Aboriginal Australians:*

"Their small size, tightly curled hair, child-like faces, peculiarities in their tooth dimensions and their blood groupings showed that they were different from other Australian Aborigines and had a strong strain of Negrito in them. Their faces bore unmistakable resemblances to those of the now extinct Tasmanians, as shown by photographs and plaster casts of the last of those people"

The University of Sydney academic consensus - the 'Sydney School' position - was that all Aboriginal people descended from a handful of individuals. Prominent anthropologists such as Stan Larnach and N. W. G. Macintosh were insistent on this theory. As Larnach wrote:

"Three women and two or three men may have initiated the peopling of Australia. They probably arrived here by chance after being blown off course, or they may have been seeking refuge"

Tindale and Birdsell were academic outsiders, and they failed to change any minds in Sydney. Despite their work being popular elsewhere and contributing to a number of children's books on the prehistory of Australia, it was the Sydney School position which fed into the 60's Aboriginalism and overshadowed the existence of the Barrineans. Chris Ballard goes so far in his paper, *Strange alliance: Pygmies in the colonial imaginary,* as to describe such preoccupations with Negritos and short-statured peoples as ultimately rooted in an extreme racialist vision of the world, a charge most modern academics would baulk at receiving. Better not to tread those paths.

Today most researchers dismiss any speculations of Aboriginal Negritos as a political attack on the indigeneity of Aboriginal peoples, with the malicious intent of justifying Western colonialism. The Australian Museum online has a section refuting the existence of Pygmies, referring to it as a myth and a 'political weapon'. We'll see next time as to the genetic evidence used to claim a single origin for Aboriginal people.

Conclusions

This article has unravelled far beyond what I anticipated, both in writing and research. My intention was to produce one article with all the problems, but I couldn't do justice to the remaining problems - earliest dates of occupation, spread of languages, arrival of the dingo and new stone tools, the genetic connection between

253

Aboriginals and Indians, the puzzle over why the Austronesians ignored Australia, and so on.

If I have kept my reader's attention then hopefully this has followed a story from the earliest discoveries of Australian fossils to the present day. We've seen how the study of these first fossils was bound up in intellectual ferment around the Javanese remains, and how this led to theories of how Australia was populated. We saw the debates over categorising phenotypes, and then genotypes, and how they went back and forth between multiple origins or a single one.

Ultimately the questions come down these:

> Aboriginal Australians are phenotypically distinct from the rest of the human family - why?

> Did they emerge from a separate lineage of hominins?

> How many colonisation events led to the modern population?

> Aboriginal Australians and Australian fossils show great variation:

> Were the Tasmanians a separate population?

> How many colonisation events do the fossils show?

What can DNA evidence tell us about Aboriginal ancestry?

Were/Are there any Australian Negritos?

Next time we'll build on the evidence presented here and see if the Single Origin consensus can continue to hold water for much longer.

References & Further Reading

Roger Blench (2008) The Languages of the Tasmanians and Their Relation to the Peopling of Australia: Sensible and Wild Theories, Australian Archaeology, 67:1, 13-18, DOI: 10.1080/03122417.2008.11681875

https://www.peterbrown-palaeoanthropology.net/

Andrew Kramer. American Journal of Physical Anthropology. (1991) Modern Human Origins in Australasia: Replacement or Evolution?

Theories of Modern Human Origins: The Paleontological Test Author(s): David W. Frayer, Milford H. Wolpoff, Alan G. Thorne, Fred H. Smith and Geoffrey G. Pope Source: American Anthropologist , Mar., 1993, New Series, Vol. 95, No. 1 (Mar., 1993), pp. 14-50

Darren Curnoe, "A 150-Year Conundrum: Cranial Robusticity and Its Bearing on the Origin of Aboriginal Australians", *International Journal of Evolutionary Biology*, vol. 2011, Article ID 632484, 18 pages, 2011. https://doi.org/10.4061/2011/632484

Curnoe, D., 2009. Possible causes and significance of cranial robusticity among Pleistocene–Early Holocene Australians. *Journal of Archaeological Science*, *36*(4), pp.980-990.

Brown, Peter. "Artificial Cranial Deformation: A Component in the Variation in Pleistocene Australian Aboriginal Crania." *Archaeology in Oceania*, vol. 16, no. 3, 1981, pp. 156–67, http://www.jstor.org/stable/40386565.

https://quadrant.org.au/opinion/history-wars/2002/06/the-extinction-of-the-australian-pygmies/

Tuniz, C., Gillespie, R. and Jones, C., 2009. The bone readers: atoms, genes and the politics of Australia's deep past.

Adcock, G.J., Dennis, E.S., Easteal, S., Huttley, G.A., Jermiin, L.S., Peacock, W.J. and Thorne, A., 2001. Mitochondrial DNA sequences in ancient Australians: implications for modern human origins. *Proceedings of the National Academy of Sciences*, *98*(2), pp.537-542.

Trueman, J.W.H., 2001. Does the Lake Mungo 3 mtDNA evidence stand up to analysis?. *Archaeology in Oceania*, *36*(3), pp.163-165.

Adcock, G.J., Dennis, E.S., Easteal, S., Huttley, G.A., Jermiin, L.S., Peacock, W.J. and Thorne, A., 2001. Lake Mungo 3: A response to recent critiques. *Archaeology in Oceania*, *36*(3), pp.170-174.

Heupink, T.H., Subramanian, S., Wright, J.L., Endicott, P., Westaway, M.C., Huynen, L., Parson, W., Millar, C.D., Willerslev, E. and Lambert, D.M., 2016. Ancient mtDNA sequences from the First Australians revisited. *Proceedings of the National Academy of Sciences*, *113*(25), pp.6892-6897.

Bowler, J.M., Johnston, H., Olley, J.M., Prescott, J.R., Roberts, R.G., Shawcross, W. and Spooner, N.A., 2003. New ages for human occupation and climatic change at Lake Mungo, Australia. *Nature*, *421*(6925), pp.837-840.

Forster, P., Torroni, A., Renfrew, C. and Röhl, A., 2001. Phylogenetic star contraction applied to Asian and Papuan mtDNA evolution. *Molecular biology and evolution*, *18*(10), pp.1864-1881.

Stringer, C., 1999. Has Australia backdated the human revolution?. *Antiquity*, *73*(282), pp.876-879.

Dubois, E., 1937. 1. On the fossil human skulls recently discovered in Java and Pithecanthropus erectus. *Man*, pp.1-7.

Burr, W.A. and Gerson, D.E., 1965. Venn diagrams and human taxonomy. *American Anthropologist*, *67*(2), pp.494-499.

Coon, C.S., 1962. The origin of races.

Thorne, A.G., 1971. Mungo and kow swamp: morphological variation in Pleistocene Australians. *The Australian Journal of Anthropology*, *8*(2), p.85.

Wolpoff, M.H. and Lee, S.H., 2014. WLH 50: How Australia informs the worldwide pattern of Pleistocene human evolution. *PaleoAnthropology*, *2014*, pp.505-564.

Habgood, P.J., 1986. The origin of the Australians: a multivariate approach. *Archaeology in Oceania*, *21*(2), pp.130-137.

Thorne, A. and Sim, R., 1994. The gracile male skeleton from late Pleistocene King Island, Australia. *Australian Archaeology*, *38*(1), pp.8-10.

Freedman, L. and Lofgren, M., 1979. The Cossack skull and a dihybrid origin of the Australian Aborigines. *Nature*, *282*(5736), pp.298-300.

The Problems of Australia's Deep Past - Part Two

Dravidians, The Pama-Nyungan Expansion, Dingoes and Other Mysteries

In my last article I left the exploration of Australia's prehistory unresolved - which it still largely remains today - but in only covering the fossil record and the discussion of Aboriginal Pygmies/Negritos we have missed swathes of evidence for post-Pleistocene migration into Australia. As it stands the consensus is that *one and only one migration has ever taken place into Australia before the colonial period.* This is reinforced in museums, lectures, textbooks and social commentary in Australia and around the world. At least one generation has been raised on this. The competing or even complicating evidence remains largely in the realms of lone academics, marginal journals and fields and online discussion groups.

This second article will dive into later evidence for external contact with Australia, after the rising sea levels cut the continent off from the world. We will cover languages, genetics, animal and plant movements, flint tools and oral history. Hopefully I will be able to show how an old Victorian idea about migration to Australia from India has been resurrected and reinvigorated; how Aboriginal languages hold some secrets about the past and how their oral history contains intriguing tales of exotic 'fox-coloured' sailors from distant

259

lands long ago. I'll try to piece all these lines of evidence together and see what picture is painted at the end.

The Dravidian Question

One of the more confusing and almost esoteric proposals of the Victorian era was the Dravidian-Aboriginal connection and the possibility that a wave of migrants from India arrived in Australia at some point in the distant past. To quote John Mathew in his 1899 work *Eaglehawk and Crow: a Study of the Australian Aborigines, including an Inquiry into their Origin and a Survey of Australian Languages:*

> "Then followed one invasion, if not two, by hostile people. Of these the Dravidian was the first to arrive, the Malay coming later… Coming as a later offshoot from the first home of humanity, this invading band was of higher intelligence and better equipped for conflict than the indigenes of Australia. Physically, they were more lithe and wiry, and of taller stature. They were lighter in colour, though a dark race; less hirsute; and the hair of their head was perfectly straight"

To the modern ear this sounds profoundly strange, how did people come to believe that a group of south Indians invaded Australia? What was their proof? To answer this we return to the fossil record and to Huxley.

The term Dravidian is one of those 'kitchen sink' descriptors which seems to fulfil whatever role is asked of it. Generally it refers to the people of South India, and depending on how you interpret the history, could be narrowed down to: remnants of the Pleistocene Southern Dispersal populations; Pleistocene and Holocene migrant mixtures; incoming Neolithic Zagros farmers; the founders of the Mehrgarh; the founders of the Indus Valley civilisation or a mixture of all of these, sometimes called Ancestral South Indians (ASIs). This confusion was plainly evident in the 19th century, as one reviewer of Mathew's work noted:

> "There is also some ambiguity in the use of the term "Dravidian," as, from the researches of Thurston, it would appear that there is a dark, broad nosed, curly-haired primitive race in Southern India which may for the present be termed the pre-Dravidian race. The typical Dravidians (Telugus, Kanarese, &c.) are regarded by some as a later immigrant people. In his " Man : Past and Present," Keane states that "all attempts to affiliate this group [the Australian languages] to the Dravidian of Southern India, or to any other, have signally failed.""

Huxley was the first to make the connection between the 'Dravidians' and the Aboriginal Australians. During his time aboard HMS Rattlesnake's voyage to Australia (1846-50) he observed the phenotypic and linguistic relationship between the southern Indians and the Aboriginal peoples. In publications dating across 1865 -

1870 Huxley developed his theory that the Dravidian and Australian peoples represented a single pure racial type, along with the ancient Egyptians. This did little to solve the problem of Australian origins however, as anatomists and natural scientists argued for years over whether Aboriginal people were a single race, a mixed race of Tasmanian and Dravidian stock or a triple combination of 'Oceanic Negro', Dravidian and Tasmanian. In 1909 two skulls were excavated at Adichanallur, Tamil Nadu. A full analysis of their features and condition was published in 1930 by the Madras Government Museum, comparing them with Aboriginal craniometric features. At least one skull was considered to be definitely of Australoid origin, strengthening the argument that some Aboriginal peoples descended in part from a recent wave of southern Indian incomers.

This theme was picked up and expanded over the decades, reaching its full flowering in Joseph Birdsell's 1993 work *Microevolutionary patterns in Aboriginal Australia.* Here he makes the argument that a south Indian derived phenotype is visible within the Aboriginal population. But as with most of Birdsell's work, it was ultimately dismissed and by the turn of the millennium, the 'Dravidian Question' had been largely forgotten.

The Genetics Steps In

In a running theme throughout much of the genetic revolution, the older theories which had largely been dismissed came back to the fore. In 2002 a paper was published entitled: *Gene Flow from the Indian Subcontinent to Australia: Evidence from the Y Chromosome.* The researchers, working from Huxley and Birdsell, set out to test the connection between the south Indians and the Aboriginals. Working on common elements from the Y-chromosome, they concluded that there was an overlap suggestive of Indian introgression between 3-5k years ago. This meant that not only were south Indians and Aborginal people connected via the Pleistocene migration path, but that an incoming group of south Indians arrived in Australia relatively recently.

Since then a number of contradictory studies have been conducted:

> mtDNA & Y-chromosome analysis finds deep separation rather than external contact (2007)

> Microsatellite DNA marker study finds connection between Arrernte people of Australia and south Indians (2007)

> Genome wide SNP study showed Holocene introduction of Indian genetics to Australia dated circa 4kya

A particularly curious study was performed in India in 2011 - an isolated Dravidian speaking tribe, the Soliga, were found to not only be very distinct from their surrounding neighbours, but also to share close genetic affinities with at least two Aboriginal peoples:

"The Soliga tribe was found to be remarkably different from other Indian populations including other southern Dravidian-speaking tribes. In contrast, the Soliga people exhibited genetic affinity to two Australian aboriginal populations. This genetic similarity could be attributed to the 'Out of Africa' migratory wave(s) along the southern coast of India that eventually reached Australia. Alternatively, the observed genetic affinity may be explained by more recent migrations from the Indian subcontinent into Australia."

Overall the case being built by the genetic studies partially reinforces the earlier views on Dravidian migrations, but also narrows down considerably the time frame in question. The studies which positively identify a connection between south India and Australia converge on the same time period: **The Mid Holocene**. So what else happened during the Holocene which could reinforce the Dravidian connection?

Of Dingos and Stones

A topic of intense curiosity to archaeologists is the question of how and when the dingo arrived in Australia. Dingos are a very unusual canid with some unprecedented historical features:

Dingos are essentially 'feralised' dogs. Having split from a lineage of domestic dog known as the 'New Guinea singing dog', they entered Australia and reverted back towards a feral canid.

This feralisation process shows up in their inability to process starch (alpha-amylase locus) and their ability to hunt animals such as kangaroos in packs, much like wolves.

Uniquely it seems, the Aboriginal Australians made no attempt to selectively breed the dingo. Their morphology has remained consistent for at least 3,500 years.

There isn't space in this article to dive into the arguments around dingo genetics, what we are concerned with is the question of when they arrived and who brought them. The earliest dingo fossil places them in Australia 3,450 years ago, but several genetic analyses show they diverged from the singing dog around 8,300 years ago. We currently have several models now based on these studies:

8,300 years the dingo split from singing dog and crossed the land bridge between New Guinea and Australia independently

3,450 years ago the dingo was brought to Australia by humans using boats

At least one paper indicates there are two deeply split dingo populations - northwestern and southeastern

A combination of independent crossings and human movement

Another unexplained mid Holocene phenomenon is the sudden appearance of a new type of stone tool. The so-called '*backed artefacts*' or '*backed blades/tools*' first appear around 8,500 years and then proliferate rapidly around 3,500 years ago. As above with the dingo, these two dates are perfectly aligned.

Together these two lines of evidence support two major periods of change in Australia, or at least the beginning of a change and the following intensification. Let's turn now to one of Australia's greatest enigmas - the distribution of its languages.

The Pama-Nyungan Expansion

As with so many other things, there is a unique and striking difference within the structure of Australia's language families. The continent is divided between two groups of languages - the *Pama-Nyungan* and the *Non-Pama-Nyungan*. The Pama-Nyungan languages occupy the vast majority of Australia, 306 of 400 languages, with the remaining languages squeezed into a small space in the north. This is a very unusual pattern of differentiation, typically only seen during aggressive expansions like the Indo-European and the Bantu. So what is happening here?

There are a number of confusions surrounding this language distribution. Typically languages differentiate away from one another at a generally predictable rate. This would indicate that the Pama-Nyungan family, which occupies the overwhelming majority of the continent, split fairly late in Australian prehistory and hasn't had the time to internally divide. On top of this there is absolutely no consensus amongst the few linguists who study this topic as to how Pama-Nyungan evolved - whether it is even a meaningful language category, from what proto-language or family it originated or how the remaining non-Pama-Nyungan languages should be classified.

Given that prehistoric Australians, however many waves of arrival, have been on the continent for at least 50k years, the youthfulness of the Pama-Nyungan family indicates that it differentiated and then expanded rapidly around 5-6,000 years ago. Curiously, work by Schmidt (1919) identified two major language groups - a southeastern and northwestern. This division in the Pama-Nyungan family was confirmed using computational phylogenetics, but also matches deep divides within the population genetic structures of modern Aboriginal Australians, indicating that the expansion of the Pama-Nyungan languages, along with the backed-blade stone tools, was carried out by people migrating, rather than linguistic diffusion.

Studies of the Pama-Nyungan language family have shown it to contain a number of linguistic innovations, as well as loan words from the non-Pama-Nyungan languages. This is to be expected, but rather than a blurred gradient between the non-Pama-Nyungan and Pama-Nyungan, we instead see a sharp division, indicative of rapid expansion and cultural separation. To quote Patrick McConvell:

"There are loanwords in both directions but these can be detected, along with the direction of borrowing in the vast majority of cases. This is the case all along the boundary as far as we know: despite diffusion of items and to a limited extent structures across the boundary there is a sharp divide and no sense of the smooth cline one would expect if the situation were really the result of tens of millennia of diffusion and convergence."

At present there is no agreement as to how and why the expansion occurred, other than dismissing the outdated idea of external migrations - we are left with few ideas. There was no animal domestication (quite the opposite), no horticulture, no agriculture, no pastoralism. In the absence of external interventions the standard narrative looks to the changing conditions of the climate during the mid Holocene, which prompted a greater reliance on plant foods, as elsewhere on earth. But is this really enough to explain the rapid spread of one language family?

Outside Influences

The issue of whether any other group of people has migrated to Australia in the last 50k years has proved both highly elusive but persistent. Clues, hints, suggestions, but never anything truly definitive. Alternative explanations exist for almost every piece of evidence, nevertheless it is worth examining some of these examples.

C.E.M & F.M Pearce in their book *Oceanic Migration: Paths, Sequence, Timing and Range of Prehistoric Migration in the Pacific and Indian Oceans,* outline some speculative findings which would indicate that people from the Spice Islands were travelling down the west coast of Australia. The first is the boab tree. The boab is a fascinating tree because it belongs to a larger group of trees, almost all of whom exist only in Madagascar. The question of how the boab reached Australia is yet another mystery - three possibilities exist:

> Seeds from Madagascar managed to make their way across the Indian Ocean and found a new sub-species in Australia. Considered extremely unlikely due to salt water damage and the currents being against the possibility.

> Seeds made their way with the earliest humans along the Southern Dispersal route.

> Seeds travelled back and forth with sailors across the Indian Ocean - but this would require a rapid species divergence in just a few thousand years.

In 1930 and again in 1993, members of the Australian public found strange eggshells. When examined these were revealed to belong to *Aepyornis maximus,* a now extinct Madagascan elephant bird. At least one of these was radiocarbon dated to around 2000 BP, suggestive of Austronesian sailors moving the birds across the Indian Ocean. How they ended up in Australia is then a secondary question, but we will touch on the Austronesians shortly.

Finally they list a curious idea - the mythological motif of the Moon/Lake story - which seems certain to have originated in the Maluku Spice Islands and was distributed by the Taiwanese/Filipino Lapita Culture (the ancestor to the Polynesians). The myth seems to have travelled to Lapita colonies or destinations - Japan, Vanuatu, Fiji, Samoa, Hawaii and New Zealand, and interestingly, to Western Australia. This would make sense if regular seafaring contact were made between Lapita descendants and Aboriginal Australians.

A number of objects have been recovered in the past century which suggest trade and connectivity with southeast Asia. These include greenstone polished chisels, unusual stone tools and a jade statue of Chinese origin, excavated in 1879 near Darwin.

It is well known that the Makassar people of Sulawesi made repeated contact with northern Australians during the 18th century, in particular to collect the *trepang* or sea cucumber, for sale in Chinese markets. However, in Arnhem Land the Yolgnu Aboriginal peoples have a much deeper memory of earlier contacts with outsiders.

Mentioned in their mythological epic of the *Djang'kawu,* the Yolgnu have preserved an encounter with a group of people they call the ***Baijini***. It is worth trying to unpack this myth in some detail, since the connections with the wider Indian world are on full display here.

Who are the *Baijini?*

The *Baijini* appear in the story of the *Djang'kawu* elders as people who already occupy the land when the elder ancestors arrive on the shore. Alternatively in other descriptions they arrive on a shipwreck, but in either story they are people who have come from another land. They cultivated rice, made pottery and their women wore colourful sarongs, they also built houses of stone and possessed sailing technologies far above the Aborigine's capacities.

The question of who the *Baijini* are has puzzled anthropologists and historians for generations. Proposals have included Chinese, Bajau Sea Gypsies, Makassans and pre-Makassans, Indonesians, Malays and Indians, to name but a few. Other ideas include the journeying of some Aboriginal people to Sulawesi with the Makassans - thus explaining the odd order of events in one version of the story - or just simply that the *Baijini* are fictional people of mythology and nothing more. The trope of a stranger-king or external authority arriving by the sea is common in Oceania, and some researchers have suggested the *Baijini* fit into this tradition.

What we don't know about the *Baijini* is probably more relevant to us. The stories of the Makassan trepang hunters are historic in nature to the Yolgnu, but the *Baijini* are something else entirely - mythic, powerful, secretive, beings that hold knowledge fundamental to the essence of the Yolgnu themselves. As Ian S. McIntosh in his book, *Exploring the Legacy of the 1948 Arnhem Land Expedition,* writes:

"The concealment of the stories of the Bayini beyond fleeting references to them building boats, making pottery, growing rice, or weaving on their looms was quite thorough. But then there are those even more obscure references to Bayini 'flying fox' people creating sacred waterholes, or the story of the birth of the first light-skinned baby—obviously the result of a liaison between a Yolngu woman and an Indonesian man. These stories speak to an entirely different level of significance… there is a strong suggestion that there existed in Yolngu discourse some overarching belief associated with the power and prestige of the Other—a power that rightfully belonged to the Yolngu. Specifically, the notion of a 'Dreaming Macassan' appears to provide the nucleus for Yolngu thoughts on the origin and purpose of non Aborigines… In the stories that have been shared, the Bayini are seafarers who, at the dawn of time, make their way from points south of Numbulwar in the Gulf of Carpentaria, around Dholtji and Cape Wilberforce, and into Arnhem Bay and Gurrumurru, where their journey ends as mysteriously as it began."

Glancing at a map of the Austronesian Expansion shows the connectivity of the maritime world in southeast Asia and Oceania. The Austronesians linked together the Indian and Pacific Oceans over several millennia, and yet somehow ignored Australia, which is extraordinarily close to their known sailing paths. The earliest Sanskrit inscriptions in Indonesia date to the second half of the fourth century AD at Kutai, East Kalimantan, some twenty miles from the Makassar Straits. To quote Darshi Arichige, in his recent discussion on the possibility of gene flow from India to Australia:

"As now we know that Dravidians were in the vicinity of Makassar, it would have been very easy for them to visit Arnhem Land or Kimberley region with the help of the northwest monsoonal winds. Thus, if Haviks and Mukris, who are usual inhabitants of the western side of Indian subcontinent could genetically contribute to the Australian Aboriginal genome, as the researchers suggested, the Dravidians who might have started from Coromandel Coast, also stood a similar chance of such a contribution in rather recent historical times. Thus, given the archaeological evidence from the region and the genetic connection discussed above, the probability of a Dravidian contact around the 4th Century AD is very high."

So we have here tales of foreign sailors, who likely traversed the northern coast of Australia in the deep past, who were golden brown skinned and who apparently married into the Aboriginal people of

Arnhem, who pre-date the Makassans and who had the technology to arrive and then leave with their families. A very likely date could be set as late as the fourth century AD, while earlier speculations could be hinted at by looking at how Austronesian boats and skills were acquired along the Indian coastline (a topic for another time). Either way, there is a high probability that the tales of the *Baijini* and the genetic indicators of Dravidian contact in Australia could refer to the same true event.

Pieces of the Jigsaw

Summing everything up here we can point to a few evidence clusters:

> Approx 8,500 years ago both the dingo and the first evidence for backed blade stone tools appear in Australia

> Around 5,000 years ago the Pama-Nyungan language family begins to rapidly differentiate

> 3,500 years ago a new dingo group appears, the backed blade tools and the Pama-Nyungan languages spread rapidly - the maps of both the tools and the language distribution overlap extremely well

Both the dingo population and the Pama-Nyungan languages show a deep and matching division - northwestern & southeastern

Several genetics papers point to an introgression of south Indian genes somewhere between 3-5,000 years ago

The presence of boab trees and elephant bird eggs (dated to 2000 years ago), both originally from Madagascar

Lapita mythological motifs and Aboriginal stories of (likely) Indonesian or Indian seafarers present within oral histories

None of these are suggestive of one particular episode of migration, but together they point to two or three intriguing possibilities. Firstly, one or more episodes of contact took place between northern Aboriginal Australians and southern Indian sailors anywhere between 3-5,000 years ago. This contact in some way prompted an internal split or division, resulting in one language family coming to dominate most of the continent. Secondly, that southeast Asian/Indian contact may have been periodically sustained, with meetings perhaps around 400 AD and again around 1750 AD. Finally, some minor level of integration of Australia by the Austronesians into their maritime world, suggested by Madagascan flora and fauna and mythological motifs.

The major weakness with suggesting that both the flint tools and the language spread were somehow *caused* by contact with another group is that we have no mechanism or hypothesis for what this means. Did this incoming group bring a new tool style? Teach the coastal Aboriginal people a new style? Did they invade and provoke some major group conflict? We don't know.

A major missing piece from this jigsaw is the absence and few tantalising hints of Austronesian presence on the continent. This will be a topic for the third and final instalment of this series of Australian prehistory, along with some proposed scenarios based on the evidence so far.

Bibliography (not already cited or linked)

I read nearly fifty articles and chapters for this piece, not all of them helpful. These are some of the more interesting papers and books.

Pattern and context in the Holocene proliferation of backed artifacts in Australia. Hiscock, P., 2002.

Lexical and Structural Etymology. Robert Mailhammer (Ed.)

The Language of Hunter-Gatherers. Edited by Tom Güldemann, Patrick McConvell and Richard A. Rhodes

The Prehistory and Internal Relationships of Australian Languages. Patrick McConvell and Claire Bowern. 2011

Independent Histories of Human Y Chromosomes from Melanesia and Australia. Kayser et al. 2001.

Aboriginal mitogenomes reveal 50,000 years of regionalism in Australia. Tobler, R., Rohrlach, A., Soubrier, J. *et al.* (2017).

The 'global' versus the 'local': cognitive processes of kin determination in Aboriginal Australia. Dousset, L., 2008.

'Complexity' and the Australian continental narrative: themes in the archaeology of Holocene Australia. Ulm, S., 2013.

The Problems of Australia's Deep Past - Part Three

Where are the Austronesians?

If you've followed this series all the way, you'll know that I've covered two main periods of Australian prehistory with regards to migration and influences from the outside. Firstly the fossil record and the controversial question of Aboriginal Pygmies, and secondly the disparate bits of evidence during the Holocene for external contact, including dingoes, linguistics, genetics, flora, fauna and oral history. In this final piece I want to take aim at something of an absence in Australian history - the apparent bypassing of the continent during the Austronesian Expansion - as well as sum up the evidence so far and think about plausible models for the Australian past.

The Lapita Expansion

Without spending a whole article on the Austronesian Expansion, it is worth briefly reviewing the origins and spread of the Neolithic pottery using culture which appears across Oceania but somehow misses Australia. The generally accepted model for the appearance of the Austronesian peoples is known as 'Out of Taiwan' - meaning that the founding peoples who spoke Proto-Austronesian and who brought a whole suite of technology, ceramics, crops and domesticated animals. They can be traced back to Taiwan, somewhere around 5-6000 years ago. Genetic testing of fossilised remains in Vanuatu and Tonga confirm that the first inhabitants are of Taiwanese descent. In places like the Bismarck Archipelago a new archaeological horizon appears instantaneously around 3,500 years ago - red slipware with unique stamps and evidence for novel horticulture:

> "Our analyses of phytoliths and starch in sediments and on pottery has found evidence for burning, food preparation and cooking in conjunction with a suite of wild and domesticated plants indicative of horticulture. Starch and phytoliths from seeded Australimusa (syn: Callimusa) bananas as well as domesticated Eumusa (syn: Musa) bananas were recovered, as well as Colocasia esculenta (taro) starch, and Metroxylon sp. (sago palm) phytoliths"

The Lapita peoples seemed to move from the Philippines to the Bismarck Archipelago, then outwards to Vanuatu, Fiji and Tonga. On the New Guinea mainland, Lapita ceramics have been dated to around 2,900 - 2,500 years ago, along with stone adzes, obsidian tools and shell armbands. This westward movement along the coast across the south of the island seems to stop at Australia.

The Lapita peoples carried what appears to be an entire package of cultural and domesticate technology, including stilted houses, sophisticated outrigger sailing boats, taro, sago, bananas, rice, pigs, dogs, chickens and new types of stone tools. Their intermixing with local Papuan populations produced the Polynesian peoples and they passed on Austronesian languages across the region.

Despite this rapid and extensive migration there is no evidence for Lapita pottery or activity on the Australian mainland, the closest locations are islands off the shore:

Lapita on the Edge

"On an anecdotal level, Australian archaeologists regularly complain amongst themselves about the dismissive or cursory way Australian archaeology is dealt with in global surveys of human prehistory. Yet for the most part, Australianists largely ignore the outside world, positing that the ancestors of today's Aboriginal Australians came, saw and conquered about 65 000 years ago, and then, with the exception perhaps some 3000–5000 years ago of adopting the dingo, a canine that as a non-marsupial had to come from elsewhere, remained cut off from the outside world until seasonally visiting Macassan sea-slug gatherers from Indonesia began exploiting the northern coastline just before Europeans appeared on the scene. Extraordinarily, most general surveys of Australian prehistory do not even acknowledge more than in passing (if at all) that the continent was joined to New Guinea by dry land from the time of initial colonisation until the early Holocene"

This unusually frank statement comes from a book chapter entitled *Lapita: The Australian connection,* by Ian Lilley in *Debating Lapita.* His point sums up my frustrations with Australian archaeology and why I chose to write three articles on the subject - why do we allow this one continent and people the special position of total isolation prior to European colonisation? The two main areas of contention to focus on here are the Torres Straits and a tiny speck of land called Lizard Island.

Australia has over 8000 islands, a legacy of the Holocene sea level rise which separated the continent from New Guinea, the majority of which have not been comprehensively excavated. The Torres Strait islands are a natural place to look for connections between the Aboriginal and Austronesian worlds, indeed many of the modern inhabitants of the islands are Austronesian speaking and descendants of the maritime Neolithic culture which spread throughout the Pacific. Lizard Island on the other hand seems an unremarkable place, but well positioned to receive visitors from the rest of the Lapita world.

Lizard Island belongs to the chain of islands in the Great Barrier Reef and seems to have been intermittently occupied from the Australian mainland as far back as 4000 years ago. One key marine resource, which we will return to, were turtles. These seem to have been a major draw factor from Australia, and between 5-3000 years ago a flurry of activity is documented across the reef, which stabilises as the sea level settled. Some island chains were permanently occupied (Whitsunday and Keppel Islands) and others periodically visited (Shoalwater Bay Group). Many of these were then abandoned for around 2000 years, in particular the Cumberland Group, Keppel Islands, and Northumberland Group. Lizard Island seems to be highly unusual in possessing pottery and potentially stone arrangements which link both Aboriginal and Austronesian cultures.

The pottery from Lizard Island has yet to be properly dated, but analysis of the temper shows it was manufactured on the island, rather than brought there as some speculated. Examinations of the stone structures show cultural expressions which match both Torres Strait and wider Lapita material culture, but also Aboriginal styles of stonework:

> "available ethnographic analyses and archaeological evidence supports the view that visitors from Torres Strait and the southwest Pacific visited the Lizard Island Group. To what extent and on what terms these visitors interacted with local Dingaal people and their ancestors remains to be determined."

This accords with well documented connections between the Torres Islanders from Warraber and Poruma Islands who would sail to Lizard Island to source 'clubstone' and mythology from Rossel, which mentions pigs, taro and a special canoe brought by 'light-skinned' ancestral peoples. Extensive simulations of the wind patterns between the Solomon Islands and Lizard Islands conclude that travel between them was almost certain:

"In this paper we have investigated the question of seafaring between Lizard Island and the Melanesian Islands of the Solomon Sea. More accurate climate data, better information on canoe performance and a refined rationale of simulation demonstrate that the potential for navigation in the Solomon Sea is extensive, **and that sailing to Lizard Island not only is possible, but has most likely occurred**. In addition, seasonal variations of wind conditions show that journeys to Lizard Island were followed by at least several months of visit or even settlement on the island before having the opportunity to return north or north-eastwards"

What some researchers have dubbed 'The Solomon Sea Interaction Sphere' seemed to predict this connection between the Lapita world and the edges of Australia, in particular the Torres Strait. As Lilley notes:

"Combined with factors such as the presence of obsidian from Fergusson Island in the Massim in both the Reef Islands' Lapita site SE–RF–2 and at Teouma in Vanuatu to the south-east of the main Solomons and in the Post-Lapita Oposisi site on Yule Island on the edge the Papuan Gulf far to the west, the Woodlark finding led Sheppard and colleagues to hypothesise the existence of an east–west interaction sphere that also facilitated the appearance of

283

Late Lapita on the Papuan coast and the presence of Late Lapita ceramics in Torres Strait."

So what we are looking at here is the presence of Austronesian voyagers and traders moving around a well connected maritime world which included the fringes of Aboriginal Australia, most likely prompted by hunters following the hawksbill turtles which nest in the Solomon Islands but travel to forage in Australian waters. In at least two locations, these Lapita peoples left behind ceramics and traces of cultural intermixing with Aboriginal peoples. But, what is remarkable is the absence of Austronesian presence on the mainland itself - despite the huge networks of connections between tiny Pacific islands and larger land masses like New Guinea, the Neolithic juggernaut that was the Austronesian Expansion stopped right at the beaches of the Australian continent.

A Closer Look At Torres

The Torres Strait is one of the richest areas to look at when trying to understand the deep history and division between the Aboriginal peoples and the Papuans. Despite Australia being connected to a 'Greater Australia' - the Sahul landmass - the genetic differentiation of the Papuans and the Aboriginals is vast. To quote from one of the most comprehensive genetics papers on Aboriginal prehistory:

"We find a relatively old divergence between the ancestors of Pama–Nyungan speakers and Highland Papuans, only ~10%

younger than the European–East Asian split time. With the assumed rescaling parameters this corresponds to ~37 kya, implying that the **divergence between sampled Papuans and Aboriginal Australians is older than the disappearance of the land bridge between New Guinea and Australia** ~7–14.5 kya, and thus suggests ancient genetic structure in Sahul"

Why this might be is again something of a mystery. The authors speculate that the environment of the Sahul land bridge helped create a spatial and genetic separation between the populations. The modern day Gulf of Carpentaria did once contain a palaeo-lake, when the water levels were at their lowest during the Last Glacial Maximum. This lake and the surrounding rivers and marshlands may have been partially responsible for the early difference between the ancestral Australians and Papuans.

The early archaeology of the Torres region is complex but hugely interesting regarding how Australian, Papuan and Austronesian peoples interacted. The Torres Islands are made up of four main groups - the Western, Top-Western, Central and Eastern. Ethnographically the island populations are a mixture of cultural and linguistic influences. The hugely successful anthropological survey of the islands - the 1898 'Cambridge Anthropological Expedition to Torres Straits', run by Alfred Cort Haddon - revealed that the Eastern group spoke a Papuan language, Meriam, whilst the remaining islanders speak an Australian-Austronesian language known variously as Kalau Lagau Ya, Kalaw Lagaw Ya or Kala Lagaw Ya, now largely replaced by Torres Strait Creole.

The earliest archaeological occupation phase dates to between 8000 - 6000 years ago, when the island of Badu was still connected to 'Greater Australia'. This is associated with Australian, rather than Papuan peoples. As the island became cut off with rising sea levels, the occupation became sporadic, with visits from Australia between 3500 and 3000 years ago. After this a permanent settlement was established. Given that Lapita pottery does not appear in the region until between 2500 and 2000 years ago, it is reasonable to assume that these early settlers of at least the Western group were Australians, an observation borne out by early ethnographic studies of the islands. This also matches the general expansion into marine habitats across the Queensland and Great Barrier Reef regions noted by Lilley:

> "Expansion of island use commencing around 3000–3500 years ago is linked to population increases sustained by synchronous increases in marine resources … The viability of risky offshore canoe voyaging was underwritten by two key high-return subsistence pursuits—hunting green turtles and collecting turtle eggs."

Fascinatingly though, there is no evidence of Lapita/Austronesian population or even intermarriage incursion southwards onto the Cape York peninsula mainland. As a 2021 genetics paper concludes:

"Analyses of the available genomic data of the Indigenous Australian uniparental and whole genomes have shown no detectable signature of Austronesian gene flow along the east coast of Cape York in the last 3000 years... It is perhaps time to start considering that the diffusion of culture along the east coast of Cape York may have largely been facilitated by Aboriginal seafarers in a dynamic socio-cultural space where overlapping zones of interaction occurred."

What Did The Austronesians Ever Do For Us?

We've seen so far that the Austronesian presence in Australia was limited to the marine environment and island chains surrounding the north-east region. This may well be as a result of increased archaeological work in this contact zone, but it makes sense that this would be the targeted area for Austronesian seafaring, trade and fishing. So did this contact and diffusion of peoples and technology have an impact back on the mainland? As far as we know there has never been an Aboriginal pottery tradition, nor any evidence for Pacific-style horticulture - no pigs, chickens, rice or other crops. (although Aboriginal horticulture does seem to have occurred on the Western Torres islands). What hints are there for any trade or diffusion?

The horticultural root crop taro, *Colocasia esculenta,* was a key species in the Austronesian Neolithic package. Curiously this plant is found across Arnhem Land, but as a feralised variant of the original -

Colocasia esculenta var. aquatilis. A female missionary to the area, Dulice Levitt, wrote a book entitled *Plants and People: Aboriginal Use of Plants on Groote Eylandt,* in which she speculates that wild taro is the remnant of a failed or abandoned horticultural experiment in northern Australia. Another plant which could have come with the Austronesians is *Bambusa arnhemica,* an Asiatic bamboo found again in the north. This obscure species is not well characterised and a debate exists over whether the plant is native to Australia, but one possibility is that it came with people from the northern Pacific. A very curious reverse case is the Polynesian field cricket, *Teleogryllus oceanicus.* This cricket is native to Australia, but somehow found its way throughout the Polynesian islands, in much the same way as rats. The authors of a 2011 paper looking at the genetics of this insect conclude that its arrival in Hawaii predated European colonisation, and could only have come from interaction between the Polynesian and Australian worlds.

Trade between the mainland Cape York area, the Aboriginal occupied Torres islands and the wider Papuan-Austronesian world did exist, but it appears to be highly asymmetrical. In a 1978 paper by David R. Moore, he lists a number of goods which flowed to the Kaurareg Torres Aboriginal people:

"This made it clear that the Kaurareg took part fully in the general informal trading system of Torres Strait, obtaining a great variety of desired goods ranging from Fly River double-outrigger sailing canoes, drums, bows-and-arrows, stone clubs and various foodstuffs to cassowary feathers and bird-of-paradise skins from the New Guinea highlands. In return they sent pearl shell, harpoons, dried fish, human heads and sometimes wives."

This information is dated to around the late 1840's and comes from a variety of sources, most notably from a young Scots girl - Barbara Thompson - who was shipwrecked in 1844. She was the only survivor and was taken in by the Kaurareg. Here she obviously witnessed a great deal about life on the Western Torres islands and the interactions between the Aboriginal middlemen and the mainlanders on both New Guinea and Australia. Crucially she reports that relations between the Kaurareg and many Cape York groups were hostile, with the exception of the Gudang people. Trade from Cape York was essentially non-existent, the only materials desired by the Torres islanders were spears and ochre. Despite this, many Cape York Aboriginals had access to cast off outrigger canoes, drums, bamboo smoking pipes and tobacco. The Kaurareg often sailed down the coastline, most likely to harvest marine foods, but also for the limited trade it offered. While these interactions are much later than the earlier Holocene Lapita-Aboriginal contacts, it gives some clues as to the state of relations and the type of trade available.

Pama-Nyungan Loanwords

Austronesian loanwords in Aboriginal languages spoken in the Torres, Cape York and surrounding regions is no great surprise. New technologies and plants clearly made their way south even without colonisation, but what is far more revealing is the presence of Austronesian words within the general Pama-Nyungan language family itself. Recall that Pama-Nyungan is the dominant group of languages spoken by the majority of Aboriginal peoples - 306 of 400 languages. The shockingly fast development and spread of Pama-Nyungan is a mysterious topic which I dealt with in the last article, although definitive explanations are thin on the ground, in no small part due to the almost total lack of interest amongst archaeologists and linguists, even in Australia.

Pama-Nyungan is estimated to have arisen from Proto-Pama-Nyungan around 4,000 -6,000 years ago somewhere in the northern Gulf Plains. Since the language has been relatively understudied compared to other major language families there is a lot of speculation and preliminary work, but a great paper by O'Grady & Tryon attempts to highlight deep Austronesian loanwords within the group. They present the following list of words with their possible roots:

Proto-Nuclear Pama-Nyungan (PNPN) *payung shelter, protection Proto-Austronesian (PAN) * payung shelter, protection, shade, cover

PNPN *taparr round object, heavenly body. PCP *daba *raba morning, sky.

PNPN *malung shade, spirit PAN *m-al J[n]u, Proto-Eastern Oceanic (PEa) *malu shade, shadow

PNPN *punga shade, shadow, spirit, darkness PAN *bEng[I], POC *mpongl night, dark, evening

PNPN *ngAlu wave, swell, current PAN *alun, *qalun, POC *(ng)alu, PPNz (Proto-Polynesian) *ngalu wave, breakers, swell, undulation ; PCP *Galu current

PNPN *jAku play, miming, dancing POC *sangka(q) step, sway, vigorous motions with hand and/or foot

PNPN *pula feather, hair POC *pulu hair, feather

PNPN *mAya language PAN(C), POCGR (OC) *maya tongue

They conclude the paper with the following observation:

"If the putative Austronesian loanwords listed above entered Nuclear Pama-Nyungan from daughter languages of the Oceanic subgroup of Austronesian, then this would have important implications for the history and dating of Pama-Nyungan. For it is generally recognised that it has its origins in the New Guinea area approximately 4,000 years ago. Participation of these fonns in

Pama-Nyungan sound shifts would appear to ensure that they have been present from an early Pama-Nyungan stage. **In this case Pama-Nyungan itself cannot be older than perhaps 5000 years. The very impulse for the spread of Pama-Nyungan may well have been provided by the contact with Austronesian speakers and culture in the north-east of the continent**. The technological innovations brought by the Austronesians would clearly have had an effect on speakers of early Pama-Nyungan both linguistically and culturally."

The Case For Austronesian Contact

If we combine the evidence I've accumulated so far, along with the two interesting points from the previous article - that Madagascan elephant bird eggs and a Lapita mythological motif both appear on the Australian mainland - then we get the following scenario:

The Australian world became separated from the rest of humanity long before the Sahel land bridge was submerged. After this we see a flurry of Aboriginal marine travel to reach the Western Torres islands and many island groups off the east coast around the Great Barrier Reef. Austronesian contact comes both from New Guinea, as Lapita voyagers reach the remaining Torres islands, and from the direction of the Solomon islands, as some form of cultural hybridisation and ceramics appear on Lizard island. Around this time (~5,000 years ago), we see the emergence and spread of Pama-Nyungan from the northern regions across the rest of Australia. Then around 3,500 years ago the dingo was introduced to Australia from New Guinea. Very limited trade and diffusion of plants and sailing technology impacts only the north of the continent and neither ceramics nor horticulture appear to have been adopted by the Aboriginal peoples.

This then is the extent of contact as far as we can tell, and certainly by the 19th century the reports from Cape York and the Torres islands suggest that trade was of minor importance and a state of hostility existed between the mainland Aboriginal peoples and the mixed groups living in the Torres Strait.

Where Does This Leave Us?

I have attempted to highlight, over three articles, some of the major mysteries and unexplained portions of Australian prehistory - the problem of analysing Palaeolithic remains; the debates over Aboriginal Pygmies and Tasmanians; the possibility of Dravidian contact; the origins and growth of Pama-Nyungan; the proliferation of a new stone tool type; the introduction of the dingo; the scattered floral and faunal evidence for Austronesian contact; the evidence for Lapita ceramics and contact on various Australian islands and so on. At present the consensus view is that the Aboriginal peoples arrived once and only once, as a result of the Southern Dispersal route out of Africa, and contact was non-existent with the outside world until the Sulawesi Macassan sailors began harvesting sea cucumbers in the mid 18th century.

An outstanding problem, which I touched on in my first article, is the deep connection between different archaic hominins, in particular the Denisovans and possibly Homo erectus, with the earliest humans to arrive in Australia. Given the very recent awareness of the Denisovans as a species we don't yet know if they made it to Australia first. To quote from the 2016 Aboriginal genome analysis paper previously mentioned:

> "We find that Aboriginal Australians and Eurasians share genomic signatures of an OoA [Out of Africa] dispersal—a common African ancestor, a bottleneck and a primary pulse of Neanderthal admixture. However, **Aboriginal Australian population history diverged from that of other Eurasians shortly after the OoA event, and included private admixture with another archaic hominin.**"

Given the decades of debate surrounding Aboriginal fossil and phenotype analysis, it is not far-fetched to suggest that Aboriginal peoples differ from their neighbours to some degree by way of Palaeolithic archaic admixture, although how this would have come about requires access to Aboriginal fossils and further excavations in southeast Asia. I propose that the earliest migrations to Australia by modern humans were not a singular event, but rather a series of arrivals which allows for the deep phenotypic diversity seen in the fossil and ethnographic record (robust, gracile and pygmoid statures). Joseph Birdsell's Trihybrid Migration theory may well be correct

Post-Pleistocene migrations to Australia do seem to be either non-existent or very limited. The genetic drift seen in the few Aboriginal genomes that have been analysed show clearly that their haplogroup differentiation is deep and profound - truly the Aboriginal peoples have been separated from the rest of humanity for many many millennia. The only possible Holocene migration could be south Indian in origin, which aligns oral testimony, the limited genetic studies and Joseph Birdsell's proposal that the northern Aboriginals looked more Dravidian than the rest of the population (the Carpentarians). The evidence for this is shaky at best but cannot be completely ruled out. Birdsell's Trihybrid Migration theory may well be correct, but I want to leave the question of Oceanic Negritos for another article.

Finally the contact with the Austronesian world seems more extensive and far better evidenced, but again, the inroads into the continent were extremely limited compared to the rest of the Oceanic world. One possibility is that a pioneering group of Lapita voyagers did land somewhere around the Gulf of Carpentaria and did settle to some degree, establishing connections which brought the dingo, a variety of crops and sparked off the Pama-Nyungan Expansion. But the details of this are speculative. If this initial contact period did occur, it left no major genetic evidence and failed to root the Lapita Neolithic way of life among the Aboriginal people. It may have ended badly, in conflict, which ultimately drove the newcomers away, after which all contact came through the Torres Strait, mediated by their Aboriginal cousins on the Western islands. The difference in temperament between the horizon gazing Austronesians and the insular conservative Aboriginals is hard to explain, coming down to a cultural and genetic cleft, a legacy of the long separation and differentiation between different peoples.

If these conclusions feel frustrating, I share your pain. I've spent months researching these topics, reading numerous books and likely several hundred papers. What is striking to me is how little curiosity there is in many of these problems within academia. Some archaeologists share this feeling, that the Australian research world has become myopic in its declaration that the Aboriginal peoples have little to nothing to do with the rest of the world. Hopefully I have at least sparked some curiosity in my readers and have been able to highlight the outstanding questions in this area. I may return one day to add some further thoughts, but certainly for the time being I'm happy to leave the subject of Australian prehistory and its many enigmas and move on.

Bibliography (not included in text)

Oceanic Explorations: Lapita and Western Pacific Settlement (Terra Australis) - Stuart Bedford, Christophe Sand and Sean P. Connaughton

Wangga: The Linguistic and Typological Evidence for the Sources of the Outrigger Canoes of Torres Strait and Cape York Peninsula (2018) - Ray Wood

The distribution, abundance and diversity of the Lapita Cultural Complex along the Great Barrier Reef coastline (2012) - M Felgate

Remapping the Austronesian expansion (2009) Roger Blench

Australia and the Austronesians (2005) - Peter Bellwood and Peter Hiscock, Australian National University

First Austronesian contacts with mainland Southeast Asia and Northern Australia (2000) - Ian Walters

Farming and Language in Island Southeast Asia. Reframing Austronesian History (2010)- Mark Donohue Tim Denham

Beyond 'Macassans': Speculations on layers of Austronesian contact in northern Australia (2021) - Antoinette Schappe

The Metaphysics Of Aztec Violence

"Truly do we live on earth? Not forever on earth; only
a little while here. Although it be jade, it will be
broken, Although it be gold, it is crushed, Although it
be quetzal feather, it is torn asunder. Not forever on
earth; only a little while here"

Attributed to King Nezahualcóyotl (1402–72)

The question of why the Aztec and other Mesoamerican cultures
were so ritualistically violent has long haunted and bothered western
observers and scholars. Revisionists and relativists deny that they
were, while others attribute it to their pagan savagery. Early accounts
of human sacrifice and racks of skulls, vigorously resisted for a long
time, seem to be borne out by continuous archaeological finds. Some
blame demons, the inherent instability of Central American ecology,
patterns and modes of governance, or the idea that Mesoamericans
were culturally behind the West, which also had older traditions of
blood offerings and brutal religious rites. What I want to do here is
to dive into the thought, philosophy, and metaphysics of the Aztec
world, to see what the foundational principles were behind these
manifestations of sacrifice and excess. The Nahuatl *Weltanschauung*
was not a mindless or unreflective cruelty, but a sophisticated body
of ideas and axioms, developed over centuries of debate and discord.
In this way, we can approach the Aztec 'mindset' on its own terms

and attempt to understand the metaphysical logic behind their civilisation.

'The People from Aztlán'

A long and rather tedious argument has raged throughout academia for decades over the issue of 'Aztec philosophy', whether a body of thought existed, and whether such a people were even capable of higher intellectual thought. In 1956 Miguel León-Portilla published *La filosofía náhuatl,* arguing that Aztec philosophy was the equal of any Western philosophical system, that they devoted huge energy to the questions of truth, rationality, cosmic order and origins, society, the individual and what eternal processes governed the natural world. Angry responses such as *The Aztec Image in Western Thought* by Benjamin Keen denounced these comparisons and dismissed Nahautl thought as the musings of an 'Upper Stone Age people'. Personally, I don't care very much about these academic back and forths and I'm happy to take Aztec ideas as they come and not worry too much about the precise definition of 'real philosophy'.

The Aztecs, the 'people from Aztlán', formed a multiethnic empire, often difficult to demarcate. The Nahautl speaking peoples - the Mexicas, Texcocans, Cholulans, Chalcans, and Tlaxcaltecs are sometimes called the 'Nahuas', despite not all belonging to the Aztec empire proper. Therefore, what can loosely be called Aztec thought is more widely shared amongst the Nahua inheritors of Toltec civilisation but the term Aztec will suffice. We have an abundance of

Nahuatl terms for philosophical thought, including *tlamatinime* - 'knowers of things' or 'sages' and *neltiliztli* - truth, arising from *nelhuáyotl* - 'base' or 'foundation'. The Aztecs in time produced several schools which served both commoner and noble, the *Tēlpochcalli* and *Calmecac,* along with a vigesimal mathematical system, pictograph manuscripts, legal codes and two calendars, expressing their own understanding of chronology. In their art, poetry, songs, mythology and metaphysics they display a deep concern for the nature of things, in particular change, motion, generation and regeneration, transformation and cosmic cycles. This anxiety over change informs everything about their civilisational superstructure.

That we know as much as we do about Aztec thought is due to the diligent and tireless work of many missionaries and scholars, including Toribio de Benavente Motolinia, Andrés de Olmos, Bernardino de Sahagún, Juan de Torquemada, Fernando de Alva Ixtlilxóchitl, Angel María Garibay K. and many others. Garibay's book *Historia de la Literatura Náhuatl* remains a classic in the field.

Ontological Monism and the Pulse of Life - *Teotl & Olin*

At the root of Aztec thought is a metaphysical claim about the nature of the universe. In his superb 2013 book *Aztec Philosophy: Understanding a World in Motion,* James Maffie lays out this vision of a single, basic, unifying energy which underlies everything in the Aztec world - *teotl*:

At the heart of Aztec metaphysics stands the ontological thesis that there exists just one thing: continually dynamic, vivifying, self-generating and self-regenerating sacred power, force, or energy. The Aztecs referred to this energy as teotl. **Teotl is identical with reality** *per se* **and hence identical with everything that exists. What's more, teotl is the basic stuff of reality.** That which is real, in other words, is both identical with teotl and consists of teotl. Aztec metaphysics, thus, holds that there exists numerically only one thing – energy – as well as only one kind of thing – energy. Reality consists of just one thing, *teotl*, and this one thing is metaphysically homogeneous. **Reality consists of just one kind of stuff: power or force**… What's more, the Aztecs regarded *teotl* as sacred. Although everywhere and in everything, *teotl* presents itself most dramatically – and is accordingly sensed most vibrantly by humans – **in the vivifying potency of water, sexual activity, blood, heat, sunlight, jade, the singing of birds, and the iridescent blue-green plumage of the quetzal bird**. As the single, all-encompassing life force of the cosmos, *teotl* vivifies the cosmos and all its contents. Everything that happens does so through *teotl*'s perpetual energy-in-motion

This striking description helps us out here by highlighting the importance of several key aspects of the Aztec mindset. There is no dualism between a transcendental sacred space and a profane earth, there is no hierarchy of substance, no binary opposition between things and processes. *Teotl* has no goals, no origin, there is no order from chaos, just an eternal dynamic, creative power. To say this is animistic is obvious, but it also echoes the Chinese concept of *qi,* as Maffie explains later in the chapter. *Teotl* is the foundation for all higher metaphysical and religious beliefs. Apparent binaries between gods and humans or between appearance and reality can be collapsed into this holism. Antagonistic pairs like male-female, hot-cold, night-day, are more akin to the ying-yang concept, where they exist as complementary pairs which create a unity, rather than static divisions. Also of note is the absence of a moral dimension to *teotl*– it is amoral, unconcerned with what is good or bad, right or wrong.

Since *teotl* is a process, like all Aztec thought it operates through change and motion. In fact, change *is* motion, like the movement of the sun, or the walk of life a human takes from birth to death. There are three kinds of motion or change that *teotl* undergoes: *olin,* *malinalli,* and *nepantla,* and we will discuss each of them as we go on. *Olin* is an important concept, linked linguistically (though this is disputed) to resin, rubber balls, and blood. Blood and resin are connected, since resin is akin to blood but from a tree, and the particular type of movement that *olin* defines is that of a bouncing ball, something which moves in a pair - up-down, back-forth, here-there, to-from. Following scholars Eva Hunt and Lopez Austin, Massie gives us this description of *olin*:

> The foregoing analyses suggest that *olin* motion-change has a specific shape: it moves up and down and to and fro; it follows an arced, rounded, or curved path; it carves out a volume; it revolves around a central axis; and it has centred. It includes the more simple rising and falling motion of an earthquake and the more complex pulsating motion of a beating heart or curving motion of stirring a liquid. *Olin*-defined processes of becoming and transformation are curvaceous and rounded like a ball, a cross-sectioned corncob, and a plump body. *Olin*-defined transformational processes unify inamic partners such as life~death, day~night, and male~female by curving, rounding, oscillating, and centering them into a single process. Indeed, this shape would seem to be an essential element of what it means to describe these processes as cyclical. *Olin* motion-change is also vitalizing. It is the shape of the life-sustaining energy of corn and the shape of the vitalizing energy of a fetus's stirring and coming into life. **In short, *olin* defines the shape of coming-into-life, of cyclical completion, of life-energy generally. Indeed, it defines the shape of life or living per se. *Olin* life**

energy rises and falls. It swings back-and-forth. It pulsates.

Olin is attached to the title *Nahui Ollin,* which refers to the Fifth Sun, the epoch the Aztecs believed they lived under. This time period was a delicate balance, destined to come to a catastrophic end, like the previous four suns. The Fifth Sun was called the Sun of Movement, *Ollintonatiuh.* A continual blood offering must be made to the gods Huitzilopochtli, Tezcatlipoca and Quetzalcoatl to stave off this apocalypse. But we get ahead of ourselves.

Olin is further linked to a huge number of other *ol*-terms, all related to the animating motion-energy of *teotl.* Of these, the term *teyolia* has great significance. It translates as 'soul', 'spirit', 'animating force' or 'vital force'. The body resonates with *teyolia* and can be felt in the *olin*-like movement of the lungs, the pulse, and importantly the heart, where the greatest concentration of *teyolia* resides. Removing the heart of a person transforms or mutates the *teotl-olin* motion of the beat to the ascending energy as it heads upwards to the sun. What appears like death in this act is in fact the transformation of power from the body to the sky as the heart beats out its last, even when separated from its owner. The *olin* of the heart then feeds the Fifth Sun. Other Nahuatl words link maize, blood, breath, fire, life and nourishment to *olin* and the *olin*-motion of *teotl.* It suffuses and animates with the vital energy we associate with life and not inert matter. This is also why rubber balls are included in the

304

semantic web of *olin*-motion, they leap and bounce in a way which seems animate and alive.

But we should not think of *olin* as a smooth and orderly form of motion. The chaos of life intrudes into this metaphysics and *olin*-motion or *olin*-change possesses the ability to become destructive at any instant. Processes like heartbeats, childbirth contractions and ball bounces can be thrown into havoc and cause death or harm. Maffie describes it thus:

> Although typically orderly, regular, and predictable, the *olin*-patterned movement of rubber balls is in the final instance chance-like, potentially disorderly, and unpredictable. A ball's regular bouncing can quickly and quite unexpectedly become chaotic upon hitting an uneven surface. The ball takes "a bad bounce," as we say. Similarly, at any given moment a regularly beating human heart can unexpectedly degenerate into chaotic fibrillating, just as the regular oscillating contractions of childbirth can unexpectedly become irregular and fatal. Analogously, at any given moment the life-sustaining, orderly *olin* motion-change of the Fifth Sun may quickly become disorderly and destructive. And at any moment disorderly earth-shaking motion may erupt, destroying the entire Fifth Age and with it, humankind.

It is worth highlighting here that the end of the Fifth Sun will come about with violent earthquakes, a perfect encapsulation of catastrophic *olin*-motion. As Bernardino de Sahagún transcribed:

> The Fifth Sun is called the Sun of Movement because it
> moves and follows its path. And as the elders continue
> to say, under this Sun, there will be earthquakes and
> hunger, and then our end shall come.

A Twisted World of Destructive Creation - *Malinalli & Nepantla*

We saw that teotl has three ways of motion, three forms of change. *Olin* is one of these, and we now turn to the other two before seeing how they give rise to the religious and theological forms of Aztec thought. *Malinalli* is a word connected to the act of twisting, spiralling, and drilling. It comes from malinalli grass, a raw material vital to the economy of the Nahuas. From the grass came fibre, rope, cordage, matting, brooms, straws and thatch, the rope and cord were used for an enormous number of basic objects like child-carriers, baskets and nets. More conceptually *malinalli* is the act of ordering from disorder. Grass is wild and chaotic, much like vines and tendrils, but they can be given order and form through twisting and coiling into a useful shape. This conceptual process is linked to hair, creating fire, animals such as snakes and spiders, the umbilical cord of a child, the act of sex, weaving and sacrificing a person.

> The foregoing also suggests twisting and spinning are
> transformative patterns of motion-change. They

transform one kind of thing (wild grass or cotton) into another kind of thing (thread or rope); something in one condition (disorderly, wild, and peripheral) into something in another condition (well ordered and centred); and one state of being into another. Indeed, in light of the centrality of twisting and spinning in weaving, and the role of weaving as organising metaphor in Aztec metaphysics, I submit twisting-spinning plays a central role in Aztec metaphysics' conception of how reality is ordered, how it processes, and how it is transformed.

An important term to add here– *teyolia* is *tonalli*. *Tonalli* is a highly animistic concept, it is the vitalising animating force associated with heat from the sun. The sun's energy bathes the earth and everything on it, suffusing beings with power, vitality and vigour. For a person *tonalli* is strongly associated with the head and with hair. According to David Carrasco in *Religions of Mesoamerica:*

The term *tonalli* has a rich range of meanings referring to its vigour, warmth, solar heat, summertime, and soul. It infiltrated animals, gods, plants, humans, and objects used in rituals. The hair that covered the head, especially the fontanel area, was a major receptacle of *tonalli*. The hair prevented the *tonalli* from leaving the body and was therefore a major prize in warfare. It was believed that the fortitude and valour of a warrior resided, in part, in the hair, and we have many pictorial scenes showing Aztec warriors grabbing the hair of enemies. The hair of warriors captured in battle was kept by the captors in order to increase their *tonalli*. The decapitated head of enemy warriors was a supreme prize for the city, which gained more *tonalli* through the ceremonial use of heads.

Thus, human hair links both the *teotl* motion-change of *malinalli* and the animating power of *tonali*. Hair was much more than decoration, disordered and tangled hair is depicted on drunkards, people who have lost their internal power and have succumbed to chaos. Keeping one's own hair in good condition and neatly braided and arranged ensured the vital *tonali* energies were preserved, and conversely, to grab an enemy warrior by their hair was to steal and liberate extra *tonali,* which could be transferred from the captive to the captor.

Malinalli motion-change was also connected to blowing, breathing, the winds and to the female activity of sweeping, a task with profound importance to the Aztec mind. The purification of the home, the street, the plaza, was performed daily by sweeping. The Florentine Codex states:

"Quetzalcoatl is "in ehecatl" ("the wind"), master of the winds, and "in tlachpancauh in tlaloque" ("road-sweeper of the rain gods"), who sweeps the earth's surface (especially the agricultural fields and paths) by blowing or breathing upon it".

Breathing is an activity linked to song, music, the bellows for forging metals, breath of a newborn infant and to blowing fire into kindling. Life is regenerative because of these *malinalli* motions, the chaos of the natural world becomes ordered through generation. Fire-making was done using a hand or pump-drill, again an action which requires twisting and drilling, the active male agent working into the passive female receptacle, but together creating heat, warmth and fire. In the Aztec New Fire Ceremony, a sacrificial victim had their heart removed and the priest would use a special fire-drill and board to create embers within the chest cavity of the person, transferring the energy of the captive upwards in a vertical spiralling motion.

In contrast to the vibrating motion of *olin* and the twisting circles of *malinalli*, the final motion-change of *teotl* is the middle ground of *nepantla*. *Nepantla* describes the condition of 'between', 'middling' or the flowing from one thing into another. Scholars such Wayne Elzey and Frances Karttunen define it as the centre, in-between or in the middle of something. 'tlah' is a suffix for terms which invoke abundance and overflowing, whereas the verb 'nepanoa' means 'for things to intersect, unite, join together'. Activities which are related to these words and concepts include sexual reproduction, marriage, cooking, the joining of smaller rivers and weaving. The semantic underpinnings describe destructive creation, something new coming from the combining of elements, a merging of ingredients, fluids, objects, people which yields something new and orderly.

Nepantla-processes such as weaving and sexual commingling serve as root or organizing paradigms in Aztec metaphysics. The cosmos is a grand weaving in progress. Nepantla is therefore ordinary – not extraordinary. The ordinary is not interrupted by nepantla; nepantla is the ordinary. Becoming and transition are the norm – not being and stasis.

Massie ultimately sees sex, war and weaving as the three foundational activities which reflect the deepest preoccupations of Aztec metaphysics. *Nepantla* does not indicate peace, but rather the generative and destructive motion-change of creation, as two things unify to become something new. War, sex and weaving are the basic struggles of existence, and we now turn to look at how the three forms of motion-change lead to the visible and ordered violence of the Aztec world.

Enter The Gods

So far, we've examined the simple metaphysical principles of the Aztec mindset - *teotl* as the animistic energy which allows for life to exist and its three forms of expression: *olin* as the pulsing, heartbeat like motion, *malinalli* as the spiralling creative motion and *nepantla* as the unifying and generative transformation of pairs. From these concepts we can start to build a theological structure on top, which starts with a look at the gods.

In Burr Brundage's book *The Fifth Sun: Aztec Gods, Aztec World,* he describes the relationship between the Aztec gods and the monistic underlying unity of the world:

> The blatant polytheism which appears to be so characteristic of ancient Mexico is simply a symbolic reference to natural phenomena. The two thousand gods were only so many manifestations of the One. In the figure of Tonacatecuhtli we find a substitute for monotheism. . . . In order to express the idea that the cosmic forces were emanations of the divine principle the gods of nature were called children of Tonacatecuhtli.

Eva Hunt, in *The Transformation of the Hummingbird: Cultural Roots of a Zinacatecan Mythical Poem,* gives us this further description:

> Mesoamerican cultures were neither polytheistic nor monotheistic. . . . Reality, nature, and experience were nothing but multiple manifestations of a single unity of being. God was both the one and the many. Thus the deities were but his multiple personifications, his partial unfoldings into perceptible experience. The partition of this experience into discrete units such as god A or god B is an artifice of iconography and analysis, not part of the core conception of the divinity.

Since the divine reality was multiple, fluid, encompassing of the whole, its aspects were changing images, dynamic, never frozen, but constantly being recreated, redefined. This fluidity was a culturally defined mystery of the nature of divinity itself. Therefore, it was expressed in the dynamic, ever-changing aspects of the multiple "deities" that embodied it. For didactic, artistic, and ritual purposes, however, these fluid images were carved in stone, painted into frescoes, described in prayer. It is here, at this reduced level of visualisation, that the transient images of a sacralized universe became "gods," with names attached to them, with anthropomorphic attributes, and so on.

Brundage's reference to Tonacatecuhtli is insightful, since Tonacatecuhtli was one of a divine pair of beings - Tonacatecuhtli and Tōnacācihuātl - also known collectively as Ōmeteōtl, on which the concept of *teotl* is built. The gods arise from an endless creative energy and are difficult to partition into distinct personalities. But in the mythological telling, we see many important deities: Tlaloc, Xlotl, Quetzalcoatl, Xipe-Totec and so on. They became associated with places, activities, substances, cosmic forces, natural events and the structure of the universe– each one a manifestation of the underlying properties of *teotl* and motion-change.

It would be beyond the scope of even a book to show how each god composes and utilises the three forms of motion-change, so we'll look at just one example of each before moving on.

The deity most associated with *olin* is Xlotl. As we've seen, it's impossible to fully separate out Aztec gods from one another and Xlotl forms a pair with Quetzalcoatl as well as having different reflections of his own. Xlotl is the *olin*-like back and forth change between life and death, the generative force of renewal, rebirth, pregnancy, the transformation of rotting earth to plant. He is often depicted as a dog and stands for the ballgame, twins, deformed and disgusting beings, dwarves, abnormal births and diseases which horrify and scar. Dogs are something like a psychopomp in Aztec thought, they accompany the dead to the underworld. Massie notes that Mesoamerican cultures were horrified by twins and often killed one at birth, thus Xlotl's twin is Queztlcoatl, the 'Precious Twin' who lives above the ground. Xlotl and Queztlcoatl govern Venus, the morning and evening star. One of Xlotl's masks or aspects is Nanahuatzin - Little Pustule Covered One - who immolates himself to become the Fifth Sun. As the Night Traveller, Xlotl helps the Sun through the underworld each night in order for it to be reborn after a battle with the female chthonic forces of darkness. Thus Xlotl reflects and enacts the violent but creative *olin*-motion, bringing forth life after death.

Next the festival of Tlacaxipehualiztli - Flaying of Men - which the Aztecs celebrated in honour of Xipe Totec, encapsulates the energy of *malinalli*. The festival was a three day event which involved the ritual sacrifice and flaying of war captives, their energies to be captured by the warriors who took them and distributed outwards. The first day involved dancing and the eating of twisted tortillas called *cocolli*. The warriors seized and twisted the hair of their victims, cut the hair off and burnt it, before yanking and wrenching the arms and necks of their captives around in a painful, unnatural posture. On the second day an extremely elaborate ceremony was conducted. Some victims were sacrificed by having their hearts ripped out and offered to the sun, their bodies then rolled down the stairs of the temple. They were decapitated and their bodies cooked with corn and served to the families of the warriors. Another set of victims underwent *Tlahuahuanaliztli* - The Striping - where five warriors, armed with obsidian clubs performed a spiralling dance around the captive. The victim was bound to a special plinth with a ceremonial cord, analogous to an umbilical cord, and was armed with rubber balls and a feather or cotton edged war club. As he whirled around trying to defend himself, the cord tightened and the warriors sliced at him, causing his blood to spin in the cardinal directions. When he fell the priests sliced open his chest and yanked out his heart, described in the manner of a hunter seizing up a rabbit. He was then skinned and these were worn by the captors for twenty days. The third day saw the skins laid out on special grasses before teams of skin-wearing warriors performed mock battles throughout the city, distributing the energy of the captives, while the women and girls performed a ceremonial spinning dance, known as the 'serpent-dance', throughout the night. The twisting motion-change of *malinalli* is so evident throughout this festival it barely needs commenting on.

Finally, *nepantla* can be seen in a specific aspect of the goddess Tlazolteotl-Ixcuina. This deity is concerned with a confusing jumble of traits - vice, purification, lust, steam baths and cotton. She eats filth, encourages sexual degeneracy but also forgives and cleans, reflecting the 'unity-through-duality' we have seen many times so far. Images of her often reflect the *nepantla* mixing and combining to generate life. Some depict her wearing a flayed sacrificial skin, whilst simultaneously conceiving and giving birth to a child. She ingests dirt and decay whilst weaving life into existence. Offerings to her would combine physical gold and urine, as a kind of liquid gold. Thus she imbibes both the sacred and profane in order to transform and create.

A Violent Animism?

At some point in the future I plan on writing more about how animism has been invented and received amongst Western scholars and how the recent 'ontological turn' in academia and art has produced a kind of 'benevolent animism', concerned with ecology, relationships of egalitarian mutualism and friendship between different beings. My own research into Amerindian animism, working from scholars of Amazonian shamanism, has turned up a far more violent and blood-soaked vision of animistic relationships.

These are sometimes hierarchical and echo ideas of trophic webs and pyramids, but on the metaphysical plane. As we have seen, Aztec metaphysics are more pantheistic than strictly animistic, but clearly there is an acceptance that the material world is suffused with spiritual power and energy and not merely inert. The violence which emerges from the Aztec mindset could be seen as the opposite of many Western metaphysical principles. Humans under the Nahua worldview are a locus for forms of motion-change - both *tonali* and *teyolia* are specific ways in which the human body manifests forms of *teotl*. Humans can 'ascend' in a sense by becoming more powerful, more vital, more abundant with energy by engaging in the activities which promote life - sex and warfare being primary among them. Warfare allows warriors to compete and struggle, and capturing enemies gives them personal energy and prestige, but also helps the Aztec state as a whole by providing sacrificial power to the sun and the shape-shifting deities. The lack of a moral dimension to the metaphysical world means humans, while a prized manifestation of life, are also vessels for the cyclical and restless energies of the cosmos. Change, struggle, motion and flow are primary, which is why scholars often describe the Aztec mindset as anxious and preoccupied by cycles and epochs, beginnings and ends. The ultimate religious and political realities of the Aztec world are clearly far more complex and often more pragmatic than just their philosophical convictions, but their conception of the Good rests upon their concerns with change, managing that change and ultimately balancing the different cosmic forces in order to flourish in an unstable world. This is far from 'simple savagery', or killing for base instincts of pleasure or revenge (although these can never be discounted in any assessment of human behaviour). The Aztecs and the wider Nahua world strived to find balance and stability through a careful assessment of the forces of the world, which never left them alone. They knew their world would ultimately end in catastrophe, the violent termination of the Fifth Sun. Their lot was warfare, both physical and metaphysical, since this divine struggle was the only means of staving off this disaster. Life begins and ends, all is conflict and strife, the battle between opposing elements is eternal. In closing, Justino Fernández wrote of the Aztec mother goddess Cōātlīcue:

> In summary, Coatlicue is the embodiment of the
> cosmic-dynamic power which bestows life and which
> thrives on death in the struggle of opposites, a struggle
> so compulsory and essential, that its fundamental and
> final meaning is war.

Part Five - Archaeology

Thoughts on the Maritime Bell Beakers, Iberian Graves & Egypt

Looking for non-steppe influences in the Copper Age

I wrote an article a while back looking at the impact of the 2015 genetics papers showing the reality of an invasion from around the Pontic-Caspian steppe circa 3000 BC. The response inside academia was hysterical in places, but more thoughtful in others. In particular I was struck by the discussion in a 2017 paper by Volker Heyd entitled '*Kossinna's Smile*'. One paragraph has been floating around my mind for a while:

> Something was changing dramatically at a Continental scale in the late fourth/early third millennium BC: the emergence of anthropomorphic stelae throughout Europe, including France and Iberia, is one indicator; the new flint and copper daggers and occasional hammer-axes in the west are a second; and the graves of men buried with such weapons— warriors—is a third.

> Especially revealing is the recently discovered funerary complex of paramount status in the PP4-Montelirio sector of the 'mega-site' of Valencina de la Concepción, deep in the Iberian south. **Several features are strongly reminiscent of Yamnaya/CWC**

graves: the date of 2875–2700 cal BC; the large barrow with burial chamber; the individual male burial, crouched on his right-side, oriented east–west; the flint dagger, and staining with red cinnabar pigment. The upper part of the chamber and the immediate surroundings offer two other significant artefacts: a long, oval African ivory 'plate' and a decorated gold sheet, both in the form of 'sandals'. **Further such sandals, sandal soles or sandal-shaped idols, as they are also called, made of ivory, bone or limestone, are recorded from four other sites in southern Iberia.**

All are key sites of the Chalcolithic and are dated to the first half of the third millennium BC. These are fascinating features/artefacts, but they would be of little wider significance if the contemporaneous European context did not have a really extraordinary parallel to offer: **foot-print/shoe/sandal-formed engravings on Yamnaya/kurgan stelae from the Ukraine, carved and erected some 4500km away**. Sandals are widely seen as symbolically loaded, with interpretations ranging from signs of status, power and property to concepts (in a burial context) of walking out of the tomb, towards the underworld in the case of sandal tips facing downwards. While we may only partly comprehend the symbolism, it is just one example of pan-European interconnectivity in the early third millennium BC, centuries before the Bell Beaker expansion around 2500 BC.

This is fascinating to me and a good example of why genetics should be integrated with traditional archaeology. Something much wider than the emergence of the Yamnaya was occurring across Europe, and the existence of parallel artefacts and styles of burial seems to suggest a continental shift during the Copper Age. I want to muse on three topics which might point to other sources of cultural influence on the time period, from outside the steppe area - Neolithic anthropomorphic stelae, Egyptian influence on Copper Age Iberia and connections between the Maritime Bell Beakers and North Africa.

Stelae, Daggers & Axes

The emergence of the anthropomorphic stelae phenomenon is an interesting case to consider, classically associated with a shift from east to west as part of the general interactions between the steppe and western Europe. But there have been a number of papers recently challenging this assumption, which itself dates back to the 1920's. The different stelae - engraved upright stone slabs - while clearly related to some degree, do show regional differences (Iberia, Trento-Adige, Lunigiana, Rouergue, Sion-Aosta, Sardinia and Languedoc). Dating them has always been a problem, and often their chronological development has been assessed by comparing the motifs within the engravings.

Stelae in both southern France and Brittany appear to be older than the appearance of the Yamnaya in the record. The Rouergue group of France can be dated to around 3500-3000 BC, while the simple Brittany stelae date to around 4500 BC, likely developing out of the standing-stone menhirs from the previous millennium. Does this mean then that, at least in some places, the stelae phenomenon predated interaction with the steppe? Or was there a much earlier connection between the areas around Ukraine and western Europe? Certainly post 3000 BC we see a common convergence on stelae motifs - belts, daggers, axes and forms of jewellery - but in which direction do these images flow? Guilaine argues in a 2018 paper that the French Rouergue axes could easily represent antler hammers or maces and that the Italian Remedello-style dagger images could have been borrowed from French Neolithic flint blades. This certainly isn't without controversy, since flint daggers and copper daggers emerge roughly at the same time, meaning flint daggers themselves may be imitations of widely traded copper versions.

The destruction and re-use of stelae seems to match the time period for cultural and human migration from the east, according to Angelika Vierzig:

> At the break between the two styles of stelae in Sion, partly also in Aosta, there was a visible cultural change, including the destruction of previous structures, reorganisation, and reconstruction. Stelae of the first phase, standing in alignment, were taken down and hewn for reuse in new tombs. For this purpose, the stone stelae were narrowed, provided with door-like entrances, or turned round. A further, second total change and

destruction also took place in Sion, less than 100 years after the younger stelae had been erected, during the Beaker period. There was not one stele from the first or second phase that remained undamaged and in its original position.

It is often assumed that the alteration of many stelae in the second half of the 3rd millennium and their reuse in new graves and other contexts shows the aggressive destruction of the previous cultural self-image and its symbols. The stone tomb in Nal´čik for instance can be interpreted in this way, as all the stelae were used upside down as supporting stones of the tomb. But the careful integration of old images into new contexts, as apparent in many cases, suggests that the original symbolism was known and often still significant. The use of old stones in contexts of new world views is more a process of appropriation than of destruction. The monuments did not lose the power ascribed to them and therefore they were integrated into new contexts.

This kind of destruction, re-purposing and semi reverence mirrors the closing up and alteration of Neolithic megalithic tombs during the Bell Beaker invasion of Britain. Partly a way of stamping their authority over sacred and important places, and partly appropriating the power of those sites to their own ends.

Sandals, Ivory & Egypt

In the opening paragraph, Heyd makes the connection between sandals found at a southern Iberian Copper Age grave and images of sandals on Yamnayan stelae. He suggests that the Iberian elites were aware of the social importance of these motifs due to some long range connections across Europe. However, other explanations exist.

The Belgian archaeologist Luis Siret (1860-1934) made great advances in studying the prehistory of southern Iberia. Amongst his ideas was a connection between these communities and those of the eastern Mediterranean, in particular with Egypt. Guilaine states:

> With regard to these observations it may be noted that, in the early twentieth century, the Belgian archaeologist Luis Siret (1913) compared several Iberian Chalcolithic cultural traits with those from Egypt—notably the 'symbolic' hoes (funerary adzes), figurines, ivory combs, ostrich eggs, alabaster vases and hippo ivory, as well as lithic artefacts.

While such observations were buried in the post-war frenzy to dismiss migration and human movement as prime factors for cultural development, they do have relevance in the light of evidence from Iberian Copper Age tombs.

Ivory artefacts are found across southern Iberia during the Copper and early Bronze ages. Biochemical analyses of these objects reveal them to be made from a mixture of Asian, African and even Pleistocene era elephant ivory, opening up the likelihood of extensive trade across North Africa and southern Spain. Some have suggested that a North African-Iberian interaction sphere dates back to the Neolithic. Studies of the objects in the 1970's indicated a stylistic connection between Levantine Ghassulian, the Naqadian and Iberian ivory figurines. Guilaine tries to link the exceptional crystal dagger and arrowheads discovered in Copper Age graves to an Egyptian prototype, but personally I think this is unconvincing.

Equally the argument that sandals were an important symbol for Egyptian royalty, and therefore the motif could be Mediterranean rather than Yamnaya in origin, seems weak. Probably the best that can be said is that Copper Age Iberian elites were particularly concerned with acquiring foreign exotic objects, including ostrich egg-shell beads, ivory figurines, gold, crystal weapons and cinnabar. This testifies to at least sporadic trade networks with Egypt or North Africa in general. Whilst this doesn't eliminate steppe influence on southern Iberia, it does open up the discussion that not every influence and cultural change around 3000 BC came from the steppe.

Maritime Bell Beakers

The emergence of the Bell Beaker phenomenon is still under intense scrutiny and research. An exact chronology and location of its development is ongoing but most agree that the rivers and coasts of western Iberia are the likely homeland. Bell Beaker pottery has become synonymous with the culture and splits into two main groups - All Over Ornamented (AOO) and Maritime style. The

Maritime pottery style is very different, with linear horizontal bands impressed into the exterior. This type of pottery is not found anywhere else except for Morocco and Algeria. How it came to be produced in Iberia is one of those very dry and dull topics which sees little attention. A single paper published in Spanish in 1964 by Pellicer suggests that Maritime Pottery could have arisen from earlier local Neolithic styles, but the similarities with North Africa are intriguing.

In 1971 an excavation in Sidi Allal, Morocco, turned up the only known copper knot-headed pin in the country. Along with bone and stone tools were also found Maritime Bell Beaker sherds and a classic Beaker Palmela copper arrowhead. The map above shows the distribution of knot-headed pins across Europe. In fact, the connections between North Africa and Iberia are overwhelming for the Maritime Beaker period - wrist guards, pottery, halberds, arrowheads, awls and daggers have all been uncovered across Morocco and Algeria. Maritime pottery has turned up in 11 Moroccan sites and 2 Algerian, while imports of Asian and African ivory seem to have come from several coastal regions.

The author of this 2014 paper notes:

> However, we have to enumerate different kinds of supposedly imported items, which confirm contact and exchange between the Iberian Peninsula and the Maghreb at that time. This refers to

Bell Beaker vessels, Palmela points, a halberd, a tanged dagger, copper awls and a wristguard, all unearthed in the Maghreb, and the presence of African ivory in the Southwest, Southeast and Centre of the Iberian Peninsula. We therefore suggest an exchange of these prestige items for ivory between elites from the Iberian Peninsula and their emerging counterparts in the Maghreb. In the Maghreb we can find this imported material especially in the North near Tangier, the Atlantic coast between Rabat and Casablanca and the region of Oran.

The parallels for these objects point especially towards the Guadalquivir and Tagus estuary, as do the above mentioned comparisons for the Bell Beakers from Aïn Smene. Especially in the Guadalquivir estuary, and also the Southeast of the Iberian Peninsula, we could detect not only African but also Asian ivory at that time. It therefore seems possible that in this framework of an import of Asian ivory from or via Syria also some eastern knot-headed pins could have reached the Iberian Southeast and Southwest.

This back and forth between Iberia and North Africa seems important for understanding the development of the Beaker phenomenon, particularly with regard to the prestige objects and elite driven social structure emerging during the Copper Age. But how much of this flow was unidirectional and what is the relationship between the Maritime pottery styles and those found in North Africa?

Guilaine notes at the end of her paper:

> Regardless of the function of the Maritime beaker, a suitable social context favouring its emergence and adoption was required in order to distinguish such a marker. In the whole of third-millennium BC Western Europe, only one region benefited from such a social environment: southern Iberia, with its unusually large sites and burials probably restricted to high-ranking leaders. **A possible hypothesis could be that these elites may have called in potters (perhaps from Africa) to produce such an original beaker type, which may also have been the expression of a particular social group**. This situation would then explain the strong and expanding presence of this marker within the existing material cultural tradition (from Almeria to Lisbon Bay), which would become completely different from that of the Iberian interior. The end of the regional Chalcolithic—marked by the progressive abandonment of its most characteristic sites—was not due to any external intrusion. Rather, the internal evolution of this society, driven by specific Bell Beaker development, finally led to its deconstruction.

This idea that Iberian Copper Age elites were displaying their power and prestige through exotic and unique objects does feel compelling, given the evidence for the trade in ivory. What is missing here is a classic problem in Beaker archaeology, which is the regional discontinuity. How do these various zones across southern and western Iberia link together during the formation of the Beaker culture? Kunst described this problem back in 2001:

> Another strange fact is that there are several regions without Bell Beakers, sometimes separating rich Bell Beaker regions from one another, such as the Algarve between the Tagus and Guadalquivir areas. In the Algarve, several Copper Age settlements like Alcalar and Santa Justa are known, and Alcalar is one of the largest Copper Age settlements of Portugal with at least the largest necropolis, and yet there are no Bell Beaker finds there, although the area has been investigated since the late 19th century. As Teira recently pointed out, only in the last excavations at Alcalar was one bell beaker potsherd found.

Conclusions

This piece was really just to get some nagging thoughts off my chest, to explore some of the ideas floating around since 2015 regarding the influence of the Yamnaya across Europe. It may well be that everything I've written here is wrong and can be explained away, but I think it's fruitful to explore non-steppe cultural expressions during the early Copper Age and look at the regional groupings of Neolithic and early copper using peoples. If nothing else the recent papers exploring outside influences during this time period shows that migration and external forces are thankfully very much back in vogue.

Between War Bands and the Woke in Today's Archaeology

On February 7th, 2018, the general public in Britain were given the news that a piece of genetic analysis had been published about a Mesolithic man who lived in Cheddar Gorge some 9000 years ago. Ordinarily this might have been a quiet news story, one that yielded nods of interest and some chatter among nerdish corners of the internet. But this was a different kind of story - for front and centre of the reporting, in gleeful triumphal tones, came the new mantra, *"our ancestors were black"*.

According to the geneticists, the Mesolithic man may have had dark-to-black skin and green or blue eyes, an image forever associated with the Western Hunter Gatherers, and now a piece of received truth within the emerging folklore of Britain's multicultural past. Oceans of digital ink have now been spilled in opinion columns, social science journals and dissertations, each declaring with a smug satisfaction - *"the British are racist", "the British still have a problem with race" and "our black ancestors destroy the myths of white Britain"*. This event isn't a one-off or a rare event, almost weekly now western media outlets report archaeological finds which somehow tally perfectly with the morals of the day: transgender skeletons, female hunters, gay Palaeoliths, non-binary Vikings, shield maidens, black Romans, the list seems endless.

So how exactly did we end up in a place where archaeology has been colonised by such politicised and obviously dubious results? What has happened to the discipline to end up with bizarre readings of gender politics being considered good osteology? I'll aim to show in this article some of the major changes and controversies that have taken place within archaeology over the last few decades and how these are likely to play out in the future.

The Old Paradigm

The post-war years in archaeology saw a major change in direction in response to the emotional and intellectual fallout of the conflict, particularly among the 'thinking' classes who pointed to nationalism and racism as driving forces behind the slaughter. Prior to the war archaeology had been developing along a trajectory which accepted the existence of defined 'cultures', identifiable through their particular type of material culture (pottery, buildings, weapons, art etc) and burial practices. This idea, that cultures could be readily observed through differences in their artefacts, had been slowly established since the mid 1700s and came to be called the 'Culture-Historical' model or approach.

Culture-History was an explanation for how particular groups of people maintained a distinctive way of life and was strongly tied to the developing notion of an ethnic identity. Scandinavian, German and British thinkers had developed a distinction between '*Kultur*' and civilisation, tying a '*Volk*' to a unique pattern of behaviours, defined by Edward B. Tylor as "that complex whole which includes knowledge, belief, art, morals, law, custom, and other capabilities and habits acquired by man as a member of society". Works such as Klemm's *General Culture-History of Humanity*, a 10 part series published between 1843-52, expanded the idea and divided the world into the 'active' and 'passive' races, the pinnacle of each being the Germans and the Negroids and Finns. Probably the most important figure of the time however was Gustaf Kossinna.

Kossinna (1858-1931) was a Professor of Archaeology at the University of Berlin and pioneered a methodological approach to archaeology known today as *'settlement archaeology'*. He believed that Europe during prehistory was a jumble of different cultures, each with a distinct type of material culture. He argued that a culture was an equivalent expression of an ethnicity, therefore not only was Europe a patchwork of distinct cultural groups, but that each group had a unique racial and ethnic origin which could be traced by following the material culture backwards and forwards in time. He postulated that the origins of the Indo-Europeans lay with a series of migrations which allowed a more creative and dominant culture to rise above the passive and weak. These ideas, more than any others, have been denounced today as pseudoscience, racist, bad scholarship and unworthy of consideration. We will return to this later in the essay to see Kossinna vindicated.

British archaeologist V. Gordon Childe took Kossinna's ideas and developed a powerful and lasting methodological approach to prehistoric archaeology. In his 1925 works *Dawn of European Civilisation* and *The Danube in Prehistory*, Childe outlined a full and complete hypothesis of European prehistory, showing the distinct cultural groups based on their material culture and how various technologies had moved into Europe from the Middle East. This was a major breakthrough and many of the cultures have passed into the standard archaeological model, including the Bell Beakers and the Hallstatt.

The triumph of the Culture-Historical approach can be seen today - it is still the dominant mode of analysis in most countries around the world. Its strengths lie in the ability for people and groups today to link themselves to past cultures and feel a sense of continuity with the past. It also allows nations to claim sections of prehistory and deliberately bind the current system to a previous and more ancient one, for good or ill. But it was precisely this quality which horrified the post-war generation of scholars and the back-lash to Culture-History has ruled the academy ever since.

Rise of the New Paradigm

It wouldn't be fair to label the rejection of Culture-History as merely squeamishness on the part of the post-war researchers. Decades of new ideas had begun to filter into the mix, including social anthropology, positivism, functionalism, ecological approaches and Marxism, to name a few. It would be boring and tedious for any reader to suffer through a blow-by-blow of how these came to eclipse and be eclipsed in turn over the next 60 years or so, but suffice to say that archaeology found itself in a decade by decade intellectual maelstrom, as one idea competed with another and the scientific technology improved exponentially.

Out went older forms of study, including craniometry and philology, and in came radiocarbon dating, scientific objectivity and a massive influx of data from the natural sciences, including geology, biology, ecology, chemistry, experimental replication and palaeontology. The horizon of possibilities for a young researcher seemed limitless, with new methods of studying soil samples, dating artefacts and examining the molecular composition of deposits left on pottery and tools. Experimental archaeologists began building ships, siege engines, knapping flint and creating entire living villages to experiment with agricultural techniques and wooden architecture. Anthropology was integrated in new and exciting ways and researchers like Marshall Sahlins, Colin Turnbull and Lewis Binford demonstrated that hunter-gatherers were not living in Hobbesian nightmares, but enjoyed rich and healthy lives, largely free of the toils of farming peoples.

The 1966 '*Man the Hunter*' symposium resulted in gender, firescaping and high quality anthropological data being placed foremost in the literature. Marxism pushed economics to the front of many debates, allowing materialism to be taken seriously and the study of trade, coinage, markets and material consumption became dominant in every field from the Neolithic to the Roman Empire.

Many of these intellectual movements of course took place in a wider social context, as the Cultural Revolution of the 1960's introduced feminism, identity, power and hierarchy, collective liberation struggles, subaltern studies, decolonisation and similar ideas into the academy. Evolutionary theories such as sociobiology and evolutionary psychology were also made use of by archaeologists and anthropologists - Napoleon Chagnon being a classic example.

However, within this brew of ideas and theories was a set of common commitments. The older intellectual traditions of Culture-History and forms of colonial and racial anthropology were denounced and largely expunged from the academy. Culture-History was an obvious candidate for ire, since many fascist thinkers and movements had made direct use of the approach, not to mention the sympathies within that generation of archaeologists for Nazism and similar ideologies.

Kossinna himself was crucial in developing the idea of a biologically superior Aryan race and that the German nation was both the inheritor of this line, but also internally and externally fragmented. The Nazis founded the '*Ahnenerbe*', an organisation dedicated to finding supporting evidence for the Aryan hypothesis. They launched expeditions to Syria, Tibet, the Antarctic, analysed runes in Scandinavia and searched for Atlantis. Given this history, the post-war archaeological discipline purged its methodologies and approaches of anything which smacked of racialism and the search for ethnically distinct and superior cultures. As the decades moved on, archaeology built a shaky but tenacious fortress of intellectual defences against part of its heritage, based on the total rejection of racial science. Part of this included the downplaying or dismissal of any theory which placed migration or invasion at the heart of its interpretation. It also involved promoting a form of fairly radical subjectivity which intended to demolish the idea of 'higher' or 'lower' stages of human life, to allow indigenous and hunter-gatherer people to be included in the human story without being denigrated to a lower level of existence.

Altogether, by the 1990's and early 2000's, Western archaeology largely prided itself on having removed the majority of racial, nationalist, patriarchal and colonialist theory and rhetoric from within the discipline.

The Two Towers: the Woke and the Steppe

Into this comfortable consensus came two earth-shattering movements. These twin challenges were the rise of a hyper-militant Americanised obsession with identity and power, and the devastating return of the Culture-Historical model in 2015. The former is well known to everyone at this point and needs little explanation, but its particular manifestation within archaeology has been difficult and awkward and has yet to be fully digested, but some obvious examples include:

The collaboration between historians and archaeologists to downplay and even deny the Saxon invasion of Britain, citing the colonial heritage of Saxon supremacy and the admission of a migration hypothesis.

The 'queering' of Viking archaeology, the interpretation of Norse mythology as pro LGBT, of burials as showing no common ancestry to Viking warriors, the existence of female fighters and non-binary or transgender individuals.

The interpretation of several high profile Roman era skeletons as sub-Saharan females.

The insistence on gender parity during Palaeolithic and Mesolithic prehistory.

The introduction of queer, disability and feminist theory within prehistoric archaeology as standard teaching practice.

A commitment among archaeologists to ensure their work does not support or uphold 'nativist' or nationalist interpretations of history.

Taken together, a number of concerns have animated recent research, including the identity politics of race and sexuality, the older feminist insistence on equality and the anxiety of bolstering a multiracial narrative in the face of mass migration, starting in the mid 1990s. Alongside the rise of these issues has been the downplaying of more traditional topics, particularly anything focused on violence, invasions, migrations and conquest.

A hybrid approach to prehistory has emerged which has largely maintained the older Culture-Histories, such as the Solutrean or the Maglemosian, but which focuses heavily on the individual, their particular lives, the lives of objects and the subjectivities of older 'lifeways'. It's noticeable how absent any large scale top down narrative is for prehistory, often leaving students bewildered about how to contextualise historical processes and change. However, the most grating part of these developments has actually been the destruction of theoretical tools in the face of the 'woke' approach. For example, the resurrection of craniometry to prove the ancestry of Roman skeletons, or the attempt to diagnose 'gender identity' from grave goods isn't a comfortable outgrowth of archaeology as presented from the 1960's onwards. It has the hallmarks of an imposed and outsider approach to archaeological interpretation, forcing researchers to twist older methods to suit the new needs.

Bioarchaeological studies of so-called 'third' or 'fourth' genders appeal to the ethnographic record for examples of men who behave as women and vice-versa, which do exist, but they then rely on diagnostic patterns on the bones of a person to reveal a contradiction between their livelihood and their sex. This is uncomfortable for a discipline which has worked tirelessly to abolish the presumption of gender roles and in other osteological examinations will attempt to subvert their own findings. For example, a female skeleton which shows wear patterns of upper limb extension interpreted as throwing would be joyfully considered a female hunter, but on being forced to consider a 'third' gender may have to conclude that this was 'actually' a man who was born into the wrong body.

While these debates and intellectual currents have been steadily working their way into the legitimate side of academic archaeology, a more frightening spectre has emerged - the ghost of 'Culture-History' has come back with a vengeance. In 2015 two papers were published, Haak et al 2015 and Allentoft et al 2015, both triumphantly holding up the severed head of post-war archaeology with the following conclusions:

A third group of Europeans existed aside from the Western Hunter Gatherers and the Early European Farmers, these were either directly descended from the Yamnaya Steppe Cultures or a very similar group, this group migrated into Europe from the Pontic-Caspian region and most likely began the spread of Indo-European languages.

Along with these two papers came several more (Mathieson et al 2015 and Poznik et al 2015) which asserted that the Yamnaya invaders were fair skinned, much larger in stature and were predominantly male.

It is difficult to overstate the distress and anxiety these results caused in the archaeological world - a theoretical bomb had just removed the foundations from underneath the entirety of modern scholarship. Invasions were real, male warriors dominated Europe, they were white, huge and aggressive, they took local women and killed or subjugated the men, they had symbols of war, they were the nightmare Aryans of earlier generations. It was all real. Before the Haatz paper was even published several co-authors quit, distressed at the implications of their own research, the main authors had to write a 141 page appendix denouncing any connections between their findings and the Culture-Historical approach, but the cat was out of the bag.

In a 2017 paper entitled '*Kossinna's Smile*', Volker Heyd summarised several years of conference tears with the following: "While I have no doubt that both papers are essentially right, they do not reflect the complexity of the past. It is here that archaeology and archaeologists contributing to aDNA studies find their role; rather than simply handing over samples and advising on chronology, and instead of letting the geneticists determine the agenda and set the messages, we should teach them about complexity in past human actions and interactions". Frustrations abounded across the global community - Ann Horsburgh, an African prehistorian railed bitterly: "*such molecular chauvinism prevents meaningful engagement. It's as though genetic data, because they're generated by people in lab coats, have some sort of unalloyed truth about the Universe*". But the bombs kept falling. In 2018 a paper by Olalde et al broke the news that up to 90% of Britain's Neolithic population were replaced by incoming Bell Beaker steppe migrants. It could not have been more devastating for the old guard, many of whom have spent their lives dedicated to a particular theory of Beaker pottery movement, summed up in the 'first lecture' phrase - "*pots are pots, not people*". The return of Kossinna and his 'settlement archaeology' has been quickly dismissed as '*Risk Board archaeology*', but despite the pleas, walk outs and demands of researchers, Kossinna is indeed smiling.

The Gathering Storm

Sharp eyed readers will have noted among the reactions to the 2015 papers this revealing phrase - "*we should teach them about complexity in past human actions and interactions*", referring to archaeologists teaching geneticists about complexity. Or in other words, *we don't like the results you're proving, we need to teach you how to produce better ones.*

This threat is likely the opening salvo in a new war to reclaim the narrative from the scientists and bring it back into the text house of traditional archaeology. This tension between genetics and older methods of interpretation is in its infancy; the first ancient skeleton to have his genome fully sequenced was a Greenlander in 2010 by Eske Willerslev, we have many years ahead of us.

A good indicator of the emerging struggle is in the 2019 paper *'Present Pasts in the Archaeology of Genetics'* by Frieman & Hofmann. In it the authors rail against the Yamnaya steppe war band interpretation of the 2015 papers. They build a laughably absurd case that the media had racialised the Yamnaya by decrying the use of the term 'thugs' as racist in North American parlance (the paper was published in Denmark) and complaining about an Armenian translation of the Indo-European war band tradition as 'Black Youth'. They demand that genetic information such as eye colour and skin tone not be reported in the literature, that home and hobby DNA testing kits have fuelled an obsession with appearance and that the fact that dominant males reproduced more in prehistory should be irrelevant in genetic reporting. They state: *"It is time to question whether the almost exclusive emphasis in our narratives of the past on successful, conquering, increasingly whiter and male individuals, the classic winners of (pre)history, is terribly well thought out, or indeed an objective representation"*.

But the real meat of their pitch comes at the end, where they make a series of further demands that archaeogenetics submit to the greater interpretive power of traditional archaeology. Hiring non-geneticists to write lengthy and complex additions to papers, altering publication standards, educating university press officers and so on - the fight is now on.

In a similarly hysterical paper Hakenbeck (2019) increases the pressure on the geneticists and looks even to pull down the commercial DNA testing companies, stating that white nationalists are taking to online forums to compare ancestry results, looking for Y-chromosome haplotypes which might identify them as Yamnaya. We should expect to see further and more institutional changes in archaeology to ensure that the results of these genetics studies are dampened and problematised. They won't be able to ban these studies entirely, almost all the money in archaeology now goes into such STEM oriented work, but they can and will double down on making the results as muddied as possible.

Conclusions

Archaeology has come full circle from the late 19th century to the early 21st. The older thinkers who looked to the material artefacts from excavations and carefully categorised them by type and age have been lifted from their obscurity and deserve wider recognition. Only with the absolute precision of genetics have their names and ideas been reinvigorated and a more interesting future for archaeology lies ahead, one where migrations, conquests and vitality are back on the table. To be a traditionally liberal academic working on archaeology today is to be hemmed in between the ghosts of Culture-History and their blue-haired students demanding that skeletons be considered queer third genders.

The latter has the institutional backing, but little public support and almost no real research outputs. The former is ploughing ahead into new territory and leaving behind the old guard with their beaker pots in their trembling hands. A real fight has broken open the consensus and the potential direction of archaeology is now up for grabs in a meaningful way. If more geneticists, interested in Culture-History and looking to determine the truth of the Indo-European and other great migrations, were to be trained and enter the profession, we could see a powerful new direction in scholarship.

Of course, this enthusiasm should be tempered by the realities of working in a captured and hostile institution, but for the first time in decades there is a breach in the walls and we should take full advantage of it.

Transgender Skeletons?

Exploring The Mess Of Modern Bioarchaeology

"Archaeologists have discovered a 5,000-year-old skeleton which they believe may be the remains of a transgender person. The male skeleton was found in a suburb of Prague and is buried in a manner previously only seen for female burials. The body is believed to date from between 2900 and 2500 BC and is from the Corded Ware culture of the Copper Age. Men's bodies from that age and culture are usually found buried with their heads towards the west and with weapons. But this skeleton was found with its head towards the east and was surrounded by domestic jugs – as women's bodies from the time are usually found. At a press conference in Prague yesterday, archaeologists theorised that the person may have been transgender or 'third sex'. Kamila Remišová, the head of the research team, said: "From history and ethnology, we know that when a culture had strict burial rules they never made mistakes with these sort of things.""

Pink News, April 6th, 2011

A question I sometimes get asked on podcasts or in messages is "is there such a thing as a transgender skeleton?", usually referring to human remains found in the prehistoric and early historic periods. On one level this question is ridiculous, of course not, the skeleton is an accurate reflection of biological sex, regardless of how its owner may have dressed it in life. But despite any rational attempt at a pushback, trans advocates and activists have successfully pushed themselves and their ideas into bioarchaeology and forensic anthropology, resulting in a semi open conflict within the disciplines over the meaning and characterisation of sex, once considered an immutable feature of the human body. So let's examine the current state of play.

Gender Wars

Since at least the publication of Judith Butler's *Gender Trouble* in 1990, most academics have become comfortable with the idea that sex and gender are two distinct phenomena - one related to your biology, the other as a kind of 'performance' of the social role your sex class is expected to play. To some degree this seems obvious, to be a man in Masaai culture is not quite the same thing as being a man in Mohawk culture. Yet only the most obstinate denialist of reality would argue that the roles men and women play have *nothing* to do with their biology.

Still, this split between sex and gender has become all pervasive. The National Health Service in the UK lists the definitions of both, along with a more modern term *gender identity*. This rather more radical concept is the idea that a person experiences an internal state which corresponds to a particular gender, and that this is more important than the biological sex one was born with. If the language sounds slippery and tricky, it is meant to be. Gender identity has no real definition, just a circular argument trying to describe what gender actually means.

This aside, the sex/gender difference has become well established in bioarchaeology and forensic anthropology. A standard introduction would run like this:

> "To accomplish these goals, we first have to define a set of key concepts. We define **sex** as the biological state of being male, female or intersex, as indicated by sex chromosomes, gonads, internal reproductive organs, and external genitalia, amongst other features (Fausto-Sterling et al., 2012a). Sex, like developmental age, can be estimated from the skeleton through several mostly morphometric methods with varying degrees of accuracy (Milner and Boldsen, 2012). **Gender** is the culturally contingent range of biological, physical, behavioral, and psychological characteristics associated with a given sex."

The effect of this has been relatively minimal, since the divide neatly maps onto the physical remains (sex) vs the clothing/grave goods/mortuary rites etc (gender). But this distinction seems almost reactionary when confronted with the more nebulous gender identity and 'queer theory' of more fringe approaches to bio and osteoarchaeology.

'Destabilising' the Category

A standard method in 'queer' and critical theory is to take concepts devised in literary and postmodern theory and apply them to the sciences. Bioarchaeology seems ripe for the taking in this regard since it contains a classic target category type - binary sex.

Binaries have long been attacked in postmodern literary theory; ideas such as 'man vs woman', 'civilised vs uncivilised' and 'occident vs orient' were deconstructed in the earlier postmodern waves and found to contain an implicit hierarchy, one is naturally assumed to be more important than the other. Queer theory takes this approach much further and actively seeks to 'destabilise' the binary, deliberately blurring the poles, deconstructing terminology and setting out to undermine firm social categories.

Naturally the biological distinction between male and female comes under particular ire for the queer activist. They seek to destroy the concept of binary biological sex (a trait which emerges so far back in evolutionary history it is shared by protists, plants and animals) and replace it with a constantly shifting messy series of uncertainties. A piece typical of this genre of thought notes:

> "The perception of a hard-and-fast separation between the sexes started to disintegrate during the second wave of feminism in the 1970s and '80s. In the decades that followed, we learned that about 1.7 percent of babies are born with intersex traits; that

behavior, body shape, and size overlap significantly between the sexes, and both men and women have the same circulating hormones; and that there is nothing inherently female about the X chromosome. Biological realities are complicated. People living their lives as women can be found, even late in life, to be XXY or XY."

I don't intend to use this article to outline a defence of basic biology, I assume my readers haven't fallen for this kind of sophistry and accept the validity of biological sex as a given. However, the attack on the sex binary has come from multiple angles and it is worth outlining the main approaches and refuting what needs to be refuted:

Claim One: Sex is a spectrum because a number of chromosomal, gonodal, endocrine and phenotypic disorders exist which don't easily fit into either sex (eg Turner Syndrome & Klinefelter Syndrome)

Claim Two: Sexing a skeleton is an imprecise, subjective and biased process which is often ambiguous at best and prejudiced at worst

 Claim Three: The sex/gender binary in bioarchaeology often reverts to privileging the biological category as true and the mortuary evidence for gender as interpretative

I have little interest in arguing with the first claim, since even entertaining the idea that sex is a spectrum, not a binary, is to engage with an analytical approach that favours a critical textual and philosophical method rather than anything based in reality. The other two I will explore next.

Sexing A Skeleton

A fundamental task of the bioarchaeologist or forensic anthropologist is to identify the skeleton or human remains as either male or female. Knowledge of this fact is obviously crucial for a criminal case and is invaluable information for any archaeological assessment - but without a chromosomal test, how can a skeleton be identified as either male or female with any confidence?

The methods for sexing a skeleton can be split into morphological (descriptive) and metric. Both are typically used in any case. Metric methods rely on large population studies where averages can be created to check against, while morphological methods derive from well established differences in skeletal shape and structure. Morphological methods include assessing the skull, pelvis, jaw and long bones, often on a 1-5 scale. Metric methods take these measurements and can statistically test them against population data sets.

The anthropologist or archaeologist will create a report based on the conditions of the remains and provide a 'sex estimation' which reflects their skill, experience and any metric or digital assistance they may have used. The opacity of the person's identity is an epistemological problem for anyone working with human remains, you have a former person in front of you who was a male or a female, but you have a gap of mortality between you and, while the tools of forensics and osteology help the dead to speak, they aren't always accurate.

To give forensic scientists and archaeologists their due - there is an enormous literature of blind testing to help refine models, techniques and winkle out any biases over morphological approaches. Some of these are truly amazing, to quote from one paper:

> "The material involved in the study comprises 262 pelvic bones and 180 skulls of male individuals from two mass graves in Serbia. The material was examined separately by an experienced and an inexperienced physical anthropologists. Sex was correctly estimated by the experienced anthropologist in 100% of individuals using all of the 16 pelvic and cranial criteria."

New automated digital imaging methods combined with 'deep learning' algorithms and other limited artificial intelligence programs are equally as impressive, with papers reporting up to 97% accuracy in estimation.

However, the majority of sex estimation cases are not subject to blind tests where the answer is known beforehand. In these cases estimation carries with it a level of imprecision, which is now called the '*zone of uncertainty*' in the literature.

This is no surprise really, humans have a natural level of variation within any given population, and physical markers for sex, assuming they are even all present or in a decent condition, don't always show themselves in an obvious way. Hence the room for doubt which has given wiggle space for gender activists to push back against the sex binary in estimation.

A Female Burial?

One of the classic problems of archaeology is trying to understand the identity of a buried or cremated person through the mortuary acts, grave goods and practices that can be detected. This gets far more complicated when we are looking at the prehistoric era, where our sources of analogy are ethnographic studies of forager and tribal peoples.

An absolute classic of this genre is the question of whether someone buried with a sword was a warrior in life? A good example is the reassessment of a Viking warrior grave found in Birka, Sweden. Grave Bj 581 contains martial grave goods, including swords and several horses. Osteologically the person had always been identified as a woman, but the grave goods raised doubts. Finally the issue was resolved through genetic testing, and the person found to be a woman.

Now we reach some contradictory and difficult problems:

> Giving priority to her biological sex we might interpret her as a powerful female warrior, with implications for Viking society at large

> Giving priority to the grave goods we might interpret her as transgender, and view her social gender as the more important

> Dissolving both categories we could see her as a destabilising, 'queer' figure, who disrupts the social norms and challenges the gender binary

Older feminist archaeologists are likely to opt for the former, showing how women could command important roles traditionally reserved for men. Younger archaeologists are more likely to see the mismatch between her sex and 'grave gender' as proof of her status as a transman, or some kind of non-binary figure. In the case of the latter it is crucial to have as little ambiguity as possible with both sex estimation and gender interpretation.

Precisely these conundrums are becoming routine in modern archaeology. The gay news outlet *Pink News* gleefully reported the discovery of a Czech Corded Ware Culture burial where the sex of the individual did not conform to the binary burial type. In these situations the outcome you want is the one you get - the media reported the discovery of a 'gay caveman', despite being from the early Bronze Age. Conflating age, sex, status, ethnicity, gender, sexuality and potentially spiritual role all serves to create a confusion where activist groups can claim the discovery of 'transgender skeletons'.

As we have seen, it is nigh on impossible to have the confidence in your interpretation to declare the mismatch between skeletal sex and social gender to be *only possible* in the case of a transgender person. Even this simple analysis overlooks the wealth of information for how gay men and women have been perceived culturally throughout history.

Forensics & Bone Surgery

A final wrinkle in this complicated mix of theory and practice is a niche concern among forensic anthropologists dealing with modern homicide cases - managing and working with skeletal remains that have undergone bone surgery to make them look visibly like the opposite sex, in almost all scenarios these are biologically men.

Some of this conversation has been framed through the tiresome critical language of 'centering' and 'marginalisation', such as this article from 2021:

"Due to disproportionate violence impacting the transgender community, forensic anthropologists may encounter the remains of trans individuals; however, it is unknown how often trans

individuals are represented in casework and if practitioners have
sufficient knowledge about trans bodies... The results indicate
that 28.9% of respondents have worked with trans individuals in
casework, but most forensic anthropologists were unfamiliar with
forms and evidence of gender affirming procedures"

Other more level-headed papers merely approach the problem as an
interesting but highly unusual problem in osteological examination,
how to make sense of a skeleton that has been deliberately modified?

The most pertinent of these osteological problems is the existence of
'Facial Feminisation Surgery' (FFS). FFS refers to a series of
procedures whereby the masculine attributes of the mandible and
cranium can be surgically altered to be more in line with a typically
feminine face. These include but are not limited to:

Forehead reduction and contouring

Rhinoplasty

Genioplasty, chin contouring

Forehead reduction often involves cutting off the anterior portion of
bone, shaving and contouring the forehead and reattaching the
anterior section with wires by securing it to a hole made in the sinus
wall. Similarly the anterior section of the mandible can be removed

and reattached with plates and screws. Acrylic burrs can be used to reduce the gonial angle, or flares can be removed with saws and rounded off.

In a sane world the discussion of forensic FFS analysis should remain quietly within the literature of the profession and have little impact on the wider culture, much as the rest of forensic work does.

Some Thoughts

As I've shown, in the many articles referenced throughout, there is a desire and a push to make transgenderism a reality within bioarchaeology and forensic anthropology. The case of modern homicide victims displaying pins in their jaws seems clear cut, they most likely wanted to change their appearance from male to female in accordance with modern gender ideology. But the glaring bias within archaeology today is to accept wholesale progressive ideology and project it backwards as though transgenderism was not a highly contingent social practice, only made possible in the 21st century.

I don't have the space or the will to tackle gender ideology in its entirety here, but it seems straightforward that several things can be true at once:

> Modern transgenderism cannot reflect the past in any
> meaningful way

The desire for some men and women to flout their social roles, either sexually or in some other way is a universal phenomenon

Burials may indicate a unusual, deviant, celebrated, powerful, marginal or other figure without 'destabilising' the binary

Shamans, slaves, certain priestly figures such as the eunuch *galli* of ancient Rome, and others may be buried or have skeletal markers of social difference. These do not make them akin to modern trans people. Perhaps in a future article I will tackle the broader question of how sex, gender, sexuality and so-called 'third genders' have been discussed in modern anthropology. But hopefully this article has clarified some issues and explained some of the many problems that go into sex estimation and burial interpretation in today's academic research practices.

Giants of the Deep: A Prehistory of Whaling

"Whales have been evolving for thirty million years. To our one million. A sperm whale's brain is seven times the size of mine... The great size of his body has little to do with the great size of his brain, other than as a place to keep it. What if the catalyst or the key to understanding creation lay somewhere in the immense mind of the whale? ... Some species go for months without eating anything. Just completely idle.. So they have this incredible mental apparatus and no one has the least notion what they do with it. The most logical supposition, based on physiological and ecological evidence, is that they contemplate the universe... Suppose God came back from wherever it is he's been and asked us smilingly if we'd figured it out yet. Suppose he wanted to know if it had finally occurred to us to ask the whale. And then he sort of looked around and he said, "By the way, where are the whales?"

The above quote from the writer Cormac McCarthy neatly sums up our schizophrenic relationship with the giants of the ocean. We recognise that whales, dolphins, orcas and other related mammals are highly intelligent and social animals. They have been honoured and worshipped for millennia, and yet we seem driven by a deep bloodlust to eradicate them. The thrill and danger, not to mention the prestige of hunting a whale is irresistible. In almost no other way can man pit his daring and bravery against nature, against Leviathan. I want to track this strange oscillating vision of whales as powerful spiritual beings but also a target of relentless persecution.

Starting with the earliest prehistoric evidence for whaling, I want to explore how whales ended up on the verge of extinction in the 19th century, while also paying homage to the tremendous courage and fortitude of those men who endured brutal and lethal conditions to ultimately convert these stewards of the ocean into consumer goods. Human nature is not endlessly malleable, and it contains all sorts of destructive impulses, but we would do well to turn this on those destroying our seas and not on those who call it home.

The earliest potential evidence for whaling dates back to the northern European Mesolithic. As the sea levels rose with the dawn of the Holocene and the melting of the glacial ice, the landscape for European hunter-gatherers changed dramatically. Their diet altered to make use of the abundant seafood – shellfish, seals, fish, eels and larger mammals. Whale bones have been discovered on Danish Ertebølle sites, alongside their dugout canoes and harpoons. Most researchers are sceptical that they were able to hunt whales at sea from these vessels and were likely scavenging beached whales, but it nevertheless potentially marks the beginning of the human drive to hunt at sea.

By the time of the Neolithic whaling seems to have advanced around the world. In South Korea, the Bangudae rock depictions of hunting at sea are widely assumed to represent whaling activity, circa 6000 BC. At Jortveit in Norway, the bones of whale, bluefin tuna and orca have been recovered, along with numerous harpoon heads and flint tools. In North America the evidence for whale hunting seems to begin around 1000 BC. These settled permanent camps became ideal places to develop more sophisticated and specialised forms of subsistence, including deep sea fishing and hunting. The methods used at this time are assumed to be similar to known communities who still hunt whales or did so in the recent past: attaching harpoons to inflatable objects, known as drogues, or driving a group of whales towards the shore in an attempt to beach them. Harpoons made from bone and antler are a common find from the Upper Palaeolithic onwards, presumably for hunting larger animals and later seals.

Polynesian whaling was a mixture of scavenging, in the case of the Maori, and of active drives and hunting, in the case of the Tuamotu islanders. These drives would involve a *kapea*, a 'whale master', who was able to call and direct the hunt. The hunters would drum on the sides of their canoes to attract whales, porpoises and sharks before the *kapea* guided the animals into a lagoon or bay to be speared. Legend has it that the *kapea* was so attuned to the whales that he could sit on their heads and back while guiding them to their deaths. In another part of the world, the Inuit and polar peoples have a long tradition of whaling as mentioned above, indeed Palaeo-Inuit sites in Greenland show evidence of people eating bowhead whales as far back as 4000 BC, almost certainly scavenged.

Pacific Eskimo peoples developed a sophisticated hunting system using kayaks and poison tipped slate darts, fired from an atlatl (spear thrower). The monkshood based poison would cause local paralysis in the whales fins and they would drown, to be washed ashore a few days later. Ownership was claimed by the specific signature of the slate dart. These hunting technologies were fiercely guarded and were reserved for an elite group of hunters. A number of species were hunted across the polar archipelagos – grey, humpback and bowhead in particular. Every part of the whale was prized, in particular the valuable oil that could be rendered. Prior to European colonisation, the only form of fuel the Inuit had was animal fat and it was burned in stone lamps to provide small amounts of heat and light. This tiny heat source was crucial for melting snow into drinking water.

Moving into the mediaeval era, whaling was determined by the technology of the boat and the skill of the whalers. One of the first areas to become specialised at whaling was the Basque Country, who started sending out boats in the 11th century. Over time they moved into the English Channel, out into the North Sea and began whaling around Iceland, Greenland and Newfoundland. British whaling prior to the 16th century was limited, with the Crown claiming beached whales. As open water naval technology improved, the option to send out boats into the Atlantic and Scandinavian territorial waters increased. The creation of the Muscovy and later South Sea companies spurred commercial interest in whaling, with fleets recruiting skilled sailors from across northern Europe, most notably from the Netherlands. As the Industrial Revolution exploded, the demand for whale oil in manufacturing, lighting and textile production rose dramatically. Astonishingly sperm whale oil was still being used for automobile production in the US as late as the 1970s.

The methods of hunting became increasingly more mechanised and dangerous for the crew. The whale was typically harpooned, either from a smaller whaleboat or later from the main ship itself. The harpoon was thrown into the whale with the force of a man's arm, or fired into the whale with a mounted harpoon gun. This role was difficult, dangerous and often had an aura of superstition attached to it, most famously depicted by Queequeg in Melville's Moby Dick. The whale would react violently, thrashing and lashing out with its tail and head. The whaleboat was liable to be smashed or sunk. The whale would then attempt to dive and drag the boat along, whipping the harpoon line which would need to be let out rapidly to avoid the boat being dragged underwater. Once the animal was exhausted it was killed, with lances, explosive harpoons and other similar weapons, before being towed or hauled onboard a larger vessel to be processed. This unpleasant and dirty job required multiple shifts of six-hour work days, butchering the meat, draining and rendering oil, separating bone from flesh. The prize objects from different whales included – the baleen plate, used for carriage springs, umbrellas and corsets, among other objects, the blubber, removed in a process called '*flensing*' and rendered for sale, and *spermaceti*, the odourless oil from the head of the sperm whale, used for cosmetics and industry. Today a modern Japanese whaler can process an animal in around 30 minutes, combining mechanical and human labour.

It's hard to pinpoint with any accuracy what the long term effects of millennia of whaling have had on their populations. Historical whaling, from the 17th century onwards, had a devastating effect on whale numbers. In many instances, such as the eastern North Atlantic grey whale, they were driven to local extinction and pushed towards a critically low number of individuals. The Antarctic blue whale has still not recovered, nor has the North Pacific right whale, whose numbers were decimated from 30,000 individuals in 1840 to only around 300 individuals today, the vast majority of which were taken in the single decade from 1840-1850. A 2004 paper looking at the impacts of the Basque whaling industry in the 15th century concluded that a huge drop in the right whale and bowhead whale population occurred during this century. The effects of the removal of such a huge number of key species is also under investigation. The almost total loss of the Greenland right whale, around 46,000 individuals, has freed up an estimated 3.5 million tonnes of krill, providing a boom for seabirds and fish. Similarly the loss of a number of Antarctic whales has resulted in a surge of seabirds, penguins and seals.Probably the greatest ecosystem change from the loss of whales is their capacity for moving nutrients around the oceans. Their faeces and dead bodies both move and liberate crucial elements of sea food webs. Blue whale faeces contains 10 million times the iron concentration compared to the surrounding sea water, prompting phytoplankton blooms. So much carbon and nitrogen is moved through the oceans by whale migrations, deaths and births, that it is referred to as the 'whale pump' or the 'whale conveyer belt'. Even their bodies, falling into the depths, provide a huge banquet of resources for sea creatures, with potentially over 100 specialised species dedicated to scavenging from their carcasses. As one of the last surviving families of megafauna, we are able to study the impact of large animals on food webs – counter intuitively, although krill stocks temporarily increase when whales are removed, over the long term krill has yet to recover to its pre-industrial whaling mass.

It's hard to be recklessly optimistic about the future of whales, with their lives dependent on the state of the world's oceans. With the numerous threats coming from overfishing, coral bleaching, plastic and other pollution and the collapse of the marine food webs, it looks bleak for all sea life. The irony of living in late modernity is the explosion of scientific knowledge about the natural world, while the same forces also commit it to extinction. We know now that whales are highly intelligent, sensitive and deeply social. We have realised how much we don't know about them, how far and where they migrate, how they communicate and pass on information. We've pitted ourselves against them now for millennia and now possess the technology to eradicate them if we wanted, but something about them still captivates and grabs us. Their slow calming nature, massive yet peaceful frame, it's not hard to see why various groups around the world consider them as human ancestors or progenitors. They seem more likely to possess a soul than many other animals, perhaps this is why we've been drawn to hunting them over the ages. For traditional hunting peoples, the animal isn't just a creature to impose your will onto, but part of a web of contractual obligation. If a hunter is to be successful he must ultimately persuade the animal to let itself be killed, in exchange for the proper observation of taboos and rituals. Any break in the contract and negative repercussions will follow. So maybe Cormac McCarthy was right – there are secrets in the mind of the whale, being kept under lock and key until we're ready

Palaeolithic Seafaring

How We Mastered The Waves and Colonised The World

"Ships are the nearest things to dreams that hands have ever made, for somewhere deep in their oaken hearts the soul of a song is laid." - Robert N. Rose

One of the ultimate expressions of the heroic soul in primitive man is that he stared across a violently stormy body of water, and knowing all the dangers still lashed trees and branches with rawhide and set out to master his destiny. This is something of life at its most vital, most energetic, most daring and ambitious. The instinct to expand and explore. The world would be a far smaller place if our ancestors had meekly accepted their lot around the savannah watering holes.

So what do we actually know by way of real evidence of the earliest seafaring? We are hobbled by the almost total absence of organic preservation from the deepest Palaeolithic. No wood, leather or hide artefacts remain. This makes finding boats or sailing equipment virtually impossible. Instead a fruitful approach has been to combine the climatology data of which areas of land would have been islands and infer from any human remains that they must have sailed there.

One of the earliest pieces of evidence in this line comes from the Kagayan Valley in northern Luzon, an island in the Philippines. Remains of butchered megafauna and stone tools have dated the arrival of *Homo erectus*, or potentially even the Denisovans on the island to 709,000 years ago. This is an astonishingly archaic date for a sea crossing. The simian figures of erectus bands, perhaps with language, being capable enough to plan and execute such a voyage seems beyond what we understand of their capacities. Yet the entire continent of Oceania, with the Pacific to the east and the Indian ocean to the west, is the stage for a hugely complicated history of human migration.

At various points no less than five hominid species travelled and flourished in the archipelagos and warm sheltered coral bays. Potentially as late as 15,000 BC Denisovans and modern humans were breeding entirely new branches of the family tree. The sea levels around South East Asia were significantly lower than today, making it possible to either walk to Borneo or into Taiwan and cross to Luzon. But no matter how we look at it, the earliest crossings involved a deliberate and organised mission to traverse a body of water and colonise another land.

The fact that the earliest sea voyages were undertaken by *Homo erectus*, rather than our own species, has irritated archaeologists and proved controversial, with some saying that they were carried to Luzon on tsunami debris! The evidence continues to build, with stone tools found on the Arabian island of Socotra dating to anywhere between 800,000 and one million years ago, and more tools on the island of Crete, dated to around 130,000 BP. These dates don't fit anything other than erectus or perhaps in the case of Crete, Neanderthals. In the background of these arguments is the spectre of the ridiculed 'aquatic ape hypothesis', the idea that humans evolved under pressure to become fishers and seashore foragers with unique adaptations for the water.

While the academy is fiercely hostile to the idea, the evidence in favour keeps mounting. Humans have the unusual ability to voluntarily control our breathing, making it possible to dive to great depths, and with training to stay underwater for over ten minutes. We require iodine in our diets and can process high levels of omega-3 fatty acids. Our bodies are streamlined enough to swim, dive and wade with a minimum of instruction and we are born with a fatty vernix layer which is chemically similar to other sea mammals. Added to this all human infants possess an innate diving reflex for several months after birth, a deep physiological adaptation which protects the child from drowning, lowers the heart rate and releases additional red blood cells. Curiously the presence of this reflex never seems to attract much scientific attention and its existence is still a mystery. Taken together it's not difficult to make the case that early hominids were familiar and comfortable with diving and swimming. It only needs a group of young men watching birds out at sea to hatch a plot to sail on some lashed logs.

Neanderthals are another candidate for seafaring before modern humans. Their Mousterian style tools have been unearthed on the

Greek islands of Zakynthos, Kefalonia and Lemnos, as well as potentially Crete. The cope pushback has been to say that Neanderthals swam to these islands, but this seems a stretch. Given that they were capable of distilling tar in oxygen free kilns, carving fire-hardened wooden spears, crafting leather working tools from bone and identifying manganese dioxide as a fire starter, it's not too difficult to imagine them building boats and exploring the Mediterranean. Their entire way of life was based on extreme physical exertion and danger, using short spears to hunt megafauna up close. Their injuries are still gruesome to think about millennia later - multiple limb fractures, broken facial bones, rounds of rib breaks, missing teeth, deafness and blindness. A culture forged in such immense hardships seems unlikely to shrink from a challenge.

By the time we reach the story of modern humans the world had already seen seafaring, but over the coming years Homo sapiens took it to new levels. With the sea levels low enough to link Borneo, Java, Sumatra and the Malay Archipelago into a landmass called Sundaland and the coast of Australia extended outwards to New Guinea in a shelf named Sahul, the shorter distances between the islands made Palaeolithic voyaging a realistic prospect. Several routes have been proposed which match with archaeological remains potentially as early as 76,000 BP. Despite this evidence there have been some truly ridiculous attempts by archaeologists to fend off this narrative, including the scenario involving a pregnant woman washed out by a strong current or people clinging to bamboo mats caught up in ferocious waves.

The presence of deep sea fish such as tuna, mackerel and shark at many sites should finally dispel such idiocy and most researchers accept that the Palaeo-Papuans/Australians intentionally colonised their island chains. What cultural impetus drove them to push further and further into Oceania we'll never know, but an expansive energy compelled them outwards and downwards. This first wave of migrants reached Tasmania in roughly 40,000 BP. This culture was evidently exploiting a broad spectrum of foods, from nuts and tubers inland to deep sea fishing and coastal foraging. We don't know what kind of boats and vessels were used, as none have survived in the record. What we do know is that by the time of European contact, the boat technology of southern Australia was too simple to make their ancestral voyages, suggesting that they had lost or forgotten a more sophisticated sailing culture. Intriguing hints of these vanished vessels may have been preserved, etched into the walls at Gwion Gwion, possibly as early as 20,000 BP.

The second wave of migration in Oceania occurred around 3000-1500 BC, a much later time period, corresponding to the Asian Neolithic. These settlers brought pottery, rice and new sailing technologies with them and the consensus is that they expanded outwards from Taiwan, down into the Philippines and then split into both Borneo and east into New Guinea and the Pacific Islands. The migrations continued as they made contact with Sri Lanka, South India and most incredibly, Madagascar. The Austronesian maritime trade network was the world's first true era of globalisation, as the

Romans eventually made contact around the Red Sea and the Polynesians almost certainly landed in South America.

While most pursuits of prehistoric sailing and seacraft rely on glimpses and flashes of evidence, the culture which is forever a byword for voyaging is the Polynesian. Their sailing technology has survived into modern times and their skill at star and wave navigation is unparalleled given that they were a Neolithic culture. The Polynesian Pacific triangle of islands is a territory of 10 million square miles, with the remotest outcrop - Easter Island, sits alone in a circle of four million square miles. If there ever were a true 'Sea People' they would be the closest contenders. Captain Cook described the scenes as he encountered the shores of Hawaii, recalling how the islanders swam out to their boat in such numbers and with such grace that they looked like shoals of fish. European explorers routinely extolled their physical power and beauty:

> " . . as a race they were tall, shapely, and muscular, with good features and kind eyes. In symmetry of form the women have scarcely been surpassed, if equalled, while the men excelled in muscular strength"

In order to colonise the tens of thousands of islands in the Pacific, they made use of stick charts, oral compasses, noted swells, currents, the flight patterns of birds and the latitude of islands. Their stellar compasses made use of up to 150 stars. They used celestial navigation and famously even the swinging of their balls to help aid their direction. As well as making it to Hawaii and South America, there are settlements on the Auckland Islands and a tale of the Ui-te-Rangiora: a story of mountains of ice, bitter cold and snow, hinting that they may have sailed to Antarctica. The development of the catamaran and the outrigger vessels, along with the first true sails, allowed them to sail deep into the open ocean.

Meanwhile, in Europe, as the glacier ice melted and flooded Doggerland, opening up the continent as a mosaic of rivers, bogs, coastline and lakes, the people of the Mesolithic were developing their own boat building cultures. One of the earliest known production sites comes from a submerged site on the Isle of Wight. Several dugout canoe vessels have been found in Holland and Denmark, with at least one Ertebolle boat burial. Decorated paddles have been found on other Danish sites. We don't yet know how sophisticated their sailing methods were, but we know that people were able to colonise Ireland from the Scottish islands and that Ertebolle vessels were possibly bringing in whales.

Sealing became a major source of food as the ice receded around Norway and the Baltic, with hunters following the coastlines. The Holocene proved to be the impetus for sailing developments globally, as water levels rose and landscapes became wetter. Native Americans and Inuits made use of kayaks and birch bark canoes, rock art in Azerbaijan and Korea show reed boats and whaling; coracles and curraghs are invented independently. The outpouring of creativity and technology with the warmer climate spurred the creation of more complex vessels and by the time of the Bronze Age we see powerful ocean going ships, like the Dover Boat found in Kent in the UK, dated to 1500 BC and made from oak planks. Only typically British health-and-safety regulations have prevented archaeologists from sailing a replica across the Channel.

Surveying the full scope of human seafaring, starting with our ancestral cousins, it's easy to focus on the evidence that we have, which is the evidence for success. Forgotten are the innumerable attempts, partial journeys and catastrophes which must have been the norm for early sea adventures. The Neolithic ships which crossed the Indian Ocean to Madagascar must have been just one in countless years of missions. It must have been a regular sight to see young men waving from the surf as they disappeared to the horizon and were never heard of again. A brazen defiance of death and drowning must have coursed through such people, we can scarcely imagine the existential horror and excitement of a stretch of water, not knowing what might be over the waves. A reckless and restless spirit is bestowed on people who take to the sea like this and we can, and should, aspire to summon these energies into the here and now.

Part Six - Reflections

Horror & Prehistory

Deep Time and Bodies Of Stone

"Devouring Time, blunt thou the lion's paws,

And make the earth devour her own sweet brood;

Pluck the keen teeth from the fierce tiger's jaws,

And burn the long-lived phoenix in her blood …"

Possibly the most frustrating thing about the study of prehistory is how fully alien and exterior it is to the wider culture. Almost no writers, artists, sculptors, musicians or poets take up the task of the first several hundred thousand years of human existence. It feels so remote and archaic as to have little to offer us, with the exception of *The Flintstones* to remind us how much better off we are now. I want to offer a brief sketch here of a theme which, if tapped, could release immense creative wealth. That niche and under-utilised crossover between the deep past and horror.

At first glance this seems faintly ridiculous - weren't people's lives so simple and boring as to make poor fiction? How could ragged bands of mammoth hunters or flint knappers contribute to such a sophisticated genre? I will suggest several themes where prehistory could shine, all focused on the horror of encountering something so unfathomably old as to warp the mind and frustrate the senses: the discovery of a body and the realisation that living flesh can transform into stone. Ultimately the true horror of prehistory, as we shall explore, is the terror of 'deep time'; that instant when the rational faculty attempts to comprehend the sheer scale and the depth of the ages. Hopefully then, this will be a meditation and an exercise in thinking with these objects and places whose lifespan we cannot hope to understand.

Deep Time

"We felt ourselves necessarily carried back to the time when the schistus on which we stood was yet at the bottom of the sea, and when the sandstone before us was only beginning to be deposited, in the shape of sand or mud, from the waters of a superincumbent ocean. An epocha still more remote presented itself, when even the most ancient of these rocks, instead of standing upright in vertical beds, lay in horizontal planes at the bottom of the sea... **The mind seemed to grow giddy by looking so far into the abyss of time**"

John Playfair, 1788

James Hutton (1726-1797) and his friends, Playfair and Hall, famously developed the concept of 'geological time'. In an era dominated by the notion of biblical genealogies, Hutton stood quietly watching the cliffs of Berwickshire and, from his simple observation of strata, deduced the most horrifying of possibilities. Not only was the Earth older than 4004 BC, it was so incomprehensibly old, that, to paraphrase Playfair again: it was so ancient, the imagination could not keep pace with what the rational mind was saying.

This barely legible concept has been dubbed 'deep time', originally by writer John McPhee in *Basin and Range.* Physically it is used to talk about events on a geological timeline, moments which can be compressed by language but take countless human lifespans to finish, if they ever do. Continental drift, mountain formation, the immense pressures which cause minerals to alter their chemical structure. To hold a piece of flint in your hand is to make contact with silicon dioxide from billions of dead sea creatures, subject to the most immense compulsions and transfigured into a smooth, grey stone. As words these are impressive, but when you allow that sensation of encountering an object of such age to flow through you, it induces the most appalling reality of time. Deep time doesn't just have to refer to geological epochs though. Cosmological deep time is even more mind-cracking to contemplate; likewise the spans of deep prehistory can engage the same sense of dread, of existential unease at how the universe was 'meant' to operate.

Part of why deep time causes such psychological distress, I believe, is the thought that no-one or no being is capable of witnessing the unfolding actions of the earth. In the smaller and more provincial view of human affairs, starting say in 4000 BC, there is at least the sense that a narrative is being maintained. People are watching and recording, events do not go unnoticed. The seeming indifference of the world when time is stretched out to millions of years is terrifying. The slow accretions of sand or chalk or magma, coalescing their way into a structure or form, we want to imagine that these were witnessed and observed, they were recognised for the important acts they were. Instead, deep time invites us to conceive of a world where *no-one is watching, this has never been seen before*. Imagine, as some archaic forager picking their way across the landscape, you come across a patch of shale which is on fire, or a band of coloured minerals in the rock face; a patch of crystalline daggers which have grown out of the floor, or a column of granite in the iron sea, almost perfectly straight. Would this not feel like a haunted landscape, but haunted by its sheer emptiness?

Faces Of Living Rock

In the 1950's, an old Greek shepherd, Philippos Chatzaridis, was trying to encourage his friends to help him explore an unusual local rock face. For many years he had noticed a strange patch of earth which was always of a different temperature to its surroundings and emitted an unearthly 'breath' of noise on quiet days. Convinced that there was an underground spring flowing beneath the hill, the villagers eventually started digging into the ground. Finding not rock, but compacted earth, they excavated a small entrance to a subterranean world. What they found continues to rock the foundations of modern archaeology.

The interior of the cave was a time capsule of such unbelievable antiquity that researchers still argue about the dating today. Known now as Petralona Cave, geologists estimate the pinkish, cactus-like formations to have their origins in the Mesozoic, a good 200 million years ago. Preserved within this alien world were a menagerie of fossils ranging from rodents and bats to primitive forms of badger and wolf. Of greater remoteness to our minds were the bones of rhinos, leopards, jaguars, elephants and lions. But the most startling revelation of all was the discovery of a hominid skull.

Encrusted with calcite, looking far more like a face grown out of the rock itself, this skull was cemented to the cave wall, lifted clear off the floor by the growth of the stalagmites. This kind of deep time, where a human died and his inorganic remains, the stony scaffold of his flesh, were joined in an inhuman embrace with the living growing rock; it reveals to the reflective reader a deep dread of our mortal coil and the much more powerful non-human forces that we arise from. The calcium in his bones leached and hardened with a depth of age out of our understanding. Scientifically speaking this skull has proved a thorn in the side of the conventional narrative, and the heroic efforts of archaeologist Aris Poulianos, despite being banned from working on the site, have produced a nagging doubt in the minds of the orthodox:

This skull may belong to an extinct but independent group of evolved humans.

In 1993, a group of cave researchers near Altamura in Italy came across a 30ft deep limestone sinkhole. Lowering themselves down they too found themselves face to face with the terrifyingly uncanny scene - the complete skeleton of a human was encased in the walls of the cave. The limestone water which for tens of millennia had slowly dripped down the sides of the hole had enveloped the man's remains in a kind of 'popcorn-like' layer of calcite. He seemed to protrude from his lithic slumber, much as an overgrown ruin is reclaimed by the moss and the roots. Within these cold and quartzite kingdoms, the medium takes on a scale of life which has no human equivalent. To imagine a younger Palaeolithic human, flickering torch in hand, slowly inching their way through a dark and inhospitable abyss, each footfall potentially disappearing into some appalling chasm in the earth, this is to enter the world where both immanent and existential horror could have been all too real. The dancing and stuttering leaves of light might have, for an instant, illuminated the terrible hollow of an eye socket, vacant for eternity. Imagine the moment of unholy realisation, when the face finally emerges, but pockmarked and banded around with hardened stone. This is where our human might lose all their nerve, or perhaps in morbid terror, continue to stare at this monstrous form. Something both living and dead.

"Thou Shalt Set Thee Up Great Stones"

Stone has the capacity to surprise, beyond its ability to capture and ensnare the deep sleep of the human form. Across the span of prehistory, stone is the most durable of companions and we recognise this in our classification of the overwhelming majority of the human story as dominated by stone. But, what did our forebears imagine stone to actually be? Recreating taxonomic schema from hundreds of millennia ago seems a fool's errand, but there are hints in the record of a deeper appreciation for the transformative power of rock.

In the cave system of the Grotte du Trilobite at Arcy-sur-Cure, in northern Burgundy, a most remarkable but unsung discovery was made. The occupation of the caves by Magdalenian hunters has been long documented, but the presence of two strange pieces of portable artwork gives a rare insight into how they might have appreciated the transfiguration of life itself. The first was a marine arthropod, a trilobite fossil, modified and altered to become a pendant. The nearest source of such finds has been worked out to be several hundred miles away, meaning this object had been curated and preserved, either accompanying a traveller or perhaps changing hands. Alongside this was a carving of a beetle, shaped from fossilised wood - lignite - with its black and shiny surface utilised to create the exterior look and feel of an insect. Archaeologist Chantal Conneller writes (my emphasis):

"Modern scientific understandings of fossils would privilege the form over the material and see this as a beetle that has become stone – a beetle in an unfamiliar material. However the technological mimicry of this transformation – the act of making a stone into a beetle – may suggest the Magdalenians had a different view of this transformation and perceived it as a stone with an unfamiliar form. The manufactured lignite beetle suggests people recognised that **beetles might emerge from stones**. The trilobite appears to have been picked out because of the non-human agent of transformation – **perhaps conceived as the work of a supernatural being, or perhaps effected by the stone itself**"

Gironde, in southwest France, reveals yet more examples of the Magdalenian relationship with stone. The fossilised bones of *Halitherium,* a species of sea-cow, are relatively common in the sedimentary layers of the region. Foragers would have recognised in these alien forms a monstrous and potentially dangerous beast, one which may lurk out in the depths, one which could have given rise to all manner of stories and legends. The people here, and in earlier times, collected and made use of these bones. Attempts to make arrowheads, harpoons and other weapon tips lie scattered around the floor of Grottes de Jaurias, some successful, most not. It seems that the Magdalenians wished to convert the power of these bones-now-stones into the killing end of a hunter's armoury.

Both of these examples may seem interesting at such a remove, but with such imaginative effort we can perhaps think through what these might mean. That people viewed and understood the transformation of bone-stone-animal-mineral-living-dead could have been part of a benign story of the cosmos, but it could also invoke a horror of what life might actually, at bottom, be. If the living can be transformed from breathing and dancing beings composed of flesh, into the disarticulated bone of the dead, and further into the realm of the earth itself, what is life but a fleeting fleck of liberated rock? If monsters can be prised from their ancient tombs and manufactured into tools, what then is the human form but a momentary geometry, inhabited by something ephemeral but doomed to sink and be compressed into mud, shale and sand? All Palaeolithic people appreciated the subtle properties of different stones, choosing the correct one for the task - flint, chert, jasper, quartz, shale, slate, ochre… the inventory is vast.

The grinding and preparation of powders and dyes is present on the walls of the finest cave art; the knowledge that some stones can yield fire was common to Neanderthals in the use of manganese, flint and pyrite; the ability to physically modify flint through careful heating was an art perfected by the Solutreans. Human bones were routinely used, as offerings, drinking vessels, points and hooks; this world was one where life didn't just end at death, but the corporeal form could be transformed and repurposed in macabre but perhaps mundane ways. All this is to evidence the creative facts of prehistory and lay them at the feet of the would be horrorist. There is something ghastly about seeing a living being taken apart and transformed into mere objects, a dread and anxiety which we are largely spared today.

Hopefully what I've sketched out here is just an appetiser for thinking about prehistory and horror. The realisation of how deep time goes, both for the species and for the earth, offers up Lovecraftian themes of existential dread. In the more immediate discoveries of stone and bone metamorphosis there is a terror of the body and the ways it can be manipulated, but also the more eerie forces of the cosmos which can transfigure objects from one form to another. We don't appreciate enough, even as archaeologists, how much these themes might have preoccupied the lives of our ancestors. Did they fear the decay and change of death? Did they see bone and stone as a continuation of the same substance, which is why perhaps we find finger bones stuffed into the cracks of cave walls? Did they lurch in disgust seeing the skeletal remains of a long extinct monster, or worse, did their hearts skip a beat seeing a human skull, mouth agape, raised off the floor by an unearthly force and welded into a pink stalagmite? These and many more questions can be approached through fiction, and so I throw down the gauntlet dear reader, we have a world of creativity here at our fingertips. If modern life has some unique qualities, it is the stagnation of culture and cultural products. Renew and revitalise friends, and bring the disquieting horror of the primaeval back into the present.

Midwinter Melancholia

A Reflection on English Aesthetics

Once upon a time, as a boy, I found myself crossing a field in mid December. The sun had drawn down to the softest of weak glimmers underneath the dark clouds and the snow was falling, thick, soft and heavy as I trudged through the fresh drift. Silhouetted against the sky were tall and thin poplars in a row; some broader oak spreading over a line of hedgerow. The absolute silence, the dark and the snow, the semi-domesticated farmland I was standing on, the thick clouds. It gathered in me something that never quite left, a feeling that is evoked every time I sit quietly in an old church, or ponder a log fire with a warm drink. A keen pessimism and happiness all bound together.

The author Peter Ackroyd writes in *Albion: The Origins of the English Imagination:*

> "The English landscape itself seems to harbour ruins as if in an embrace, but their cultivation may also be an aspect of English melancholy. In the Anglo-Saxon poem "The Wanderer," there is an invocation of the ruined walls which are "standing beaten by the wind and covered with rime. . . . He then who in a spirit of meditation has pondered over this ruin and who with an understanding heart probes the mystery of our life down to its

depths. . . . How that time passed away, grown shadowy under the canopy of night as though it had never been!"

The winter naturally lends the atmosphere and weather towards this disposition. With Britain's gloomy, rain lashed countenance, more bound to the permanent gentle mania for discussing, analysing and grumbling each day's forecast, we lack the clean, abrupt Scandinavian minimalism or the fiery passion of the sun. Instead the gloaming provokes a strange love of the twilight and the gloom. It summons the need for heavy curtains, stone floors, and old wood polished by time. When the daylight disappears in the mid-afternoon, the Anglo finds himself drawn to the cosy glow of the pub and the tavern. Glass, steel and concrete are too harsh, too flat and visible. Where the English imagination is truly refreshed is seeing the tiny cubbyholes and niches in an old house, the crooked little table in a corner, in the piles of old books and the dusty travel trunks on top of the wardrobe.

I believe it's correct when the comparison is made with the American imagination and their love for space. The frontier, the road trip, the plains and vistas, huge forests and corn fields. The source of their vitality comes from this horizon, endlessly stretching out before them. By contrast the English have no space. We have no wilderness and no empty frontier. What we have instead is the other dimension - *time.*

The depth of time is the fuel of the English aesthetic. Aeon laid over aeon. Accretions of Roman, Saxon, Viking, Medieval, all bound together and softly whispering over one another. The lowest walls of the building may have foundations of sandstone, with mediaeval timbers like old bones resting on Edwardian supports. The energetic vitalism of the Victorians pulses through most English cities in the rebuilt walls, neo-Gothic railings and red brick archways. This, I fear, will always draw the Anglo back into himself. Caught in a sticky web of the past, every narrow corridor housing old ghosts, now with little blue placards, freezing everything in place like a wasting disease.

"There is a word in Old English which belongs wholly to that civilisation— "dustsceawung," meaning contemplation of dust. It is a true image of the Anglo-Saxon mind, or at least an echo of that consciousness which considered transience and loss to be part of the human estate; it was a world in which life was uncertain and the principal deity was fate or destiny or "wyrd."

In his 1933 work, *In Praise of Shadows,* Japanese author Jun'ichirō Tanizaki argues for the aesthetic primacy of deep, black pools of shadow in Japanese architecture and in its cultural imagination. He contrasts this with much of Western modernity's obsession with scraping every speck of dirt and history away from their smooth and shiny, well-lit spaces. I take issue with this assessment, for it has

386

always seemed to me that shadows also belong to an earlier and more culturally tight form of English aesthetic. The love of dark hardwood furniture, old crumbling manors and firelight casts its physical and metaphorical shadow across the Anglo mind. The love of '*dustsceawung*', a reminder of the fading and more impressive previous civilisation, is everywhere, even if only in a twee and sentimentalist form today.

I don't resent that millions of English tourists crowd through our ruined churches and stone circles every year - picnicking among abbey foundations and guiding their children over the stones of former times. What I dislike is that this spiritual urge to dance among the heaps of old bones has been effectively partitioned from our daily lives. Modern Britain seems to crave shiny flat new buildings, smooth driveways, minimalist interior design, open plan office spaces, glass fronted public libraries and screens to direct, inform and guide at every turn of the head. We have abandoned the much older love for the ancient as part of the quieter rhythms of the year, and in its place a rush to the two-dimensional and the surface.

Minimalism has no inner and outer, no doorway to guide one from the outside world of the fearful and cold to the warm and friendly. Anglo-Saxon cosmology, like its wider Germanic variants, prizes the care and maintenance of one's inner world against the outer. I believe this instinct to run deeply through the Anglo soul. Small windows, revealing the hearth glow; arrow-slits in castle walls; portholes in the creaking ship; a small recess in the stone balancing a family heirloom. Read any guidebook for English interior design and the same motifs appear over and again - a rejection of the minimal and neat aesthetic, a preference for clutter, casually thrown blankets, a mismatch of Oriental rugs and stags heads, a need for multiple levels of height in decoration, with no obvious guides. The feeling evoked is one of timeless occupancy, with each generation merely adding, modifying and jumbling.

"The sound of horse hooves on the road in the early morning; the smell of autumnal fires and the haze that hangs just now like a halo round faded sunflowers and dahlias and thatched barns; a tea-table of gleaming silver and the curtains drawn against the damp night; an open brown folio beside an open fire, with the soft flicker of lamp or candle-light on ancient furniture; the slow, measured march of time noted in the peaceful serenity of a grandfather clock"

Arthur Bryant, The Lion & The Unicorn

I would hardly be the first to identify this attraction and instinct to place and time with the English taste for the ghost story. As Aris Roussinos notes:

"ghosts, should they exist, seem to be curiously institutionalised figures, adhering to schools, hospitals and museums, the London Underground and military installations. The Army, in particular, has a surprisingly rich and detailed ghost lore about its various historic barracks across Britain and, formerly, Germany. In this, we can say there's something particularly British about ghosts: like our establishment, they seem doomed to wander forlornly across one Gothic quadrangle or another for eternity."

The image of the English institution lingers firmly in the heart of the Anglo, despite them being scrubbed away over the past few decades. The haunted house trope is particularly effective in Britain precisely because so many of our dwellings are ancient. Boarding schools, manor houses, palaces, cathedrals, small country churches, graveyards, farmhouses, rural estates, asylums, hotels and pubs. Each connected to the soil by some small and bounded fact of history. As a child I spent several years at a boarding school, one with as rich a folklore of ghosts as any other. A 'Red Lady' haunted the upper floors of the school, where no-one went and nothing seemed to happen. Likewise the cellar of the dormitories had a 'Grey Lady'. These architectural features seemed to create an oppressive atmosphere of so much thick time, all sitting heavily in corners and high ceilings, like I was just a visitor.

In that densely layered way, the portraits, black and white photographs and medals and trophies of former students fed into an existential feeling that 'events have happened here', and echo down the empty corridors. Younger students were sent in pairs on errands across the school, in part to prevent the sheer terror of a six year old boy looking down a dark passageway and refusing to go any further.

A true Englishman will tell you how they went into the rain and wind, maybe crossing a patch of moorland or heath, and then exclaim how it cheered them up. Their cheeks red and cold, stripping off wet wax jackets, they might go for a pint, or read a book. In an earlier time they may have smoked a pipe and skimmed a newspaper. This is archetypal. Although transformed into a 'flat cap and jacket' brand and consumer style, it's possible to be sincere and to tap into a sense of comfort and homeliness, security and familiarity. Some critics have extended this attitude of the English into their vision of a safe island and a hostile world. Perhaps this is true, I certainly don't reject it.

"Out of this land of visions emerges a poetry of the dream-world. Beowulf is in part a dream-poem; the strange elegies of the Anglo-Saxon spirit are enacted in unreal landscapes compounded of dream and vision. Beowulf himself follows Grendel's mother through "frecne fen-gelad," a terrifying fen path, towards a tarn or mere where flickers "fyr on flode" hiding an ancient terror. Perhaps only the Anglo-Saxons were capable of such horror, although the persistent taste for Gothic in English literature suggests that their influence has lingered."

John Leland (1503 – 1552), a poet and historian has the honour of being the first 'antiquarian'. Commissioned by Henry VIII to search the kingdom's monastery libraries and archives, he went "*to peruse and diligently to serche at the libraries of monasteries and collegies of this yowre noble reaulme, to the intente that the monuments of auncient writers as welle of other nations, as of this your owne province mighte be brought owte of deadely darkenes to lyvely lighte.*" In the most true of English intentions, he sought these treasures as they *"lay secretely yn corners".*

Be of no doubt that this new pastime, of poring over local documents and looking for secret, small histories in the nooks of the island, has blossomed in the Anglo soul. No town is without a historian, no household or child free from the influences of museums, endless archaeology programmes and metal detection announcements. No Remembrance Day goes past without millions of people bringing out medals, certificates, photographs of ancient family members, all buried in Flanders. We are a ghost island, permanently enthralled with portions of our history.

This is not without its dangers, as the tendency for reverence and nostalgic commemoration sinks into a sweet sentimental morass, and worse - the total fairy story of post-war Britain. Without any driving energy for expansion in some realm or other, it seems we collapse in ourselves and project out into the world only the most small-minded and timid versions of power. British 'soft power', as it has become known, can be summed up in that cloying speech given by Hugh Grant in Love Actually. Alluding to the roll-call of pop figures from Shakespeare, Churchill, the Beatles, Harry Potter and David Beckham's feet, these lines were referenced by Blair himself in a discussion about foreign policy. As painful as it is to watch a nation descend into something so small as young adult fiction and footballers, it makes sense when considering this tendency to immortalise our heritage, but now in a misty eyed and sterile way.

Some days when I see black and white timber buildings being used as wine bars, and churches stripped for dance floors, I want to burn everything to the ground. Everything that is older than 1945. I get the impulse to grind it all away into dust and obliterate the very memory of the stones. Perhaps only then will we see how much we have lost. In an ironically Anglo-Saxon way, I wish we did mourn the passing of a greater time. As Peter Hitchens once wrote:

"I had a feeling we were now a smaller people than we had been, scuttling about in the ruins of a lost civilisation."

The overbearing pretence that we still live in the same society, surrounded by all the detritus and crazed cobblestones of former years, holds us back and prevents us from generating something new with what we have. Ours is a civilisation which has been largely untouched by external powers for a millennium, renewing itself from the inside by borrowing, altering, jumbling, compromising and reforming. None of that spirit seems to have been retained, and we are driven entirely by outside modern forces. Even our industrial heritage is mostly a tourist industry now, with steam trains for children and cotton mills as foreign luxury apartments.

Of course the same impulse to burn everything away is met by an equal desire to protect everything that made England what it was, and can still be. This is probably why I'm an archaeologist, in love with the past and all the reserves of energy that it can offer. May we soon return to that source and create something new.

-

Printed in Great Britain
by Amazon

54862889R00218